# MODERN MANDARIN CHINESE

## for Beginners

**Monika Mey**

D1379249

## About the Author

Monika Mey (M.A.) specialized in Chinese Studies, Japanese Studies, and Communication Studies in Erlangen / Nuremberg and Shanghai. Since 1996 she has headed the China Coaching Center (see *www.ChinaCoachingCenter.de*) in Munich, a contact point for communication between the German and Chinese cultures. Over the past decade, while operating the center and making numerous trips through all parts of China, she has amassed a great deal of useful information and successfully incorporated it in this text.

Monika Mey offers language courses in Germany and China for people interested in learning modern colloquial Chinese. Her offerings also include cross-cultural management training programs, seminars on regional and cultural features, and interpretation and translation services. Monika Mey is vice chairperson of the China-Network e.V.

First edition for the United States and Canada © Copyright 2008 by Barron's Educational Series, Inc.
Title of the original German edition: **Monika Mey. Compact SilverLine Chinesisch fur Einsteiger**
© **Copyright 2006** by Compact Verlag GmbH, Munich, Federal Republic of Germany.

Author: **Monika Mey**
English translation: **Kathleen Luft**

*All inquiries should be addressed to:*
Barron's Educational Series, Inc.
250 Wireless Boulevard
Hauppauge, NY 11788
**http://www.barronseduc.com**

ISBN-13: 978-0-7641-3925-3 (book only)
ISBN-10: 0-7641-3925-8 (book only)
ISBN-13: 978-0-7641-9456-6 (book & CD package)
ISBN-10: 0-7641-9456-9 (book & CD package)

Library of Congress Control Number 2007929148

Printed in China
9 8 7 6 5 4 3 2

## Foreword

*Modern Mandarin Chinese* is a comprehensive self-study course that will give you a quick, expert introduction to modern colloquial Chinese as it is spoken today in the People's Republic of China. The internationally accepted Pīnyīn 拼音 system of romanization makes access to Standard Chinese, also known as Standard Mandarin, much easier. Because of the way the course is designed and the gradually increasing level of difficulty, the book is equally suitable for beginners and for those who want to refresh their skills.

As you journey in this book through the most important provinces of China, sample sentences from authentic sources of colloquial speech will help you communicate successfully in everyday situations. Essential topics of daily life are dealt with in fifteen chapters, always with reference to a particular province. Whether you're out shopping at a market, strolling around town, staying in a hotel, or visiting a Chinese family, you'll find the crucial phrases and necessary vocabulary for every situation.

Each lesson contains vocabulary words and sample sentences in Chinese characters, in Pīnyīn, in a literal English translation, and in correct, colloquial English. In addition, each chapter introduces the new characters with an indication of the way they are formed. In the semantic fields, you will find additional terms that relate to other major aspects of the province in question (places of interest, foods). "Info boxes" provide interesting background information about linguistic or regional features. At the end of each chapter, a wide variety of exercises will help you practice what you've learned. The answers are supplied in the back of the book.

You can put many of the sample sentences to immediate use in China, on the street, in restaurants, and in other everyday situations. Taxi drivers and waiters, in particular, will be delighted to hear you express your wishes in perfect Chinese—orally and in writing!

Complete phonetics, as well as a comprehensive list of elements of Chinese characters (radicals) with English translations, will help you gain an understanding of both the spoken and the written language. Key principles of grammar are placed next to the sample sentences and are repeated in the back of the book, in a compact, alphabetically arranged section.

On the two audio CDs, you will find the syllables presented in the Introduction, as well as all the vocabulary words, sample sentences, and semantic fields, so you can listen, practice pronunciation, and read along in your text.

Good luck!

# Contents

# Semantic Fields and Info Boxes

## List of Words in Semantic Fields and Info Boxes

# Introduction

## Introduction to Chinese Phonetics

Chinese is a language originally based on pictorial symbols. Each symbol, that is, each Chinese character, represents one spoken syllable and one unit of meaning, or morpheme. There are around 50,000 characters in all, but only 408 different syllables, which can be further differentiated in spoken Chinese by using the "four tones." When you add in all the unstressed syllables, the overall total of acoustically distinguishable syllables is 1,276. The individual syllables can be represented as characters or in Pīnyīn 拼音, the most common romanization system for Standard Mandarin.

Despite the differences resulting from the tones, there still are a great many syllables or characters that sound alike; therefore, correct pronunciation, first of the phonetic Pīnyīn 拼音 transcription and second of the tones, is indispensable to prevent misunderstandings.

### Pīnyīn 拼音 Transcription and Its Pronunciation

The phonetic Pīnyīn 拼音 transcription, which was introduced in the late 1950s and is now the international standard, makes it possible for anyone learning Chinese to pronounce the characters immediately. The transcription uses roman letters, although not all of them correspond exactly to English sounds or pronunciations. In the material that follows, all the initial and final sounds of Chinese are presented.

| | |
|---|---|
| a, -a | as in "father" |
| ai, -ai | similar to "eye" |
| an, an- | continental "a" plus "n" |
| ang, -ang | as in "**ang**st" |
| ao, -ao | similar to "**cow**" |
| b- | unaspirated **p**, as in "**sp**ot" |
| c- | like **ts** in "bats," but aspirated |
| ch- | as in "**ch**in," but strongly aspirated, with tongue curled upward |
| chi | **ch** + voiceless **i**, with mouth barely opened and teeth together |
| ci | **ts** + voiceless **i**, with mouth only slightly open and teeth together |
| d- | unaspirated **t**, as in "stay" |
| -e | in unstressed syllables, like the neutral vowel, or schwa, in "sof**a**" |
| e, -e | in syllables with a tone, a back, unrounded vowel, an **o** with lips spread |
| ei, -ei | as in "j**ai**l" |
| en, -en | as in "mistak**en**" |
| eng, -eng | like Chinese **e**, but with **ng** added |
| er | as in "st**ar**" |

| | |
|---|---|
| f- | as in English |
| g- | unaspirated **k** |
| h- | differs widely by region, ranging from English **h** to Scots **ch** |
| i | like **ee** in "bee" |

---

### Info Box

**Exceptions with "i":**
In the syllables "zhi," "chi," "shi," and "ri," "i" is pronounced with teeth together and tongue curled back.
In the syllables "zi," "ci," and "si," "i" is also pronounced with teeth together, but with the tongue in the same position as for the initial consonant.

---

| | |
|---|---|
| -ia, ya | If the syllable "ia" stands alone, it is written "ya" in Pīnyīn and is pronounced as i + a, with short "i." |
| -ian, yan | If the syllable "ian" stands alone, it is written "yan" in Pīnyīn and is pronounced like the Japanese word "**yen**." In combination with initial consonants, the "i" is short. |
| -iang, yang | If the syllable "iang" stands alone, it is written "yang" in Pīnyīn and is pronounced like the Chinese word "**yang**." |
| -ie, ye | If the syllable "ie" stands alone, it is written "ye" in Pīnyīn and sounds like the "ye" in "**Ye**men." |
| -ing, ying | If the syllable "ing" stands alone, it is written "ying" in Pīnyīn and is pronounced as i with **ng** added at the back. |
| -iong, yong | If the syllable "iong" stands alone, it is written "yong" in Pīnyīn and is pronounced as "**Jung**." It occurs only after "j," "q," and "x." |
| -iu, you | If the syllable "iu" stands alone, it is written "you." If it is a syllable in the third or fourth tone, then an additional "o" is heard between "i" and "u." |
| j- | as in "jeep," unaspirated. It is always followed by "i" or "u." |
| ju | j + a vowel that English lacks, like the German ü, resembling "ee" with rounded lips |
| juan | j + ü + **en**, unaspirated |
| jue | j + ü + **e**, unaspirated |
| jun | j + ü + **n**, unaspirated |
| k- | as in "**kill**," very strongly aspirated |
| l- | between English **l** and continental **r** |

| | |
|---|---|
| m- | as in English |
| n- | as in English |
| -o | starts with English "oo," ends with continental "o"; occurs only after b, p, m, and f |
| -ong | the "o" sounds like "u"; more or less like "oong." |
| ou, -ou | as in "flow" |
| p- | strongly aspirated, as in "pit" |
| q- | as in "church," strongly aspirated, always followed by j or u |
| qu | q + ü, aspirated |
| quan | q + ü + en, aspirated |
| que | q + ü + e, aspirated. |
| qun | q + ü + n, aspirated |
| r- | as in "road" |
| s- | as in "son" |
| sh- | as in "T-shirt," but with the tongue tip curled upward |
| t- | as in "tomato," but more strongly aspirated |
| -u, wu | If the syllable "u" stands alone, it is written "wu" in Pīnyīn and sounds like "oo." The "w" is not pronounced, only slightly hinted at. If "u" follows j, q, x, or y, it is pronounced as ü.. |
| -ua, wa | If the syllable "ua" stands alone, it is written "wa" in Pīnyīn and is pronounced as in "water." The "u" sound is only hinted at; the stress is on the "a." |
| -uai, wai | If the syllable "uai" stands alone, it is written "wai" in Pīnyīn and is pronounced as in "wine." Here too, the stress is on the "a." |
| -uan, wan | If the syllable uan stands alone, it is written wan in Pīnyīn and is pronounced like u + an. The stress is on the "a." If "uan" follows "j," "q," "x," or "y," the "u" is pronounced like "ü" and the "a" like "e," that is, as üen. |
| -uang, wang | If the syllable "uang" stands alone, it is written "wang" in Pīnyīn and is pronounced as u + ang, with the stress on the "a." |
| -ue, yue | After "n "and "l," pronounced as ü + e, with stress on the "e." After "j," "q," "x," and "y," also pronounced as ü + e. |
| -ui, wei | If the syllable "ui" stands alone, it is written "wei" in Pīnyīn and is pronounced like "way." Between the "u" and "i," an "e" can be heard. |
| -un, wen | If the syllable "un" stands alone, it is written "wen" in Pīnyīn and sounds like the "on" in "won." |

Info Box

Info Box

**Exception with "un":**
After "j," "q," "x," or "y," "un" is pronounced "ün."

| | |
|---|---|
| -uo, wo | If the syllable "uo" stands alone, it is written "wo" in Pīnyīn and is pronounced as "**war.**" The "u" is only hinted at; the stress is on the "o," which sounds like an "a." |
| -ü, yu | If the syllable "ü" stands alone, it is written "yu" in Pīnyīn and is pronounced as in "**mu**te" or French "**tu.**" |
| w- | as in "**w**ord," with lips rounded |
| x- | sibilant similar to English **sh**, but closer to German "i**ch**," with the tongue rounded and the tip touching the lower teeth |
| xu | like the sibilant **x** + **ü**, but written as "u" |
| xuan | like the sibilant **x** + **üen**, with stress on the "en" |
| xue | like the sibilant **x** + **üe**, with stress on the "e" |
| xun | like the sibilant **x** + **ün** |
| y | as **y** or **i** in English |
| z- | as in English "clou**ds**" |
| zh- | like English **ch** with no aspiration, similar to "**j**ungle" |

# Introduction

## The Four Tones

Chinese has four tones, which are used to distinguish the meaning of a syllable. Variations in the intonation of the same syllable occur in English words as well but without changing the meaning of the words.

This little story will help illustrate this phenomenon, using the English word "there" as an example:

Mr. Jones and Mr. Smith are trying to spot an airplane in the sky. They can't see the plane yet, they can only hear it. Suddenly Mr. Smith, who catches sight of it first, cries out, his voice at a steady pitch, "There!" Mr. Jones looks in the wrong direction and asks questioningly, his voice rising, "There?" Somewhat annoyed, Mr. Smith, his voice falling and rising in wavelike fashion, mimics him, saying "There." Then, his tone of voice decisive and falling, he points again to the part of the sky where the airplane is to be seen: "There!"

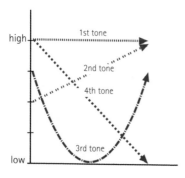

Diagram of the Four Tones

**First tone:** dì yìshēng 第一声
Pitch: a steady high sound
Represented by a horizontal bar over the stressed vowel: ā, ē, ī, ō, ū (there is no syllable with "ü" in the 1st tone).

**Second tone:** dì'èrshēng 第二声
Pitch: rising
Represented by a sharp upward accent mark over the stressed vowel: á, é, í, ó, ú, and ǘ.

**Third tone:** dì sānshēng 第三声
Pitch: falling-rising
Represented by a first falling and then rising stroke over the stressed vowel: ǎ, ě, ǐ, ǒ, ǔ, and ǚ.

**Fourth tone:** dì sìshēng 第四声
Pitch: falling
Represented by a sharp downward accent mark over the stressed vowel: à, è, ì, ò, ù, and ǜ.

If you see no tone mark on a vowel, then it is pronounced as an unstressed syllable. This can apply to one-syllable words as well as to the final syllable of two-syllable words.
Examples for one-syllable words:
de 的, ma 吗, le 了
Examples for multisyllable words:
jiǎozi 饺子, bāozi 包子,
bàba 爸爸, māma 妈妈

## Examples

The correct pronunciation is essential: horse or mother, pig or host, star or last name, snow or blood? The following examples will indicate how embarrassing it can be if you haven't really mastered the pronunciation of the tones!

That's why you first need to start with intensive practice in pronunciation. First, listen to all the syllables on the audio CD. Next, repeat them, and then memorize the correct pronunciation along with the Pīnyīn transcription.

| | | | | | | |
|---|---|---|---|---|---|---|
| (CD1 1) 妈 | mā | mother | 星 | xīng | star | |
| 麻 | má | hemp | 行 | xíng | to go | |
| 马 | mǎ | horse | 醒 | xǐng | to wake up | |
| 骂 | mà | to curse | 姓 | xìng | last name | |
| 吗 | ma | interrogative particle | | | | |
| 猪 | zhū | pig | 靴 | xuē | boot | |
| 竹 | zhú | bamboo | 学 | xué | to learn | |
| 主 | zhǔ | host | 雪 | xuě | snow | |
| 祝 | zhù | to wish | 血 | xuè | blood | |

(CD1 2) Words of single syllables

**First tone**

| | | | |
|---|---|---|---|
| yī | sān | qī | bā |
| huā | hē | chī | tā |
| fēn | qiān | zhōng | tiān |

**Second tone**

| | | | |
|---|---|---|---|
| shí | méi | chá | huáng |
| bái | nín | qián | máo |
| nián | cóng | cháng | néng |

**Third tone**

| | | | |
|---|---|---|---|
| wǔ | jiǔ | yǒu | yě |
| shuǐ | wǒ | nǐ | jǐ |
| bǎi | liǎng | qǐng | mǎi |

**Fourth tone**

| | | | |
|---|---|---|---|
| èr | sì | liù | bù |
| xìn | fàn | zài | shì |
| zuò | jìn | wèn | kuài |

**Toneless:** ma   ne   de   men

(CD1 3) Tone combinations of two syllables

**First tone**

| | | | |
|---|---|---|---|
| kāfēi | Xī'ān | Jiāngsū | jīdīng |
| Zhōngguó | huāchá | chūnjié | sīchóu |
| kāishuǐ | yēnǎi | duōshǎo | bāoguǒ |
| shēngrì | chīfàn | fāpiào | jīdàn |
| xiānsheng | tāde | shīfu | bāozi |

**Second tone**

| | | | |
|---|---|---|---|
| Nánjīng | Fúzhōu | Chéngdū | Chángshā |
| hóngchá | língqián | yóujú | chángchéng |
| píjiǔ | cháguǎn | shíjǐn | píngguǒ |
| yóupiào | búcuò | yígòng | yídìng |
| shénme | mántou | péngyou | chéngzi |

# Introduction

**Third tone**

| | | | |
|---|---|---|---|
| Běijīng | kǎoyā | shǒujī | mǎidān |
| Jǐ'nán | děngyú | cǎoméi | dǎoyóu |
| xiǎojiě | lǎobǎn | kěyǐ | shuǐguǒ |
| kělè | nǚshì | lǐmiàn | hǎiwèi |
| wǒde | nǐde | jiǎozi | lǐzi |

**Fourth tone**

| | | | |
|---|---|---|---|
| gùgōng | càidān | ròusī | yìbān |
| lǜchá | wèntí | yìzhí | sùshí |
| qìshuǐ | hàomǎ | diànnǎo | dìzhǐ |
| diànhuà | jiàoshòu | duìmiàn | Hànzì |
| zhèli | dàifu | tàitai | kuàizi |

**Tone combinations of three syllables**

| | | | |
|---|---|---|---|
| wūlóngchá | suānlàtāng | gōngchéngshī | zhōngguórén |
| nánpéngyou | niúzǎikù | nánfāngrén | hóngmáodān |
| pǔtōnghuà | xiǎolóngbāo | nǚpéngyou | shǒutíbāo |
| kuàngquánshuǐ | duìbuqǐ | diànhuàhào | zìxíngchē |

**Exercises**

Put extra effort into practicing especially difficult syllables!

| | | | |
|---|---|---|---|
| chǎng – zhǎng | jī – qī | chá – zhá | cèng – zèng |
| xiáng – jiáng | chàn – zhàn | jiān – qiān | zǎo – cǎo |
| què – juè | chī – chē | shé – shí | rè – rì |
| zǎi – zěi | chéng – zhéng | zhè – zhì | yǒu—yǎo |

**Distinguish between the tones when you listen and speak!**

| | | | |
|---|---|---|---|
| qiān – qián | liáng – liàng | sǒng – sóng | yè – yé |
| quē – què | wū – wǔ | lú – lǚ | kòng – kōng |
| xīng – xìng | óu – ǒu | cī – cì | rè – rě |
| biǎn – biàn | chéng – chēng | huǒ – huò | jī – jí |
| máo – mào | jiǔ – jiù | zhè – zhé | xiǎng – xiāng |
| yī – yì | péi – pěi | sì – sī | mò – mǒ |
| jìng – jīng | fēn – fěn | è – é | duō – duǒ |

## Introduction to Chinese Characters

After you've practiced the pronunciation of the individual syllables with the help of the Pīnyīn transcription, you need to carry over this knowledge to the Chinese characters. This is not altogether easy, because Chinese characters represent ideographic symbols, not a phonetic alphabet, as is true in the case of English. Unfortunately, Chinese characters have a very loose relationship with phonetics, so you have to learn each character independently, along with the correct pronunciation and proper written form.

If you can already speak Chinese, that will help you learn the writing system because it will be easier for you to remember the components of the characters, which give an approximation of the characters' pronunciation and are repeated in characters that are pronounced in a similar way. But whether you already speak Chinese or not, it is necessary to learn the writing system separately from the colloquial language, starting with the basics.

### The Eight Basic Strokes

The formation of Chinese script is based on eight basic strokes. The character yǒng 永 (eternal) contains all the basic strokes.

| | | |
|---|---|---|
| a | diǎn | dot |
| b | héng | horizontal |
| c | shù | vertical |
| d | gōu | hook |
| e | tí | rising |
| f | zhé | turning |
| g | piě | slanting to the left |
| h | nà | slanting to the right |

Write the character by making the strokes in the designated order and direction!
Follow these four basic rules when you write:
1. Horizontal strokes before vertical strokes. Example: 十
2. Strokes slanting to the left before strokes slanting to the right.
Example: 小
3. Write the characters from top to bottom. Example: 三
4. Write from left to right.
Example: 你
These four basic rules are a basic guideline for learning to write by yourself. In the following fifteen lessons, however, when you do the writing exercises, you'll see that there are exceptions here as well. Be persistent, and learn them by memory!

### Radicals

Chinese characters are listed in dictionaries under character components known as radicals. They are arranged in the table of radicals (部首目录 bùshǒu mùlù) according to the number of strokes in each.

This means that if you can quickly and reliably identify the radical and the number of its strokes, you'll be ahead of the game when searching for unknown characters in a dictionary.

The following character components (radicals) must be memorized. The list contains the ra-

# Introduction

dical, the name of the radical in Chinese, the explanation and/or translation of the radical, and its placement in more complex characters.

| Radical | Name | Explanation/Translation | Position in Characters |
|---|---|---|---|
| **1 stroke** | | | |
| 丶 | diǎn | dot | (variable) |
| 一 | héng | horizontal stroke | (variable) |
| 丨 | shù | vertical stroke | (variable) |
| 丿 | piě | stroke slanting to the left | (variable) |
| 乙 | gōu | sickle; secondly | (variable) |
| **2 strokes** | | | |
| 二 | èr | two | (variable) |
| 十 | shí | ten | (variable) |
| 亠 | wénzìtóu | "lid"; to protect | (top) |
| 冖 | tǔbàogài | to cover | (top) |
| 人 | rén | human being | (top) see also 亻 |
| 亻 | dānlìrén | human being | (left) see also 人 |
| 入 | rù | to enter | (top) see also 人 |
| 儿 | ér | child; son | (bottom) |
| 八 | bā | eight | (top; bottom) |
| 冂 | tóngzìkuàng | free country | (outside) |
| 凵 | xiōngzìkuàng | pit | (outside) |
| 匚 | sānkuàng | suitcase | (outside) |
| 冫 | liǎngdiǎnshuǐ | ice | (left) |
| 讠 | yánzìpáng | language | (left) see also 言 |
| 几 | jǐ | small table | (variable) |
| 力 | lì | power | (variable) |
| 刀 | dāo | knife | (variable) see also 刂 |
| 刂 | lìdāopáng | knife | (right) see also 刀 |

| 勹 | bāozìtóu | to embrace | (two sides) |
| 匕 | bǐ | spoon | (left; right) |
| 阝 | ěrdāopáng | city | (right)   see also 邑 |
| 阝 | ěrdāopáng | hill | (left)   see also 阜 |
| 卜 | bǔ | to soothsay, tell fortunes | (variable) |
| 卩 | dān'ěrpáng | hunched person; seal | (right) |
| 厂 | chǎng | slope; cave dwelling today: factory | (two sides) |
| 厶 | sī | private | (top, bottom) |
| 又 | yòu | right hand; today: also | (variable) |

3 strokes

| 口 | kǒu | mouth | (left) |
| 囗 | dàkǒukuàng | framing; enclosure | (outside) |
| 土 | tǔ | earth | (variable)   see also 士 |
| 士 | shì | term for respected persons | (left, bottom)   see also 土 |
| 忄 | shùxīnpáng | heart | (left)   see also 心 |
| 纟 | jiǎosīpáng | silk | (left)   see also 糸 |
| 爿 | jiāngzìpáng | something thin and flat; bamboo strip | (left)   see also 爿 |
| 饣 | shízìpáng | food; nourishment | (left)   see also 食 |
| 扌 | tíshǒupáng | hand | (left)   see also 手 |
| 氵 | sāndiǎnshuǐ | water | (left)   see also 水 |
| 犭 | fǎnquǎnpáng | animal with claws, dog | (left)   see also 犬 |
| 宀 | bǎogàitóu | roof | (top) |
| 夂 | zhéwén | to follow | (variable) |
| 艹 | cǎozìtóu | grass | (top) |
| 夕 | xī | sunset | (variable) |
| 大 | dà | big | (top; bottom) |
| 女 | nǚ | woman | (left) |
| 子 | zǐ | child; son | (left; bottom)   see also 子 |
| 孑 | zǐzìpáng | child | (left)   see also 子 |
| 寸 | cùn | thumb (1/3 decimeter) | (right; bottom) |
| 马 | mǎ | horse | (left; bottom) |
| 小 | xiǎo | small | (top) |
| 尸 | shī | body; corpse | (two sides) |
| 门 | mén | gate | (outside) |

| 山 | shān | mountain | (variable) |
| 工 | gōng | work | (variable) |
| 己 | jǐ | personal | (top) |
| 巾 | jīn | cloth; scarf | (variable) |
| 广 | guǎng | canopy; far; to extend | (two sides) |
| 廴 | jiànzhīpáng | to go; structure | (two sides) |
| 辶 | zǒuzhīpáng | to run | (two sides) |
| 彳 | shuānglìrén | to go; standing double person | (left) |
| 飞 | fēi | to fly | (two sides) |
| 弋 | yì | arrow | (right) |
| 弓 | gōng | bow | (left) |
| 彡 | xiésānpiě | beard; adornment | (left; right) |

## 4 strokes

| 心 | xīn | heart; feeling | (bottom)    see also 忄 |
| 戈 | gēzìpáng | pick; halberd | (left; right) |
| 户 | hù | family; door; account | (two sides) |
| 韦 | wéi | leather | (left; right) |
| 见 | jiàn | to see | (right; bottom) |
| 贝 | bèi | shell; money | (left; bottom) |
| 手 | shǒu | hand | (bottom)    see also 扌 |
| 攵 | fǎnwénpáng | hand that holds a stick | (right)    see also 攴 |
| 文 | wén | writing | (left, top) |
| 王 | wáng | king; jade | (left) |
| 车 | chē | wagon | (left; top) |
| 斗 | dòu | bushel (measurement for grain); to fight | (right) |
| 斤 | jīn | axe; pound | (right; left) |
| 方 | fāng | rectangle; direction | (left; bottom) |
| 日 | rì | sun | (variable) |
| 曰 | yuē | to say | (variable) |
| 月 | yuè | moon, meat | (right, left) |
| 木 | mù | tree | (variable) |
| 欠 | qiàn | to owe; to be lacking; to yawn | (right) |
| 止 | zhǐ | to stand still; to stop | (left; top) |
| 歹 | dǎi | bones; bad, evil | (left) |

| 礻 | shìbǔpáng | rites; to revere; to show | (left)　see also 示 |
| 殳 | shū | stick; lance made of bamboo | (right) |
| 比 | bǐ | to compare | (top; bottom) |
| 毛 | máo | hair; feather; down | (left; bottom) |
| 氏 | shì | family; surname; clan name | (right, top) |
| 气 | qì | gas; air | (two sides) |
| 水 | shuǐ | water | (bottom; top)　see also 氵 |
| 火 | huǒ | fire; anger; rage | (variable)　see also 灬 |
| 灬 | sìdiǎndǐ | fire | (bottom)　see also 火 |
| 爪 | zhuǎ; zhǎo | claw; talon; paw | (left) |
| 父 | fù | father | (top) |
| 风 | fēng | wind | (left; right) |
| 爿 | pián | something thin and flat; strip of bamboo | (left)　see also 丬 |
| 片 | piàn | something thin and flat; strip of bamboo | (left) |
| 牙 | yá | tooth | (left) |
| 牛 | niú | cow, ox | (left; bottom) |
| 犬 | quǎn | dog | (bottom)　see also 犭 |
| 瓦 | wǎ | brick; ceramics | (right; bottom) |

## 5 strokes

| 衤 | yībǔpáng | clothing | (left)　see also 衣 |
| 玉 | yù | jade | (bottom) |
| 瓜 | guā | melon; pumpkin | (right) |
| 钅 | jīnzìpáng | metal, gold | (left)　see also 金 |
| 甘 | gān | sweet | (top) |
| 鸟 | niǎo | bird | (right) |
| 母 | mǔ | mother | (left; bottom) |
| 田 | tián | field | (variable) |
| 疒 | bìng | disease | (two sides) |
| 龙 | lóng | dragon | (top; bottom) |
| 白 | bái | white | (variable) |
| 皮 | pí | skin; leather | (right; left) |
| 皿 | mǐn | container, vessel | (bottom) |
| 目 | mù | eye | (variable) |

| | | | |
|---|---|---|---|
| 矛 | máo | lance | (left; top) |
| 矢 | shǐ | arrow | (left) |
| 石 | shí | stone, rock | (left) |
| 示 | shì | altar; to revere; to show | (bottom)   see also 礻 |
| 禾 | hé | plant producing grain | (left) |
| 穴 | xué | cave; hole | (top) |
| 立 | lì | to stand erect | (variable) |

6 strokes

| | | | |
|---|---|---|---|
| 竹 | zhú | bamboo | (top) |
| 米 | mǐ | rice | (left) |
| 糸 | mì | silk | (bottom)   see also 纟 |
| 缶 | fǒu | pottery; urn | (left; bottom) |
| 页 | yè | book page; leaf | (right) |
| 齐 | qí | proper, near | (left; top) |
| 羊 | yáng | sheep | (variable) |
| 羽 | yǔ | feather | (variable) |
| 老 | lǎo | old; to get old | (top) |
| 而 | ér | to attach; additional; and | (top; left) |
| 耳 | ěr | ear | (variable) |
| 臣 | chén | minister; subject | (left) |
| 自 | zì | nose; self | (top) |
| 至 | zhì | to reach | (left) |
| 臼 | jiù | mortar | (top) |
| 舌 | shé | tongue | (left) |
| 舟 | zhōu | ship; boat | (left) |
| 艮 | gěn | frank, sincere | (left; top) |
| 虍 | hǔzìtóu | tiger | (top) |
| 虫 | chóng | insect; worm | (left) |
| 血 | xiě; xuè | blood | (left) |
| 衣 | yī | clothing | (bottom; top)   see also 衤 |
| 西 | xī | nest; lid; west | (top) |
| 亚 | yà | abbreviation for Asia | (top) |

7 strokes

| | | | |
|---|---|---|---|
| 麦 | mài | wheat | (left) |
| 角 | jiǎo | horn; angle; corner | (left) |

| 言 | yán | language | (variable)   see also 讠 |
| 谷 | gǔ | valley | (left; right) |
| 豆 | dòu | bean | (left) |
| 豕 | shǐ | pig | (bottom; left) |
| 豸 | zhì | worm | (left) |
| 龟 | guī | tortoise, turtle | (bottom) |
| 赤 | chì | red; loyal | (left) |
| 走 | zǒu | to go | (left) |
| 足 | zú | foot; enough | (variable) |
| 身 | shēn | body | (left) |
| 辛 | xīn | suffering | (variable) |
| 辰 | chén | time, day | (top) |
| 邑 | yì | city | (right)   see also 阝 |
| 酉 | yǒu | wine jug | (left; bottom) |
| 采 | cǎi | to pick, pluck | (top; left) |
| 里 | lǐ | village; traditional Chinese measure of length (0.5 km) | (left) |
| 卤 | lǔ | thick sauce | (left) |

**8 strokes**

| 金 | jīn | metal; gold | (bottom)   see also 钅 |
| 鱼 | yú | fish | (variable) |
| 阜 | fù | hill | (left)   see also 阝 |
| 齿 | chǐ | teeth | (left) |
| 雨 | yǔ | rain | (top) |
| 青 | qīng | green; blue | (left) |
| 非 | fēi | not | (top, bottom) |
| 其 | qí | this; such; that | (top, left) |

**9 strokes**

| 面 | miàn | face | (right) |
| 革 | gé | leather; pelt; to change | (left) |
| 音 | yīn | noise | (top, left) |
| 食 | shí | food; nourishment | (bottom; right)   see also 饣 |
| 香 | xiāng | scent | (left; bottom) |
| 鬼 | guǐ | spirit; ghost | (variable) |
| 骨 | gú; gǔ | bone | (left) |

10 strokes

| | | | |
|---|---|---|---|
| 高 | gāo | big; tall | (left; top) |
| 鬲 | lì | clay pot with three feet | (bottom) |

11 strokes

| | | | |
|---|---|---|---|
| 鹿 | lù | roebuck; stag | (variable) |
| 麻 | má | hemp; smallpox scars | (two sides) |

12 strokes

| | | | |
|---|---|---|---|
| 黑 | hēi | black | (variable) |

13 strokes

| | | | |
|---|---|---|---|
| 鼓 | gǔ | drum | (top) |
| 鼠 | shǔ | mouse; rat | (left) |

14 strokes

| | | | |
|---|---|---|---|
| 鼻 | bí | nose | (left) |

## Using a Chinese Dictionary

In most dictionaries there are basically two different ways to look up a Chinese character: either by the pronunciation, that is, the Pīnyīn transcription, or under the radical of a character.

If you know the pronunciation of the character you're looking for:

First, you have to convert the pronunciation correctly into the Pīnyīn transcription, and then you can look up the word in the alphabetically arranged dictionary, keeping the four tones in mind.

If you don't know the pronunciation of the character you're looking for:

**Step 1:** Try to identify the radical of the character under which it is listed in your dictionary, and count its strokes. In the table of radicals, all the radicals are arranged according to the number of their strokes and provided with numbers. If you don't have any experience with radicals yet, then you can go through the table of radicals in your dictionary until you find similarities with the character you're looking for.

**Step 2:** Once you've found the radical, note the number that follows it! Under this number, you will find in the table for looking up Chinese characters (检字表 jiǎnzìbiǎo) every character that contains this radical. If there are a large number of characters with this radical, simply count the remaining number of strokes (number of strokes minus the presumed radical), and then you can search more quickly and more selectively.

**Step 3:** If you still haven't found the character, either you haven't looked under the correct radical or you miscounted the remaining number of strokes. You need to start over at Step 1, continuing your search with another radical. If you still haven't found the character after several attempts, then it is also possible that it was not included in the dictionary.

**Step 4:** You've guessed the correct radical and have also found the complete character in the second list, the table for looking up Chinese characters (检字表 jiǎnzìbiǎo). Now all you have to do is look for the page number given or the Pīnyīn transcription in the dictionary.

Exercise

Try to find the character 茶 by following the four steps just described.

## Checklist for Learning Chinese Systematically

**Really put your mind to it, and divide your study sessions into smaller blocks!**

1.  First, skim the entire book, and at the same time read a travel guidebook for China that also contains background information about the country.
2.  Practice the correct pronunciation, using the phonetics exercises in the introduction to this book.
3.  Keep looking at the list of radicals in the introduction. That will help you develop a feeling for the structure of the characters.
4.  Write the characters from the vocabulary lists, using the appropriate list for the sequence and direction of the strokes. It is best to use a calligraphy brush or a soft pencil for this purpose.
5.  Write characters every day—until your hand has "memorized" the character.
6.  For words of more than one syllable, also memorize the meaning of the individual characters. They will crop up repeatedly in other combinations.

7.  Make little vocabulary cards, and learn to read the words from the "vocabulary section" and write them from memory. The cards will give you a good overview of what you have just learned.
8.  Buy a modern Chinese-English, English-Chinese dictionary, so you can independently look up characters that occur in the vocabulary lists or in the semantic fields.
9.  On the two audio CDs, you will find examples of syllables from the introductory chapter, as well as all the vocabulary words, sample sentences, and semantic fields contained in the book. Use the CDs to practice your pronunciation, but also to test your knowledge of vocabulary and thus improve your listening comprehension.
10. Finally, commit the individual sample sentences to memory. Link them with places such as Chinese cities or provinces in order to memorize them more easily. The sample sentences are presented in the same way in each lesson.
    **Example**
    Characters
    > 中国有啤酒，也有绿茶。
    Pīnyīn transcription
    > Zhōngguó yǒu píjiǔ, yě yǒu lǜchá。
    Literal translation
    > *China / have / beer, / also / have / green tea.*
    Correct translation
    > In China, there is beer and green tea.
11. The grammatical explanations that are important for you to learn are integrated into the "Sample Sentences" section. In the back of the book, you will find a summary of the most important phenomena of Chinese grammar.

12. Keep repeating the sample sentences. In that way you will automatically learn the grammar.
13. Use the semantic fields to enlarge your personal vocabulary and practice your pronunciation. Write the characters that appear in the semantic fields only when you are sure of the sequence of the strokes. Otherwise, you will simply be memorizing mistakes in writing.
14. Use the semantic fields when you visit a Chinese restaurant and want to order authentic Chinese dishes.
15. Take the book along when you travel. Each lesson is paired with an administrative unit of China, to make it easier for you to find specific places of interest and other destinations by taxi and train when you're on a trip.
16. Do the exercises contained in each chapter. You will find the answers in the back of the book.

People's Republic of China
中华人民共和国
Zhōnghuá Rénmín Gònghéguó
Area: 3.7 million square miles
Population: 1.3 billion
Time: Central European Time (CET) + 7 hours
National holiday: October 1

When bargaining in markets, ordering in restaurants, and purchasing tickets at ticket windows, you will find that written Arabic numerals are understood and sometimes even displayed on pocket calculators. To allow for all contingencies, however, you should not only learn to say the numbers from 1 to 10, but also learn to use the hand signs shown here.

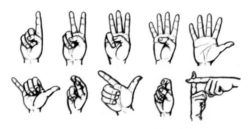

## Vocabulary

| | | |
|---|---|---|
| 一 | yī | one; pronounced yāo in telephone and room numbers |
| 二 | èr | two |
| 三 | sān | three |
| 四 | sì | four |
| 五 | wǔ | five |
| 六 | liù | six |
| 七 | qī | seven |
| 八 | bā | eight |
| 九 | jiǔ | nine |
| 十 | shí | ten |
| 中国 | Zhōngguó | China (*middle / land, kingdom*) |
| 有 | yǒu | to have, there is/are |
| 酒 | jiǔ | alcohol |
| 啤酒 | píjiǔ | beer (*beer / alcohol*) |
| 也 | yě | also, too |
| 茶 | chá | tea |
| 绿茶 | lǜchá | green tea (*green / tea*) |
| 和 | hé | and (does not link clauses) |
| 这里 | zhèli | *here* (southern Chinese variant; *this / suffix*), synonymous with 这儿 zhèr |
| 这儿 | zhèr | *here* (northern Chinese variant; *this / suffix*), synonymous with 这里 zhèli |
| 没 | méi | not (have); negates the verb yǒu 有 |
| 没有 | méi yǒu | not have, there isn't/aren't; without (*not / have*) |
| 吗 | ma | interrogative particle at end of sentence |
| 花茶 | huāchá | flavored green tea, usually jasmine tea (*flower, blossom / tea*) |

| | | |
|---|---|---|
| 可口可乐 | kěkǒu kělè | Coca-Cola (*can / mouth / can / pleasure*); colloquial 可乐 kělè |
| 开水 | kāishuǐ | boiled water (*boil, cook / water*) |

## Sample Sentences

**Topic 1: Declarative sentence with yǒu 有**
(see Grammar)

中国有啤酒。
Zhōngguó yǒu píjiǔ.
*China / have / beer.*
There is beer in China.

The most common word order in simple declarative sentences is subject–predicate–object. In this case, you always use the basic form of the verb and the noun, because Chinese has neither conjugation nor declension. The English word "there" is not translated because it does not contribute to the meaning of the sentence.

**Topic 2: The Adverb yě 也**

中国有啤酒，也有绿茶。
Zhōngguó yǒu píjiǔ, yě yǒu lǜchá.
*China / have / beer, / also / have / green tea.*
There is beer and green tea in China.

In clauses that English would link with "and," Chinese often uses yě 也 as a conjunction. Yě 也 is an adverb; it always precedes a verb or an adjective.

> ### Info Box
>
> When two third tones occur together, as in the case of yě yǒu 也有, the first "third tone" is pronounced as a second tone. The spelling does not change, however.

**Topic 3: The Conjunction hé 和**

中国有啤酒和绿茶。
Zhōngguó yǒu píjiǔ hé lǜchá.
*China / have / beer / and / green tea.*
There is beer and green tea in China.

The conjunction hé 和 can be used to link individual nouns in enumerations but not to connect clauses.

> ### Info Box
>
> **Tone change with** yī 一, qī 七, **and** bā 八
> yī, qī, and bā in dates and numbers
> yí, qí, and bá before a syllable in the fourth tone or before a toneless syllable that originally had the fourth tone
> yì, qì, and bà before a syllable in the first, second, or third tone

**Topic 4: Negation with méi yǒu 没有**

这里没有花茶。
Zhèli méi yǒu huāchá.
*Here / not (have) / have / flavored tea.*
There is no flavored tea here.

If you want to negate a sentence that is formed with the verb yǒu 有, place the adverb méi 没 directly before yǒu 有. Méi 没 can be used in all tenses.

这里没有花茶，也没有可口可乐。
Zhèli méi yǒu huāchá, yě méi yǒu kěkǒu kělè.
*Here / not (have) / have / flavored tea, / or / not (have) / have / Coca-Cola.*
There is neither flavored tea nor Coca-Cola here.

## Writing Exercises

Write the characters with the correct sequence and direction of strokes, and mark the radical. It's a good idea to lay a transparent sheet of paper over the characters first, and then go over the strokes before you try to write freehand.

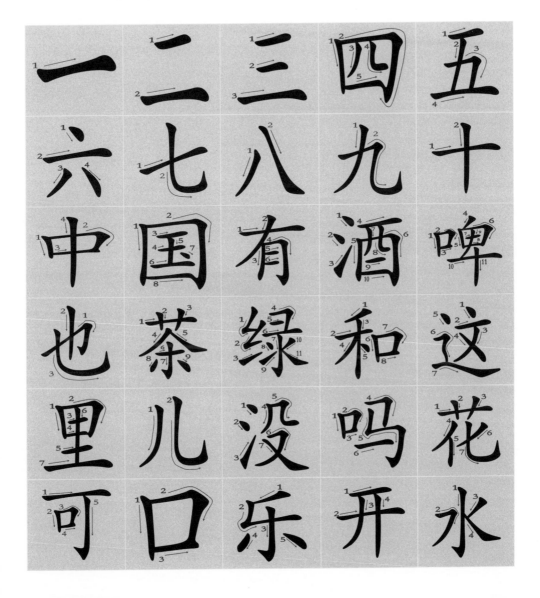

Two negated parts of a sentence can also be linked with yě 也.

In this case, the verb absolutely must be repeated; otherwise, the sentence is incomplete and incomprehensible.

这里没开水。
Zhèli méi kāishuǐ。
*Here / not (have) / boiled water.*
There is no boiled water here.

Méi 没 can also be used without yǒu 有, if an object follows.

### Topic 5: Interrogative Sentences with the Interrogative Particle ma 吗
(see Grammar)

这里有开水吗?
Zhèli yǒu kāishuǐ ma?
*Here / have / boiled water / interrogative particle?*
*Is there boiled water here?*

In an interrogative sentence with ma 吗, the structure of the declarative sentence is retained. Only the addition of ma 吗 at the end of the declarative sentence makes it into a question..

### Topic 6: Interrogative Sentence with the Positive-Negative Question yǒu méi yǒu 有没有

这里有没有开水?
Zhèli yǒu méi yǒu kāishuǐ?
*Here / have / not (have) / have / boiled water?*
Is there boiled water here?

In this type of question, the positive (affirmative) form comes first, followed immediately by the negative (negated) form of the verb. It is also known as a "verb-not-verb" construction. The particle ma 吗 is no longer required. The meaning is the same as that of a question with ma 吗, however.

### Topic 7: Positive Answer
有。
Yǒu。
*There is/are; have.*
Yes.

Chinese lacks a word for "yes." Instead, the verb used in the question is repeated in the answer, in this case yǒu 有.

### Topic 8: Negative Answer
没有。
Méi yǒu。
*Not (have) / have.*
No.

In a negative answer, generally the verb used in the question is negated. If no object follows, méi 没 cannot be used alone in the meaning "No."

## Info Box

Use the semantic fields to practice your pronunciation. There is no need for you to learn how to write the characters yourself, but passive knowledge of them will help you find your way around a Chinese menu and feel at ease in other "danger zones" that you may encounter as a tourist.

## Semantic Fields

Nonalcoholic Beverages

| | | |
|---|---|---|
| cappuccino | pàomò kāfēi | 泡沫咖啡 |
| Dragon Fountain tea | lóngjǐngchá | 龙井茶 |
| iced tea | bīngchá | 冰茶 |
| iced coffee | bīngkāfēi | 冰咖啡 |
| espresso | nóngsuō kāfēi | 浓缩咖啡 |

| | | |
|---|---|---|
| hot chocolate | rè qiǎokèlì | 热巧克力 |
| instant coffee | sùróng kāfēi | 速溶咖啡 |
| jasmine tea | mòlìhuāchá | 茉莉花茶 |
| coffee | kāfēi | 咖啡 |
| coconut milk | yēnǎi | 椰奶 |
| soft drink | qìshuǐ | 汽水 |
| milk | niúnǎi | 牛奶 |
| milkshake | nǎixī | 奶昔 |
| mineral water | kuàngquánshuǐ | 矿泉水 |
| Oolong tea | wūlóngchá | 乌龙茶 |
| orange juice | chéngzhī | 橙汁 |
| Pepsi-Cola | bǎishì kělè | 百事可乐 |
| juice | guǒzhī | 果汁 |
| black tea | hóngchá | 红茶 |
| soy milk | dòujiāng | 豆浆 |
| Sprite | xuěbì | 雪碧 |
| "Eight Treasures" tea | bābǎochá | 八宝茶 |

| Alcoholic Beverages | | |
|---|---|---|
| draft beer | zhāpí | 扎啤 |
| cocktail | jīwěijiǔ | 鸡尾酒 |
| dark beer | hēipí | 黑啤 |
| fermented millet beverage or "wine" | gāoliángjiǔ | 高粱酒 |
| Maotai (liquor) | Máotáijiǔ | 茅台酒 |
| Qingdao/Tsingtao beer | Qīngdǎo píjiǔ | 青岛啤酒 |
| rice wine | huángjiǔ | 黄酒 |
| red wine | hóng pútaojiǔ | 红葡萄酒 |
| baijiu, rice alcohol | báijiǔ | 白酒 |
| sparkling wine | xiāngbīnjiǔ | 香槟酒 |

| | | |
|---|---|---|
| wine | pútaojiǔ | 葡萄酒 |
| beer brewed from wheat | báipí | 白啤 |
| white wine | báipútaojiǔ | 白葡萄酒 |
| whiskey | Wēishìjìjiǔ | 威士忌酒 |

## Exercises

### Exercise 1

Play mahjong (mah-jongg), and say the numbers in Chinese. You'll find the rules of the game at *www.ChinaCoachingCenter.de.*

### Exercise 2

Which synonymous component do the following characters have:
茶，花，茉，莉，葡，萄？

### Exercise 3

Write the sample sentences in different versions, using the words from the vocabulary list.

### Exercise 4

Say the sample sentences out loud, using words from the semantic fields. Form sentences with the pyramid method: Take any word and add one word at a time to it until you've made a complete sentence.

Example:
pí jiǔ
yǒu pí jiǔ
zhèli yǒu pí jiǔ
zhèli yǒu pí jiǔ ma

### Exercise 5

On the audio CD, listen to the vocabulary words, sample sentences, and semantic fields and repeat them after the speaker.

## Exercise 6

First, write the following sentences in Pīnyīn, including the marks for the tones, and then translate them into English.

1. 这儿有绿茶吗？
2. 这里没有可口可乐。
3. 中国有没有花茶？
4. 没有啤酒，也没有开水。

## Exercise 7

Using the Pīnyīn transcription in the (online) dictionary, find the meaning of the following words.

1. Fēngshuǐ 风水
2. Gōngfu 功夫
3. Qìgōng 气功
4. Tàijíquán 太极拳

## Exercise 8

Translate the following sentences into Chinese.

1. There is green tea in China.

_ _ _ _ _ _ _ _ _ _ _ _ _ _ _ _ _ _ _ _ _ _ _

2. There is Coca-Cola and beer here.

_ _ _ _ _ _ _ _ _ _ _ _ _ _ _ _ _ _ _ _ _ _ _

3. There is no water here.

_ _ _ _ _ _ _ _ _ _ _ _ _ _ _ _ _ _ _ _ _ _ _

4. There is also flavored tea here.

_ _ _ _ _ _ _ _ _ _ _ _ _ _ _ _ _ _ _ _ _ _ _

5. Is there alcohol here?

_ _ _ _ _ _ _ _ _ _ _ _ _ _ _ _ _ _ _ _ _ _ _

6. No, there is neither boiled water nor tea here.

_ _ _ _ _ _ _ _ _ _ _ _ _ _ _ _ _ _ _ _ _ _ _

Běijīng 北京

Abbbreviation: Jīng 京

Capital of the People's Republic of China

Directly subordinate to central government,
  with five counties

Area: 6,486 square miles

Population: 13.82 million

Number of persons / square mile: 2,108

## Vocabulary

| | | |
|---|---|---|
| 我 | wǒ | I |
| 的 | de | particle for indicating attribution or possession (genitive) |
| 我的 | wǒde | my, mine (I / attributive particle) |
| 你 | nǐ | you |
| 你的 | nǐde | your (you / attributive particle) |
| 他 | tā | he |
| 他的 | tāde | his (he / attributive particle) |
| 她 | tā | she |
| 她的 | tāde | her (she / attributive particle) |
| 电话 | diànhuà | telephone (electricity / speech) |
| 号码 | hàoma | number (number / number) |
| 电话号码 | diànhuà hàoma | telephone number (electricity / speech / number / number) |
| 是 | shì | to be |
| 零 | líng | 0, zero |
| 多 | duō | much |
| 少 | shǎo | little |
| 多少 | duōshǎo | how much? (much / little) |
| 不 | bù | no, not |
| 什么 | shénme | what? what kind of ... (diverse / suffix) |
| 喝 | hē | to drink |
| 喝酒 | hē jiǔ | to drink alcohol (drink / alcohol) |
| 吃 | chī | to eat |
| 吃饭 | chī fàn | to eat (eat / boiled rice) |
| 几 | jǐ | how many (pieces)?; some (pieces); always followed by a measure word (MW), or "counter" |
| 个 | gè | generic measure word (MW) |
| 北京 | Běijīng | Beijing, Peking (north / capital) |
| 烤鸭 | kǎoyā | roast duck (grill, roast in oven / duck) 只 |
| 北京烤鸭 | Běijīng kǎoyā | Peking duck (north / capital / grill / duck); MW: zhī 只 |
| 在 | zài | to be (located) in a place, in, at |
| 李 | Lǐ | Li (Chinese surname: Plum) |
| ... 女士 | nǚshì | Ms. ...; form of address for women, regardless of marital status (woman / respected person, scholar) |

| 王 | Wáng | Wang (Chinese surname: *King*) |
| ...先生 | xiānsheng | Mr. ...; husband (*before, first / bear, give birth*) |
| 马 | Mǎ | Ma (Chinese surname: *Horse*) |
| ...小姐 | xiǎojie | Miss ... (*little / older sister*) |

## Info Box

**The Measure Word (MW) gè 个**

The measure word (MW), or counter, gè 个 is one of many. It is used before nouns that have no more specific measure words. In the course of working with this book, you will come across several other measure words (see Grammar in the back of the book). If you ever forget the appropriate MW, however, you can substitute gè 个 for it.

## Sample Sentences

Topic 1: Declarative Sentence with shì 是

我的电话号码是零八九八八九七一五九九。

Wǒde diànhuà hàoma shi líng-bā-jiǔ-bā-bā-jiǔ-qī-yāo-wǔ-jiǔ-jiǔ。

*My / telephone number / be*
*08988971599.*

My telephone number is 089-88 97 15 99.

The subject of the sentence is "telephone number." To express "my telephone number," the personal pronoun wǒ 我 and the attributive particle de 的 must be placed in front of the subject. Thus "wǒde diànhuàhàomǎ" 我的电话号码 is a possessive attributive construction with diànhuàhàomǎ 电话号码 as the word modified.

## Info Box

Caution: When you read sentences with attributive constructions, always look for the word modified first, and then start to translate.

The word modified always follows the attributive particle de 的.

Sentences with shì 是 and another expression (here: combination of numerals) as a predicate are called shì 是-sentences; in such cases, shì 是 is pronounced as toneless.

With combinations of numerals such as telephone numbers and room numbers with more than three places, all the numerals are spoken separately, and no numbers are formed.

Topic 2: Interrogative Sentence with shì 是 and Question Word

你的电话号码是多少？

Nǐde diànhuà hàoma shi duōshǎo?
*Your / telephone number / be / how much?*
What is your telephone number?

The structure of the question is identical to that of the declarative statement.

Topic 3: Negation with bú shì 不是 (see Grammar)

我的电话号码不是零八一零五三七七一六一。

Wǒde diànhuà hàoma bú shi líng-bā-yāo-líng-wǔ-sān-qī-qī-yāo-liù-yāo。
*My / telephone number / not / be /*
*08105377161.*
My telephone number is not 08105-377161.

To negate shì 是, use bù 不. Then bù 不 precedes shì 是 and is pronounced here in the second tone, as bú 不.

Bù 不 always changes from the second tone to the fourth tone when it directly precedes a word in the fourth tone.

## Writing Exercises

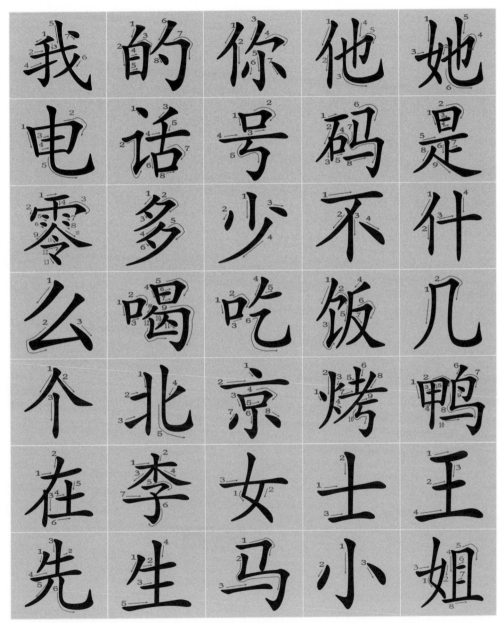

我 的 你 他 她
电 话 号 码 是
零 多 少 不 什
么 喝 吃 饭 几
个 北 京 烤 鸭
在 李 女 士 王
先 生 马 小 姐

Topic 4: Interrogative Sentence with Verb and Question Word
他喝什么？
Tā hē shénme？
*He / drink / what?*
What is he drinking?

Here too, the question has the same structure as the declarative sentence. The interrogative particle ma 吗 is not required here because a question word is already present.

**Answer**
他喝酒，不喝茶。
Tā hē jiǔ，bù hē chá。
*He / drink / alcohol, / not / drink / tea.*
He is drinking alcohol, not tea.

Clauses that are joined with "and" in English require no direct equivalent of "and" in Chinese. Instead, only a comma or a short pause in speaking is necessary. However, in Chinese the verb of the sentence must be repeated. Under no circumstances should you use hé 和 here.

> **Info Box**
>
> For the polite form of address on official occasions, nín 您 is used instead of nǐ 你 to mean "you." However because only 你 nǐ is generally used in colloquial speech, especially in southern China, this book does not use nín 您.

Topic 5: Interrogative Sentences with shénme 什么 in Adjective Position
(see Grammar)
他喝什么茶？
Tā hē shénme chá？
*He / drink / what kind of / tea?*
What kind of tea is he drinking?

Shénme 什么 can also be used as an adjective directly before a noun.

**Answer**
他喝绿茶。
Tā hē lǜchá。
*He / drink / green tea.*
He is drinking green tea.

The sentence structure remains the same as in the question.

Topic 6: The Question Word jǐ 几 and the Generic MW ge 个
(see Grammar)
她吃几个北京烤鸭？
Tā chī jǐge Běijīng kǎoyā？
*She / eat / how many MW / Peking roast duck?*
How many Peking ducks does she eat?

As soon as you count things by the piece, you have to put the MW ge 个 between the number and the object counted, and thus also between the question word and the object to be counted. (This is analogous to English "three sheets of paper" or "How many sheets of paper?")

**Answer**
她吃一个。
Tā chī yíge。
*She / eat / one MW.*
She eats one.

If the context makes it clear which object is under discussion, it is sufficient to give only the number and the MW, without the noun.

> **Info Box**
>
> In colloquial speech, ge 个 may be added as a measure word even if there were to be a more suitable MW. In the case of ducks, the MW would be zhī 只 (see semantic field "Animals," page 96).

### Topic 7: Declarative Sentences with zài 在

他在。
Tā zài。
*He / be located.*
He is in.

If nothing follows zài, then it means "to be in."

他在中国。
Tā zài Zhōngguó。
*He / be located / China.*
He is in China.

If a variation of the infinitive "to be" can be translated into English with "to be located / situated," then zài 在 is used in Chinese.

### Negation

他不在北京。
Tā bú zài Běijīng。
*He / not / be located / Beijing.*
He is not in Beijing.

The negation of zài 在 is accomplished by using bù 不，which always precedes zài 在 and is then spoken in the second (rising) tone because a fourth tone follows.

李女士和王先生在北京吃饭。
Lǐ nǚshì hé Wáng xiānsheng zài Běijīng chī fàn。
*Li / Ms. / and / Wang / Mr. / be located / Beijing / eat / boiled rice.*
Ms. Li and Mr. Wang are eating in Beijing.

If zài 在 XXXX is followed by another verb, it is translated simply as "in, at." To express merely that Ms. Li is in Beijing and it is not important what she is eating, you attach the noun fàn 饭 as an object to chī 吃。

马小姐在北京吃北京烤鸭，也喝啤酒。
Mǎ xiǎojie zài Běijīng chī Běijīng kǎoyā, yě hē píjiǔ。
*Ma / Miss / be located / Beijing / eat / Peking roast duck, / also / drink / beer.*
Miss Ma is eating Peking duck in Beijing and drinking beer.

If a specific dish is mentioned, then fàn 饭 is omitted and replaced with the name of a dish or a food item.

| Semantic Fields | | |  |
|---|---|---|---|
| Places of Interest | míngshèng gǔjī | 名胜古迹 | |
| Chinese "court-yard residence" | Sìhéyuàn | 四合院 | |

| | | |
|---|---|---|
| ancient alleys or lanes in Beijing | Hútòng | 胡同 |
| Great Wall | Chángchéng | 长城 |
| Temple of Heaven | Tiāntán | 天坛 |
| Forbidden City (Palace Museum) | Gùgōng | 故宫 |
| Lama Temple | Yōnghégōng | 雍和宫 |
| Ming Dynasty Tombs | Míng Shísān Líng | 明十三陵 |
| Tiananmen Square | Tiān'ānmén Guǎngchǎng | 天安门广场 |
| Summer Palace | Yíhéyuán | 颐和园 |

| Means of Communication | | |
|---|---|---|
| answering machine | liúyánjī | 留言机 |
| letter | xìn | 信 |
| stamp | yóupiào | 邮票 |
| browser | liúlǎnqì | 浏览器 |
| CD-ROM | guāngpán | 光盘 |
| computer | diànnǎo | 电脑 |
| printer | dǎyìnjī | 打印机 |
| eMail | diànzǐ yóujiàn | 电子邮件 |
| fax | chuánzhēn | 传真 |
| photocopier | fùyìnjī | 复印机 |
| cell phone | shǒujī | 手机 |
| home page | zhǔyè | 主页 |
| illustrated magazine | huàbào | 画报 |
| Internet | yīntèwǎng | 因特网 |
| map | dìtú | 地图 |
| laptop / notebook | bǐjìběn diànnǎo | 笔记本电脑 |
| mouse | lǎoshǔ | 老鼠 |
| modem | māo | 猫 |
| MP3 player | MP3-bōfàngqì | MP3-播放器 |
| PDA, personal digital assistant | zhǎngshàngbǎo | 掌上宝 |

| | | |
|---|---|---|
| package | bāoguǒ | 包裹 |
| post office | yóujú | 邮局 |
| postcard | míngxìnpiàn | 明信片 |
| radio | shōuyīnjī | 收音机 |
| calculator | jìsuànjī | 计算机 |
| scanner | sǎomiáoyí | 扫描仪 |
| daily newspaper | rìbào | 日报 |
| telephone | diànhuà | 电话 |
| (tele)phone card | diànhuàkǎ | 电话卡 |
| business card | míngpiàn | 名片 |
| dictionary | cídiǎn | 词典 |
| magazine | zázhì | 杂志 |
| newspaper | bàozhǐ | 报纸 |

| Terms of Address | | |
|---|---|---|
| doctor | dàifu | 大夫 |
| mayor | shìzhǎng | 市长 |
| boss | lǎobǎn | 老板 |
| director | zhǔrèn | 主任 |
| doctor (academic title) | bóshì | 博士 |
| Ms./Mrs., wife | tàitai | 太太 |
| Miss | xiǎojie | 小姐 |
| chief executive, managing director | zǒngjīnglǐ | 总经理 |
| Mr. | xiānsheng | 先生 |
| teacher | lǎoshī | 老师 |
| manager | jīnglǐ | 经理 |
| master | shīfu | 师傅 |
| uncle | shūshu | 叔叔 |
| party secretary | shūjì | 书记 |
| professor | jiàoshòu | 教授 |
| aunt | āyí | 阿姨 |
| deputy manager | fùzǒngjīnglǐ | 副总经理 |

## Exercises

### Exercise 1

Write your telephone number, including the area code, in Chinese characters and in Pīnyīn and learn to say it from memory in Chinese.

### Exercise 2

Which synonymous components do the following characters have:
他，你，信，件，传，傅？

### Exercise 3

Write different versions of the sample sentences, using the words from the vocabulary list.

### Exercise 4

Read the sample sentences aloud, using words from the semantic fields. Create sentences by using the pyramid method.

Example:
Běijīng
zài Běijīng
wǒ zài Běijīng
wǒ zài Běijīng chī
wǒ zài Běijīng chī Běijīng
wǒ zài Běijīng chī Běijīng kǎoyā

### Exercise 5

Listen to the sample sentences on the audio CD, and then repeat them after the speaker.

### Exercise 6

First write the following sentences in Pīnyīn, marking the tones, and then translate them into English.

1. 你的电话号码不是零一七九三八六二五四二。
2. 北京在中国。
3. 马先生吃我的北京烤鸭，喝我的啤酒。
4. 你喝什么？
5. 我在这里。

### Exercise 7

Using the Pīnyīn transcription in the (online) dictionary, find the meanings of the following words.

1. Máo Zédōng 毛泽东
2. Dèng Xiǎopíng 邓小平
3. Jiāng Zémín 江泽民
4. Hú Jīntāo 胡锦涛

### Exercise 8

Translate the following sentences into Chinese.

1. She is eating Peking duck and drinking flavored tea.

_ _ _ _ _ _ _ _ _ _ _ _ _ _ _ _ _ _ _

2. What kind of beer is he drinking?

_ _ _ _ _ _ _ _ _ _ _ _ _ _ _ _ _ _ _

3. Ms. Wang doesn't drink alcohol.

_ _ _ _ _ _ _ _ _ _ _ _ _ _ _ _ _ _ _

4. I also eat Peking duck in China.

_ _ _ _ _ _ _ _ _ _ _ _ _ _ _ _ _ _ _

5. I don't have a telephone.

_ _ _ _ _ _ _ _ _ _ _ _ _ _ _ _ _ _ _

6. Is there a telephone here?

_ _ _ _ _ _ _ _ _ _ _ _ _ _ _ _ _ _ _

7. Mr. Li is in.

_ _ _ _ _ _ _ _ _ _ _ _ _ _ _ _ _ _ _

# 3    Shǎnxī 陕西

Province: Shǎnxī 陕西

Abbreviations: Shǎn 陕 or Qín 秦

Capital of province: Xī'ān 西安

88 counties, 13 cities

Area: 79,383 square miles

Population: 36.05 million

Number of persons / square mile: 449

## Vocabulary

| | | |
|---|---|---|
| 百 | bǎi | hundred |
| 千 | qiān | thousand |
| 笼 | lóng | bamboo steamer that fits over a pot |
| 包子 | bāozi | steamed, filled yeast buns (*wrap up / suffix*) |
| 钱 | qián | money |
| 多少钱 | duōshǎo qián | How much does it cost? (*much / little / money*) |
| 元 | yuán | yuan (largest unit of a currency) |
| 块 | kuài | kuai, colloquial term for yuan (*piece*) |
| 角 | jiǎo | jiao, 10 cents (*horn*) |
| 毛 | máo | mao, 10 cents, colloquial term for jiao (*hair, wool*) |
| 分 | fēn | fen, cent (*part*) |
| 买 | mǎi | to buy |
| 这 | zhè | this |
| 这个 | zhège | this (*this / MW*) |
| 两 | liǎng | two; liang (50 grams) |
| 饺子 | jiǎozi | crescent-shaped dumplings made of noodle dough (*jiaozi / suffix*) |
| 太 | tài | too, far too, overly |

| | | |
|---|---|---|
| 贵 | guì | expensive |
| 太贵 | tài guì | too expensive (*overly / expensive*) |
| 欧元 | Ōuyuán | euro (*Europe / unit*) |
| 人民币 | Rénmínbì | renminbi, RMB (*person / people / currency*) |
| 请 | qǐng | to request; to invite; please |
| 便宜 | piányi | cheap (*favorable / suitable*) |
| 一点 | yìdiǎn | a little (*one / dot*) |
| 便宜一点 | piányi yìdiǎn | cheaper (*favorable / suitable / one / dot*) |
| 们 | –men | plural suffix |
| 我们 | wǒmen | we (*I / plural suffix*) |
| 我们的 | wǒmende | our (*I / plural suffix / attributive particle*) |
| 你们 | nǐmen | you (pl.) (*you sg. / plural suffix*) |
| 你们的 | nǐmende | your (pl.) (*you sg. / plural suffix / attributive particle*) |
| 他们 | tāmen | they (*he / plural suffix*) |
| 他们的 | tāmende | their (*he / plural suffix / attributive particle*) |
| 她们 | tāmen | they (*they / plural suffix*) |
| 她们的 | tāmende | their (*they / plural suffix / attributive particle*) |

## Writing Exercises

| 百 | 千 | 笼 | 包 | 子 |
|---|---|---|---|---|
| 钱 | 元 | 块 | 角 | 毛 |
| 分 | 买 | 两 | 饺 | 太 |
| 贵 | 欧 | 人 | 民 | 币 |
| 请 | 便 | 宜 | 点 | 们 |

## Info Box

The character 子 has two basic pronunciations: stressed zǐ or unstressed zi. Thus it is pronounced in the third tone when it occurs in its original meaning as a pictogram for "child" or "son" or as an honorific for a learned man, as in Kǒngzǐ 孔子 (Confucius). In the compound words "jiaozi" and "baozi," 子 is a suffix for nouns and remains unstressed.

## The Chinese Numbers

### Numbers from 10 to 999

| | 10–19 | 20–29 | ... | 100–109 | 110–119 | 120–129 |
|---|---|---|---|---|---|---|
| 0s | shí 十 | èrshí 二十 | | yìbǎi 一百 | yìbǎi yìshí 一百一十一 | yìbǎi èrshí 一百二十 |
| 1s | shíyī 十一 | èrshíyī 二十一 | | yìbǎi língyī 一百零一 | yìbǎi yìshíyī 一百一十一 | yìbǎi èrshíyī 一百二十一 |
| 2s | shí'èr 十二 | èrshí'èr 二十二 | | yìbǎi líng'èr 一百零二 | yìbǎi yìshí'èr 一百一十二 | yìbǎi èrshí'èr 一百二十二 |
| 3s | shísān 十三 | èrshísān 二十三 | | yìbǎi yìbǎi língsān 一百零三 | yìbǎi yìshísān 一百一十三 | yìbǎi èrshísān 一百二十三 |
| 4s | shísì 十四 | èrshísì 二十四 | | yìbǎi língsì 一百零四 | yìbǎi yìshísì 一百一十四 | yìbǎi èrshísì 一百二十四 |
| 5s | shíwǔ 十五 | èrshíwǔ 二十五 | | yìbǎi língwǔ 一百零五 | yìbǎi yìshíwǔ 一百一十五 | yìbǎi èrshíwǔ 一百二十五 |
| 6s | shíliù 十六 | èrshíliù 二十六 | | yìbǎi língliù 一百零六 | yìbǎi yìshíliù 一百一十六 | yìbǎi èrshíliù 一百二十六 |
| 7s | shíqī 十七 | èrshíqī 二十七 | | yìbǎi língqī 一百零七 | yìbǎi yìshíqī 一百一十七 | yìbǎi èrshíqī 一百二十七 |
| 8s | shíbā 十八 | èrshíbā 二十八 | | yìbǎi língbā 一百零八 | yìbǎi yìshíbā 一百一十八 | yìbǎi èrshíbā 一百二十八 |
| 9s | shíjiǔ 十九 | èrshíjiǔ 二十九 | | yìbǎi língjiǔ 一百零九 | yìbǎi yìshíjiǔ 一百一十九 | yìbǎi èrshíjiǔ 一百二十九 |

When 2 appears in the ones or tens place, it is read as "èr":
2 èr, 12 shí'èr, 22 èrshí'èr.
In the hundreds place, it can be read as "èr" or „liǎng": 200 èrbǎi/liǎngbǎi.

In the thousands place and above, it should be read as "liǎng":
2,222 liǎng qiān èrbǎi èrshí'èr
or
liǎng qiān liǎngbǎi èrshí'èr

Numbers from 1,000 to 9,999

| | 1000 – 1009 | 1010 – 1019 | 1020 – 1029 | ... | 1100 – 1109 | 1110 – 1119 |
|---|---|---|---|---|---|---|
| 0s | yìqiān<br><br>一千 | yìqiān líng yìshí<br><br>一千零一十 | yìqiān líng èrshí<br><br>一千零二十 | | yìqiān yìbǎi<br><br>一千一百 | yìqiān yìbǎi yìshí<br><br>一千一百一十 |
| 1s | yìqiān líng yī<br><br>一千零一 | yìqiān líng yìshíyī<br><br>一千零一十一 | yìqiān líng èrshíyī<br><br>一千零二十一 | | yìqiān yìbǎi líng yī<br><br>一千一百零一 | yìqiān yìbǎi yìshí yī<br><br>一千一百一十一 |
| 2s | yìqiān líng èr<br><br>一千零二 | yìqiān líng yìshí'èr<br><br>一千零一十二 | yìqiān líng èrshí'èr<br><br>一千零二十二 | | yìqiān yìbǎi líng èr<br><br>一千一百零二 | yìqiān yìbǎi yìshí'èr<br><br>一千一百一十二 |
| 3s | yìqiān líng sān<br><br>一千零三 | yìqiān líng yìshísān<br><br>一千零一十三 | yìqiān líng èrshísān<br><br>一千零二十三 | | yìqiān yìbǎi líng sān<br><br>一千一百零三 | yìqiān yìbǎi yìshísān<br><br>一千一百一十三 |
| 4s | yìqiān líng sì<br><br>一千零四 | yìqiān líng yìshísì<br><br>一千零一十四 | yìqiān líng èrshísì<br><br>一千零二十四 | | yìqiān yìbǎi líng sì<br><br>一千一百零四 | yìqiān yìbǎi yìshísì<br><br>一千一百一十四 |
| 5s | yìqiān líng wǔ<br><br>一千零五 | yìqiān líng yìshíwǔ<br><br>一千零一十五 | yìqiān líng èrshí wǔ<br><br>一千零二十五 | | yìqiān yìbǎi líng wǔ<br><br>一千一百零五 | yìqiān yìbǎi yìshíwǔ<br><br>一千一百一十五 |
| 6s | yìqiān líng liù<br><br>一千零六 | yìqiān líng yìshíliù<br><br>一千零一十六 | yìqiān líng èrshíliù<br><br>一千零二十六 | | yìqiān yìbǎi líng liù<br><br>一千一百零六 | yìqiān yìbǎi yìshíliù<br><br>一千一百一十六 |
| 7s | yìqiān líng qī<br><br>一千零七 | yìqiān líng yìshíqī<br><br>一千零一十七 | yìqiān líng èrshíqī<br><br>一千零二十七 | | yìqiān yìbǎi líng qī<br><br>一千一百零七 | yìqiān yìbǎi yìshíqī<br><br>一千一百一十七 |
| 8s | yìqiān líng bā<br><br>一千零八 | yìqiān líng yìshíbā<br><br>一千零一十八 | yìqiān líng èrshíbā<br><br>一千零二十八 | | yìqiān yìbǎi líng bā<br><br>一千一百零八 | yìqiān yìbǎi yìshíbā<br><br>一千一百一十八 |
| 9s | yìqiān líng jiǔ<br><br>一千零九 | yìqiān líng yìshíjiǔ<br><br>一千零一十九 | yìqiān líng èrshíjiǔ<br><br>一千零二十九 | | yìqiān yìbǎi líng jiǔ<br><br>一千一百零九 | yìqiān yìbǎi yìshíjiǔ<br><br>一千一百一十九 |

Before a MW, 2 is read as "liǎng" except before the unit of measure 两 liǎng (50 grams): 二两饺子 èrliǎng jiǎozi (100 grams of jiaozi)

As in English, the unit always follows the number. The tens unit (jiao or mao) is named separately here; that is, instead of 50 fēn, the Chinese say 5 máo.

---

**Info Box**

**Numbers with More Than One Zero:**
No matter how many zeros precede a numeral, only one is ever read:
1001 yìqiān líng yī

---

**Info Box**

In Chinese cuisine, steaming is a commonly used method of cooking. To steam foods, the Chinese use bamboo baskets with a woven bottom and lid (笼 lóng)), which they simply stack on top of a tightly closed water-filled wok. The rising steam penetrates the bamboo baskets and cooks the dumplings, yeast buns, and other delicacies.

---

In colloquial Chinese, the last unit often is omitted in speech:
150 yìbǎi wǔ statt yìbǎi wǔshí
3700 sānqiān qī statt sānqiān qìbǎi

## Sample Sentences

### Topic 1: Asking the Price without a Verb

一笼包子多少钱？
Yì lóng bāozi duōshǎo qián?
*One MW / baozi / how much / money?*
How much does one serving of baozi cost?

A question about price is formed with duōshǎo qián 多少钱. It is the equivalent of "cost."
    Word order in the interrogative sentence corresponds to that in the declarative sentence.

### Topic 2: Declarative Sentence with No Verb

一笼包子八块五毛。
Yì lóng bāozi bā kuài wǔ máo.
*One MW / baozi / eight / kuai / five / mao.*
One serving of baozi costs 8.50 RMB.

Chinese currency (RMB) has three units: yuan (colloquially: kuai), jiao (colloquially: mao), and fen. One yuan is the equivalent of 10 jiao or 100 fen.

### Topic 3: Question with No Subject

(我)买这个多少钱？
(Wǒ) mǎi zhège duōshǎo qián?
*(I) / buy / this MW / how much / money?*
How much does this (one) cost?

If understanding the sentence correctly does not require that you know who wants to buy something, the subject of the sentence can be omitted.

### Topic 4: The Unit of Measure liǎng 两

一两饺子两块钱。
Yì liǎng jiǎozi liǎng kuài qián.
*One liang / jiaozi / two kuai / money.*
One liang of jiaozi costs 2 kuai.

The traditional unit of measure liǎng 两 is used with noodle dishes, according to Chinese custom.
    If it is clear which currency is being used, frequently only the word qián 钱 is added to the sum of money, without giving the exact currency designation.

## Topic 5: Exclamations

我不买，太贵！
Wǒ bù mǎi, tài guì!
*Not / buy, / too / expensive!*
I'm not buying that! It's too expensive for me!

In exclamatory sentences, too, word order remains the same as in a declarative sentence.

不是欧元，是人民币！
Bú shi Ōuyuán, shi Rénmínbì!
*Not / be / euro, / be / renminbi!*
It's not euros, but renminbi!

In contrasts using "but (rather)," Chinese does not require a conjunction.

## Topic 6: Polite Request with qǐng 请

请你便宜一点！
Qǐng nǐ piányi yìdiǎn!
*Request / you / cheap / a little!*
Could you make it a little cheaper?

One way of creating the comparative degree of an adjective in Chinese is to attach yìdiǎn 一点.

请吃我们的饺子！
Qǐng chī wǒmende jiǎozi!
*Please / eat / our / jiaozi!*
Please eat our jiaozi!

To express a polite request, place qǐng 请 at the beginning of the sentence. If it is clear who is asking whom, there is no need to mention the parties involved.

## Topic 7: Issuing Invitations with qǐng 请

(我)请你们喝酒！

(Wǒ) qǐng nǐmen hē jiǔ?
*(I) / invite / you / drink / alcohol.*
I'm inviting you to have a drink.

In this case, qǐng 请 means "invite someone."

| Semantic Fields | | | CD1 15 |
|---|---|---|---|
| **Places of Interest** | | | |
| Xi'an (city) | Xī'ān | 西安 | |
| Tomb of Qin Shi Huhuangdi | Qín Shǐhuángdì Líng | 秦始皇帝陵 | |
| Big Wild Goose Pagoda | Dàyàntǎ | 大雁塔 | |
| Huhaqing Hot Springs | Huáqīng Chí | 华清池 | |
| mosque | Qīngzhēnsì | 清真寺 | |
| Banpo Museum | Bànpō Bówùguǎn | 半坡博物馆 | |
| Ming Dynasty city wall | Xī'ān Chéngqiáng | 西安城墙 | |
| Stele Forest Museum | Bēilín | 碑林 | |
| Terracotta Army | Bīngmǎ Yǒng | 兵马俑 | |
| Yan'an (city) | Yán'ān | 延安 | |
| Yellow Emperor's Tomb | Huángdì Líng | 黄帝陵 | |
| Eighth Route Army Head-quarters | Bālùjūn Sīlìngbù | 八路军 司令部 | |
| former residence of Mao | Máo Zhǔxí Gùjū | 毛主席故居 | |
| former residence of Zhou Enlai | Zhōu Ēnlái Gùjū | 周恩来故居 | |
| **Dumplings** | | | |
| jiaozi, boiled | shuǐjiǎo | 水饺 | |
| jiaozi, served in soup | tāngjiǎo | 汤饺 | |

| jiaozi, pan fried (pot stickers) | guōtiē | 锅贴 |
|---|---|---|
| huntun / wonton (in soup or fried) | húntun | 馄饨 |
| baozi filled with ground meat | ròubāo | 肉包 |
| baozi filled with vegetables | càibāo | 菜包 |
| baozi with sweet red bean paste | dòushābāo | 豆沙包 |

| Currencies | | |
|---|---|---|
| renminbi | Rénmínbì | 人民币 |
| euro | Ōuyuán | 欧元 |
| U.S. dollar | Měiyuán | 美元 |
| Hong Kong dollar | Gǎngbì | 港币 |
| Japanese yen | Rìyuán | 日元 |
| English pound | Yīngbàng | 英镑 |
| Swiss franc | Ruìshì Fǎláng | 瑞士法郎 |

## Info Box

### Numbers on Official Forms

Numbers are written in a more complicated way on receipts, checks, and banknotes, to prevent mistakes and forgeries:

| 壹 | yī | one |
|---|---|---|
| 贰 | èr | twp |
| 叁 | sān | three |
| 肆 | sì | four |
| 伍 | wǔ | five |
| 陆 | liù | six |
| 柒 | qī | seven |
| 捌 | bā | eight |
| 玖 | jiǔ | nine |
| 拾 | shí | ten |
| 佰 | bǎi | hundred |
| 仟 | qiān | thousand |

## Exercises

### Exercise 1

Translate the following numbers into English.
1. 三十
2. 五十六
3. 九百九十九
4. 四百五十
5. 八千零八
6. 六百零三
7. 八百一十二
8. 五千零七
9. 一千八百
10. 二百五十

### Exercise 2

Which synonymous components do the following characters have:
饺，饭，馄，饨，馆？

### Exercise 3

Write the sample sentences in different versions, using the words from the vocabulary list.

### Exercise 4

Say the sample sentences aloud, using words from the semantic fields. To do so, use the pyramid method to form sentences.

Example:
qián
duōshǎo qián
jiǎozi duōshǎo qián
sānliǎng jiǎozi duōshǎo qián
mǎi sānliǎng jiǎozi duōshǎo qián
wǒ mǎi sānliǎng jiǎozi duōshǎo qián

## Exercise 5

Listen to the sample sentences on the audio CD, and then repeat them after the speaker.

## Exercise 6

First, write the following sentences in Pīnyīn, indicating the tones, and then translate them into English.

1. 五个包子多少钱？
2. 三两饺子八块钱。
3. 你买什么？
4. 我请你吃饭！
5. 王小姐喝什么茶？
6. 请你便宜一点！

## Exercise 7

Find the meaning of the following words by using the Pīnyīn transcription in the (online) dictionary.

1. zǎofàn 早饭
2. wǔfàn 午饭
3. wǎnfàn 晚饭

## Exercise 8

Translate the following sentences into Chinese.

1. How much do two liang of jiaozi cost?

_____

2. How many baozi are in a steamer?

_____

3. There are 10 baozi in a steamer.

_____

4. Three liang of jiaozi cost 7.50 yuan.

_____

5. Here a Peking duck costs 42 dollars.

_____

6. In China, a Peking duck costs 110 RMB.

_____

# 4    Hénán 河南

Province: Hénán 河南
Abbreviation: Yù 豫
Capital of province: Zhèngzhōu 郑州
112 counties, 38 cities
Area: 64,479 square miles
Population: 92.56 million
Number of persons / square miles: 1,420

## Vocabulary

| 今天 | jīntiān | today (present / day) |
| ...年 | nián | year (needs no MW)) |
| ...月 | yuè | month; moon |
| ...日 | rì | day; sun |
| ...号 | hào | number (colloquial term for rì 日) |
| 过 | guò | to experience, pass, celebrate; to cross |
| 过年 | guò nián | to celebrate the New Year or Spring Festival (pass / year) |
| 春节 | chūnjié | traditional Chinese New Year's festival, Spring Festival (spring / festival) |
| 哪 | nǎ | which |
| 出生 | chūsheng | to be born (out of / give birth) |
| 生日 | shēngrì | birthday (give birth / day) |
| 星期 | xīngqī | week (star / period) |
| 星期五 | xīngqīwǔ | Friday (star / period / five) |
| 好 | hǎo | good |
| 早上 | zǎoshang | in the morning (morning / on) |
| 上午 | shàngwǔ | before noon, A.M. (on / noon) |

| 中午 | zhōngwǔ | at noon / midday (middle / noon) |
| 下午 | xiàwǔ | in the afternoon, P.M. (under / noon) |
| 晚上 | wǎnshang | in the evening (evening / on) |
| 面条 | miàntiáo | spaghetti-shaped noodle made of wheat flour (flour, noodle / narrow, long object) |
| 很 | hěn | very |
| 好吃 | hǎochī | delicious (good / eat) |
| 好喝 | hǎohē | delicious (good / drink) |
| 祝 | zhù | to wish; to congratulate |
| 快乐 | kuàilè | happy; cheerful (delighted / joy) |
| 圣诞节 | shèng-dànjié | Christmas holiday (the wise one / give birth / festival) |
| 岁 | suì | year of life |
| 大 | dà | big; old |
| 多大 | duōdà | how old? (many / old) |
| 问 | wèn | to ask |
| 请问 | qǐng wèn | Excuse me, may I ask ... (request / ask) |
| ...点 | diǎn | ... o'clock (dot; full hour) |
| 钟 | zhōng | time measured in hours or minutes (bell / clock) |

| | | |
|---|---|---|
| 半 | bàn | half |
| 一刻 | yíkè | a quarter of an hour (one / quarter hour) |
| 三刻 | sānkè | three quarters of a hour (three / quarter hour) |
| …分 | fēn | … minute(s) (part) |
| 差 | chà | to lack; shortly before |
| 现在 | xiànzài | now (now / be located) |
| 坐 | zuò | to sit; to sit down |
| 进 | jìn | to enter |

## Info Box

**The Chinese Calendar**
The Chinese year is based on the old lunar or farmers' calendar. Although China introduced the Western calendar long ago, the New Year's Festival, also known as the Spring Festival, is still the most important celebration in the Chinese calendar. The entire family gets together for the Lunar New Year, even if they live far apart all year long.

## Sample Sentences
Topic 1: Time Designation

### Declarative Sentences with the Date
今天是二零零六年十二月一号。
Jīntiān shi èr líng líng liù nián shí'èr yuè yí hào.
*Today / two zero zero six year / December / one number.*
Today is December 1, 2006.

Giving the date follows the pattern "from large to small": first the year, then the month, and finally the day.

When giving the year, the numerals are listed separately and then defined with nián 年. The months are simply counted in Chinese, using the numbers from 1 to 12, and defined with yuè 月. In the case of days, in written Chinese, rì 日 is added to the numbers from 1 to 31; in spoken Chinese, hào 号 is added.

### Names of the Months

| | | |
|---|---|---|
| January | yíyuè | 一月 |
| February | èryuè | 二月 |
| March | sānyuè | 三月 |
| April | sìyuè | 四月 |
| May | wǔyuè | 五月 |
| June | liùyuè | 六月 |
| July | qíyuè | 七月 |
| August | báyuè | 八月 |
| September | jiǔyuè | 九月 |
| October | shíyuè | 十月 |
| November | shíyíyuè | 十一月 |
| December | shíèryuè | 十二月 |

他们二零零七年二月十七号在北京过春节。
Tāmen èr líng líng qī nián èr yuè shíqī hào zài Běijīng guò Chūnjié.
*They / two zero zero seven year / February / 17 number / be located / Beijing / pass / Spring Festival.*
They celebrate the Spring Festival in Beijing on February 17, 2007.

The date generally is placed directly after the subject of the sentence, that is, before the verb. If a place is given in the sentence, it follows the date.

## Writing Exercises

| | | | | |
|---|---|---|---|---|
| 今 | 天 | 年 | 月 | 日 |
| 过 | 春 | 节 | 哪 | 出 |
| 星 | 期 | 好 | 早 | 上 |
| 午 | 下 | 晚 | 面 | 条 |
| 很 | 祝 | 快 | 圣 | 诞 |
| 岁 | 大 | 问 | 钟 | 半 |
| 刻 | 差 | 现 | 坐 | 进 |

## Asking the Date

你哪年几月几号出生?

Nǐ nǎ'nián jǐyuè jǐhào chūsheng?

*You / which year / how much month / how much number / born?*

When were you born?

To ask the date, the numbers are replaced by question words. With the lower numbers, for month and date, use jǐ 几; for the year, use nǎ 哪.

我一九八二年三月二十号出生。

Wǒ yī jiǔ bā èr nián sānyuè èrshí hào chūsheng。

*I / one nine eight two year / March / 20 number / born.*

I was born on March 20, 1982.

The structure of the interrogative sentence is retained in the answer.

我星期五过生日。

Wǒ xīngqīwǔ guò shēngrì。

*I / Friday / pass / birthday.*

I have a birthday coming up on Friday.

The verb guò 过 is translated here, depending on the context, as "celebrate" or simply as "have." Thus the sentence does not necessarily mean that a party is being held.

## Days of the Week

The days of the week, like the names of the months, are numbered consecutively. Only Sunday has the name "day of the week."

| Monday | xīngqīyī | 星期一 |
| Tuesday | xīngqīèr | 星期二 |
| Wednesday | xīngqīsān | 星期三 |
| Thursday | xīngqīsì | 星期四 |
| Friday | xīngqīwǔ | 星期五 |
| Saturday | xīngqīliù | 星期六 |
| Sunday | xīngqītiān | 星期天 |
| weekend | zhōumò | 周末 |

Topic 2: Sentences with No Verb

## Greeting

你好!

Nǐ hǎo!

*You (sing.) / good!*

Good day/afternoon!!

This greeting formula can be used twenty-four hours a day. All you need to do is place the adjective hǎo 好 t the end of the sentence as a predicate. An additional verb would be incorrect here.

你们好!

Nǐmen hǎo!

*You (pl.) / good!*

Good day/afternoon!

Use this variant when greeting more than one person at the same time.

早上好!

Zǎoshang hǎo!

*Morning / good!*

Good morning!

晚上好!

Wǎnshang hǎo!

*Evening / good!*

Good evening!

Depending on the time of day, there are two other possible ways of greeting someone (see above). Here the personal pronoun is omitted.

## Interrogative Sentences (with No Verb)

你好吗?
Nǐ hǎo ma?
*You (sing.) / good / interrogative particle?*
How are you?

李女士好吗?
Lǐ nǔshì hǎo ma?
*Li / Ms. / good / interrogative particle?*
How is Ms. Li?

Questions with adjectives as a predicate can be formed with ma 吗.

面条贵不贵?
Miàntiáo guì bú guì?
*Noodles / expensive / not / expensive?*
Are noodles expensive?

Questions with an adjectival predicate can also be expressed by using the positive and negative forms of the adjective.

## Declarative Sentence with Modified Adjective

我很好。
Wǒ hěn hǎo.
*I / very / good.*
I'm fine.

Apart from the greeting nǐ hǎo 你好, for grammatical reasons an adjective generally must be qualified or modified by hěn 很 if the adjective is the only predicate in the sentence. If it also is intended to convey the meaning "very," then it must be given special emphasis when spoken.

你们的饺子很好吃,绿茶很好喝。
Nǐmen de jiǎozi hěn hǎochī, lùchá hěn hǎohē.
*Your / jiaozi / very / delicious, / green tea / very / delicious.*
Your jiaozi and the green tea are/taste (very) good.

The rule "add hěn 很" also applies when the adjective consists of an adjective-verb combination.

北京烤鸭贵,饺子便宜。
Běijīng kǎoyā guì, jiǎozi piányi.
*Peking duck / expensive; / jiaozi / cheap*
Peking duck is expensive; jiaozi are cheap.

If a contrast is being expressed, hěn 很 is not needed to support adjectives in either clause.

面条不贵。
Miàntiáo bú guì。
*Noodles / not / expensive.*
Noodles are not expensive.

In negated sentences with an adjectival predicate, hěn 很 is also not required.

## Topic 3: Expressing Good Wishes / Congratulations

祝你生日快乐!
Zhù nǐ shēngrì kuàilè!
*Wish / to you / birthday / happy!*
Happy Birthday!!

祝你圣诞节快乐!
Zhù nǐ shèngdànjié kuàilè!
*Wish / to you / Christmas festival / happy!*
I wish you a Merry Christmas!

Good wishes can be introduced with zhù nǐ 祝你. The subject of the sentence is usually omitted in this case.

## Topic 4: Asking Someone's Age

你几岁?
Nǐ jǐsuì?
*You / how many years of life?*
How old are you?

When you use jǐ 几 in formulating the question, you assume a low number in the answer; therefore, this question can be directed only to children and teenagers, never to adults.

你多大?
Nǐ duōdà?
*You / how old?*
How old are you?

This type of question can be addressed to a person of any age. Here duō 多, preceding the adjective dà 大, is the actual question word; it leaves all numerical possibilities open in the answer.

我三十岁。
Wǒ sānshí suì。
*I / thirty years of life.*
I am 30 years old.

Topic 5: Time

### Asking the Time
请问,现在几点钟?
Qǐng wèn, xiànzài jǐ diǎn zhōng?
*Request / ask, / now / how much full hour / clock?*
Excuse me, what time is it now?

Polite questions can be introduced with qǐng wèn 请问.

A question about the time does not require a verb but only the question word jǐ 几 and diǎn 点; that is, jǐ diǎn 几 点 alone would be sufficient to ask what time it is.

Zhōng 钟 explains only that the sentence deals with the time. It can also be omitted.

### Giving the Time
王先生下午三点二十分在这里喝绿茶。
Wáng xiānsheng xiàwǔ sāndiǎn èrshí fēn zài zhèlǐ hē lǜchá。
*Wang / Mr. / in the afternoon / three full hour / twenty minutes / be located / here / drink / green tea.*
Mr. Wang drinks green tea here at 3:20 in the afternoon..

The same rule applies to the time as to the date: "from large to small"—first the time of day, then the hour, and finally the minutes. If the number of minutes exceeds ten, the word fēn 分 can also be omitted.

现在上午九点三刻。
Xiànzài shàngwǔ jiǔdiǎn sānkè。
*Now / in the morning / nine full hour / three quarter hours.*
It is now 9:45 A.M.

Chinese has a separate character for the quarter hour: kè 刻.
yíkè 一刻 (one quarter hour) and sānkè 三刻 (three quarter hours) frequently are used in place of shíwǔ fēn 十五分 (15 minutes) und sìshíwǔ fēn 四十五分 (45 minutes).

The words "it" and "is" do not need to be translated.

今天中午十二点半。
Jīntiān zhōngwǔ shí'èrdiǎn bàn。
*Today / at midday / twelve full hour / half*
Today at midday, at 12:30.

Instead of saying "30 minutes," the Chinese use the word bàn 半. It is always added on to the full hour.

现在三点差五分。
Xiànzài sāndiǎn chà wǔfēn.
*Now / three full hour / lack / five minutes.*
It's now five to three.

Use chà 差 to tell how many minutes (or at most one quarter of an hour) it is before the next hour.

## Topic 6: Polite Request

请坐！
Qǐng zuò!
*Please / sit.*
Please have a seat.

请进！
Qǐng jìn!
*Please / enter.*
Please come in.

Polite requests can be introduced with qǐng 请. Personal pronouns or names need not be mentioned if the context makes it clear who are the persons being addressed.

**CD1 18**

## Semantic Fields

### Places of Interest

| | | |
|---|---|---|
| Luoyang (city) | Luòyáng | 洛阳 |
| Dragon Gate Grotto | Lóngmén Shíkū | 龙门石窟 |
| Shaolin Temple | Shǎolín Sì | 少林寺 |
| Kaifeng (city) | Kāifēng | 开封 |
| Imperial Song Street | Sòngjiē | 宋街 |
| Iron Pagoda | Tiětǎ | 铁塔 |

### Noodles

| | | |
|---|---|---|
| wheat noodles | miàntiáo | 面条 |
| fried noodles | chǎomiàn | 炒面 |
| fried noodles with bean sauce | zhájiàngmiàn | 炸酱面 |
| fried noodles with vegetables | shūcài chǎomiàn | 蔬菜炒面 |
| noodle soup | tāngmiàn | 汤面 |
| noodles with beef | niúròu miàn | 牛肉面 |
| noodles with shredded meat | ròusī miàn | 肉丝面 |
| noodles with chili sauce | dàndànmiàn | 担担面 |
| rice noodles | mǐfěn | 米粉 |
| rice noodles (broad cut) | mǐxiàn | 米线 |
| "crossing the bridge" noodles | guòqiáo mǐxiàn | 过桥米线 |
| glass noodles (made of mung beans) | fěnsī | 粉丝 |
| glass noodles (broad-cut) | fěntiáo | 粉条 |

### Rice

| | | |
|---|---|---|
| boiled or steamed rice | mǐfàn | 米饭 |
| plain white rice (with no foods added) | báifàn | 白饭 |
| fried rice | chǎofàn | 炒饭 |
| fried rice with egg | jīdàn chǎofàn | 鸡蛋炒饭 |
| fried rice with beef | niúròu chǎofàn | 牛肉炒饭 |

### Methods of Preparation

| | | |
|---|---|---|
| bake, in the oven (bread, for example) | kǎo | 烤 |
| roast, grill (Peking duck, for example) | kǎo | 烤 |
| stir-fry, stir-cook (scrambled eggs, for example) | chǎo | 炒 |

| fry in a pan (fried egg, for example) | jiān | 煎 |
| steam (baozi, for example) | zhēng | 蒸 |
| deep-fry (banana, for example) | zhá | 炸 |
| cook (soup, for example) | zhǔ | 煮 |
| smoke (ham, for example) | xūn | 熏 |
| stew, braise (meat, for example) | huì | 烩 |

| Official Holidays | | |
| New Year's Day (January 1) | Yuándàn | 元旦 |
| International Women's Day (March 8) | Sān Bā Fùnǚjié | 三八 妇女节 |
| International Labor Day (May 1) | Wǔ Yī Láodòngjié | 五一 劳动节 |
| Youth Day (May 4) | Wǔ Sì Qīngniánjié | 五四 青年节 |
| Founding Day of Chinese Communist Party (July 1) | Dǎngde shēngrì | 党的生日 |
| Founding Day of People's Liberation Army (August 1) | Bā Yī Jiànjūnjié | 八一 建军节 |
| National Day (October 1) | Guóqìngjié | 国庆节 |

| Traditional Holidays (based on the lunar calendar) | | |
| Spring Festival (January / February; Chinese 12th full moon) | Chūnjié | 春节 |
| Festival of Lanterns (15th day of first lunar month) | Dēngjié | 灯节 |

| Tomb Sweeping Day (April 4/5; Chinese beginning of 3rd lunar month) | Qīngmíngjié | 清明节 |
| Dragon Boat Festival (5th day of 5th lunar month) | Duānwǔjié | 端午节 |
| Ghost Festival (15th day of 7th lunar month) | Zhōngyuánjié | 中元节 |
| Moon Festival (15th day of 8th lunar month) | Zhōngqiūjié | 中秋节 |
| Confucius' Birthday (27th day of 8th lunar month) | Kǒngfūzi de dànchén | 孔夫子的 诞辰 |
| Ancestors' Sacrifice Festival (1st day of 10th lunar month) | Zǔxiānjié | 祖先节 |

## Exercises

### Exercise 1

Write down your own date of birth and those of your family members, and practice saying them aloud until you can say them fluently in Chinese.

### Exercise 2

Which synonymous components do the following characters share:
炒，炸，烤，煎，蒸，煮，黑？

### Exercise 3

Write different versions of the sample sentences, using the words from the vocabulary list.

### Exercise 4

Say the sample sentences aloud, using words from the semantic fields. To form the sentences, use the pyramid method.

Example:
sāndiǎn
xiàwǔ sāndiǎn
xiàwǔ sāndiǎn zài zhèli
Wáng xiānsheng xiàwǔ sāndiǎn zài
zhèli
Wáng xiānsheng xiàwǔ sāndiǎn zài
zhèli hē chá

## Exercise 5

Listen to the sample sentences on the audio
CD, and then repeat them after the speaker.

## Exercise 6

First, write the following sentences in Pīnyīn,
indicating the tones, and then translate them
into English.

1. 请问，李先生好吗？
2. 你们的面条很好吃。
3. 今天中午我请你吃饭。

## Exercise 7

Find the meaning of the following words,
using the Pīnyīn transcription in the (online)
dictionary.

1. luànqī bāzāo 乱七八糟
2. Liù Sì Yùndòng 六四运动
3. wǔxiāng 五香
4. sānlúnchē 三轮车
5. bāzhé 八折

## Exercise 8

Translate the following sentences into Chinese.

1. I was born on July 25, 1988.

_____

2. Are Peking ducks expensive?

_____

3. How are you (sing.)?

_____

4. I wish you a happy birthday.

_____

5. This evening at 7:30 (19:30), I'm celebrating
my birthday.

_____

6. Are you having a birthday?

_____

7. Please, drink (some) tea.

_____

Province: Shāndōng 山东
Abbreviation: Lǔ 鲁
Capital of province: Jǐ'nán 济南
94 counties, 48 cities
Area: 60,502 square miles
Population: 90.79 million
Number of persons / square mile: 1,485

 CD1 19

## Vocabulary

| | | |
|---|---|---|
| 人 | rén | person, human being |
| 美国 | Měiguó | United States (*beautiful / country*) |
| 美国人 | Měiguórén | American (*beautiful / country / person*) |
| 英国 | Yīngguó | England (*hero / country*) |
| 从 | cóng | from, away from |
| 哪里? | nǎli? | where?; where to? (southern Chinese variant; *which / suffix*) |
| 哪儿? | nǎr? | where?; where to? (northern Chinese variant; *which / suffix*) |
| 来 | lái | to come |
| 从 … 来 | cóng … lái | from … to come |
| 那 | nà | that one (over there) |
| 那个 | nàge | that one (over there) |
| 说 | shuō | to speak, say |
| 语 | -yǔ | language |
| 语言 | yǔyán | language (*speech / word*) |
| 英语 | Yīngyǔ | English (abbr. of *England / speech*) |
| 汉语 | Hànyǔ | Chinese (*Han nationality / speech*) |

| | | |
|---|---|---|
| 美语 | Měiyǔ | American (abbr. of *United States / speech*) |
| 还是 | háishi | or (*still / be*) |
| 写 | xiě | to write |
| 文 | -wén | writing (written language); language |
| 英文 | Yīngwén | English (abbr. of *England / writing*) |
| 中文 | Zhōngwén | Chinese; Chinese script (written Chinese); (abbr. of *China / writing*) |
| 用 | yòng | to use; with, in |
| 去 | qù | to go (there) (movement in a certain direction) |
| 早饭 | zǎofàn | breakfast (*early / boiled rice*) |
| 午饭 | wǔfàn | lunch (*midday / boiled rice*) |
| 晚饭 | wǎnfàn | dinner (*late / boiled rice*) |
| 饭馆 | fànguǎn | restaurant (*boiled rice / store*) |
| 常常 | chángcháng | often, frequently (*usual / usual*) |
| 不常 | bùcháng | not often (*not / usual*) |

| 葡萄酒 | pútaojiǔ | wine (*grape / grape / alcohol*) |
| 白 | bái | white |
| 红 | hóng | red |
| 杯 | bēi | MW for glasses, goblets, and cups |
| 瓶 | píng | MW for bottles |
| 黑 | hēi | black |
| 黑啤 | hēipí | dark beer (*black / beer*) |

**CD1 20**

## Sample Sentences

### Topic 1: Asking Where Someone Is From

**The Question Word** nǎ 哪

你是哪国人？

Nǐ shi nǎguórén?

*You / be / which-country-person?*

Where are you from?/Where do you come from?

This question refers to a person's nationality, not to the place he or she has just come from. The structure of this interrogative sentence corresponds to that of the following declarative sentence.

我是美国人。

Wǒ shi Méiguórén。

*I / be / American*

I'm an American.

One way of stating your nationality is by forming a shì sentence and attaching rén 人 to the country name. Such sentences are known as sentences with a nominal (noun) predicate.

**Question with** cóng nǎli lái 从哪里来

你们从哪里来？

Nǐmen cóng nǎli lái?

*You (pl.) / from / where / come?*

Where are you (pl.) coming from?

If you want to know where a person has just come from, include cóng nǎli lái 从哪里来 in your question. Here the nationality can also be given as an answer.

A question word or a place designation must always be used between cóng 从 and lái 来.

我们从美国来。

Wǒmen cóng Měiguó lái。

*We / from / America / come.*

We are coming/come from America.

### Topic 2: Asking about Knowledge of Languages

你说英语吗？

Nǐ shuō Yīngyǔ ma?

*You (sing.) / speak / English / interrogative particle?*

Do you speak English?

With country names ending in guó 国, such as England Yīngguó 英国, the guó 国 is replaced with yǔ 语 if it has to do with the spoken language.

In colloquial Chinese, however, wén 文 is also often added to the country name, although yǔ 语 would be correct.

那个人说什么语言？

Nàge rén shuō shénme yǔyán?

*That MW / person / speak / what kind of / language?*

What language does that person over there speak?

那个人员在那讲中文或英语吗？

Nàge rén shuō Hànyǔ háishi shuō Yīngyǔ?

*That MW / person / speak / Chinese / or / speak / English?*

Does that person over there speak Chinese or English?

## Writing Exercises

| | | | | |
|---|---|---|---|---|
| 人 | 德 | 美 | 英 | 从 |
| 来 | 那 | 说 | 语 | 言 |
| 汉 | 还 | 写 | 文 | 用 |
| 去 | 馆 | 常 | 葡 | 萄 |
| 白 | 红 | 杯 | 瓶 | 黑 |

There are several words for "or." In questions, háishì 还是 is used. In this case, the verb must be repeated. Only if the verb is shì is there no need to repeat it.

## Topic 3: Imperatives
请你写英文！
Qǐng nǐ xiě Yīngwén!
*Request / you (sing.) / write / English!*
Please write in English!

If the sentence has to do with the written form of a language, then wén 文 is attached to the country name.

请你用英文写！
Qǐng nǐ yòng Yīngwén xiě!
*Request / you (sing.) / use / English / write!*
Please write in English!

If the English word "in" can be replaced with "use," Chinese has the option of using yòng 用. Yòng 用 and the noun then function as an adverbial modifier and precede the main verb of the sentence.

## Topic 4: The Verb qù 去
我们去哪里吃晚饭？
Wǒmen qù nǎli chī wǎnfàn?
*We / go / to where / eat / dinner?*
Where are we going for dinner?

The verb qù 去 already contains the notion of direction toward a goal. Chinese needs no additional prepositions such as "to" or "into."

## Topic 5: Formation of Attributes with Adjectives
(see Grammar)
我们去中国饭馆吃饭。
Wǒmen qù Zhōngguó fànguǎn chī fàn.

*We / go / China / restaurant / eat / boiled rice.*
We're going to a Chinese restaurant to eat.

To form a term such as "Chinese Restaurant," the two words can be directly combined.

我常常在中国饭馆吃午饭。
Wǒ chángcháng zài Zhōngguó fànguǎn chī wǔfàn.
*I / often / in / China / Restaurant / eat / lunch.*
I often eat lunch at the Chinese Restaurant.

As usual, the time is the second element in the sentence; that is, it directly follows the subject. The place designation comes before the main verb.

你们喝什么葡萄酒？
Nǐmen hē shénme pútaojiǔ?
*You (pl.) / drink / what kind of / wine?*
What kind of wine do you drink (are you drinking)?

If shénme 什么 is used attributively in the meaning "what kind of ...," it can be placed directly before the word it refers to.

你们喝白葡萄酒还是喝红葡萄酒？
Nǐmen hē báipútaojiǔ háishi hē hóngpútaojiǔ?
*You (pl.) / drink / white / wine / or / drink / red / wine?*
Do you drink (are you drinking) white wine or red wine?

Monosyllabic and often-used adjectives are placed directly before nouns. Even if a compound noun (such as "red wine") results from putting the attribute ("red") first, there is no need to use de 的.

她喝一杯德国的白葡萄酒，也喝一瓶英国的黑啤。

Tā hē yìbēi Déguóde báipútaojiǔ, yě hē yìpíng Yīngguóde hēipí。

*She / drink / one MW / Germany / attributive particle / white / wine, / also / drink / one MW / England / attributive particle / black / beer.*

She is drinking a glass of German white wine and also a bottle of dark beer from England.

As soon as two attributes occur before a noun, the attributive particle de 的 must be used as a link between the first attribute and the word modified. Except in the case of possessive pronouns, the attributive particle is designated as such in the literal translation of the sample sentences.

## Semantic Fields

**(CD1 21)**

### Places of Interest

| | | |
|---|---|---|
| Qingdao (city) | Qīngdǎo | 青岛 |
| beaches | Hǎishuǐ Yùchǎng | 海水浴场 |
| Mt. Laoshan | Lǎoshān | 老山 |
| Qufu (city) | Qūfù | 曲阜 |
| Temple of Confucius | Kǒngmiào | 孔庙 |
| Kong Family Forest | Kǒnglín | 孔林 |
| Kong Family Mansion | Kǒngfǔ | 孔府 |
| Tai'an (city) | Tài'ān | 泰安 |
| Taishan | Tàishān | 泰山 |

### Continents

| | | |
|---|---|---|
| Europe | Ōuzhōu | 欧洲 |
| Asia | Yàzhōu | 亚洲 |
| Africa | Fēizhōu | 非洲 |
| America | Měizhōu | 美洲 |
| Australia | Àozhōu | 澳洲 |

### Countries and Nationalities

| | | |
|---|---|---|
| Country/State | guójiā | 国家 |
| China | Zhōngguó | 中国 |
| Germany | Déguó | 德国 |
| Austria | Àodìlì | 奥地利 |
| Switzerland | Ruìshì | 瑞士 |
| France | Fǎguó | 法国 |
| Italy | Yìdàlì | 意大利 |
| Spain | Xībānyá | 西班牙 |
| Greece | Xīlà | 希腊 |
| Turkey | Tǔ'ěrqí | 土耳其 |
| Arab States | Ālābó guójiā | 阿拉伯国家 |
| England | Yīngguó | 英国 |
| USA | Měiguó | 美国 |
| foreign countries | wàiguó | 外国 |

| | | |
|---|---|---|
| Nationality | guójiā + rén | 国家 + 人 |
| Chinese | Zhōngguórén | 中国人 |
| German | Déguórén | 德国人 |
| Austrian | Àodìlìrén | 奥地利人 |
| Swiss | Ruìshìrén | 瑞士人 |
| French | Fǎguórén | 法国人 |
| Italian | Yìdàlìrén | 意大利人 |
| Spanish (person), Spaniard | Xībānyárén | 西班牙人 |
| Greek | Xīlàrén | 希腊人 |
| Turkish (person), Turk | Tǔ'ěrqírén | 土耳其人 |
| Arab | Ālābórén | 阿拉伯人 |
| English (person) | Yīngguórén | 英国人 |
| American | Měiguórén | 美国人 |
| foreigner | wàiguórén | 外国人 |

### Colors

| | | |
|---|---|---|
| beige | mǐsè(de) | 米色(的) |
| blue | lánsè(de) | 蓝色(的) |
| brown | zōngsè(de) | 棕色(的) |
| yellow | huángsè(de) | 黄色(的) |
| golden | jīnsè(de) | 金色(的) |

# 5   Shāndōng  山东

| gray | huīsè(de) | 灰色(的) | purple, violet | zǐsè(de) | 紫色(的) |
| green | lǜsè(de) | 绿色(的) | white | báisè(de) | 白色(的) |
| orange | júzisè(de) | 橘子色(的) | multicolored | cǎisè(de) | 彩色(的) |
| pink | fěnhóngsè(de) | 粉红色(的) | solid colored, | dānsè(de) | 单色(的) |
| red | hóngsè(de) | 红色(的) | single colored | | |
| black | hēisè(de) | 黑色(的) | | | |

## Info Box

**Languages**

| language | spoken language + 语 | | written language + 文 | |
| Chinese | Hànyǔ | 汉语 | Zhōngwén | 中文 |
| German | Déyǔ | 德语 | Déwén | 德文 |
| French | Fǎyǔ | 法语 | Fǎwén | 法文 |
| Italian | Yìdàlìyǔ | 意大利语 | Yìdàlìwén | 意大利文 |
| Spanish | Xībānyáyǔ | 西班牙语 | Xībānyáwén | 西班牙文 |
| Greek | Xīlàyǔ | 希腊语 | Xīlàwén | 希腊文 |
| Turkish | Tǔ'ěrqíyǔ | 土耳其语 | Tǔ'ěrqíwén | 土耳其文 |
| Arabic | Ālābóyǔ | 阿拉伯语 | Ālābówén | 阿拉伯文 |
| English | Yīngyǔ | 英语 | Yīngwén | 英文 |
| foreign language(s) | wàiyǔ | 外语 | wàiwén | 外文 |

## Exercises

### Exercise 1

Practice the measure words (counters) you have learned thus far, and translate the following expressions:
1. one glass of beer
2. two bottles of wine
3. three goblets of white wine
4. two glasses of dark beer
5. four bottles of German white wine
6. one glass of English beer
7. six bottles of American red wine

### Exercise 2

Which synonymous components do the following characters share:
说，语，言，讲，试，识，谢？

### Exercise 3

Write different versions of the sample sentences, using the words from the vocabulary list.

### Exercise 4

Say the sample sentences aloud, using words from the semantic fields. Create sentences by using the pyramid method.

Example:

wǒ
wǒ chángcháng
wǒ chángcháng zài
wǒ chángcháng zài Zhōngguó
wǒ chángcháng zài Zhōngguó fànguǎn
wǒ chángcháng zài Zhōngguó fànguǎn chī fàn

## Exercise 5

Listen to the sample sentences on the audio CD, and repeat them after the speaker.

## Exercise 6

First, write the following sentences in Pīnyīn, indicating the tones, and then translate them into English.

1. 你是德国人还是美国人？
2. 美国的白葡萄酒和中国的白酒很好喝。
3. 我们去喝酒。
4. 他们四个人喝一瓶葡萄酒。
5. 她喝一杯可口可乐。

## Exercise 7

Find the meaning of the following words by using the Pīnyīn transcription in the (online) dictionary.

1. hóngbāo 红包
2. báitáng 白糖
3. hēishì 黑市

## Exercise 8

Translate the following sentences into Chinese.

1. Are you Chinese?

_ _ _ _ _ _ _ _ _ _ _ _ _ _ _ _ _ _ _ _

2. I come from the United States.

_ _ _ _ _ _ _ _ _ _ _ _ _ _ _ _ _ _ _ _

3. Please write in Chinese!

_ _ _ _ _ _ _ _ _ _ _ _ _ _ _ _ _ _ _ _

4. I drink German red wine. Do you have it?

_ _ _ _ _ _ _ _ _ _ _ _ _ _ _ _ _ _ _ _

5. We're going out for a Chinese dinner this evening.

_ _ _ _ _ _ _ _ _ _ _ _ _ _ _ _ _ _ _ _

6. Dark beer from Germany tastes good and is not expensive.

_ _ _ _ _ _ _ _ _ _ _ _ _ _ _ _ _ _ _ _

7. Eating breakfast in China is not too expensive!

_ _ _ _ _ _ _ _ _ _ _ _ _ _ _ _ _ _ _ _

8. Where are you going this afternoon?

_ _ _ _ _ _ _ _ _ _ _ _ _ _ _ _ _ _ _ _

# 6 Jiāngsū 江苏

Province: Jiāngsū 江苏
Abbreviation: Sū 苏
Capital of province: Nánjīng 南京
64 counties, 44 cities
Area: 39,614 square miles
Population: 74.38 million
Number of persons / square mile: 1,859

## Vocabulary

| | | |
|---|---|---|
| 菜 | cài | vegetables, groceries, main dish, food, cuisine |
| 菜单 | càidān | menu (*dish / list*) |
| 碗 | wǎn | bowl, tureen, dish |
| 米饭 | mǐfàn | boiled rice (*rice / boiled rice*) |
| 想 | xiǎng | to want; would like; think |
| 吃荤 | chī hūn | to eat foods of animal origin (*eat / foods of animal origin*) |
| 点 | diǎn | in a restaurant: to choose, to order |
| 要 | yào | to want to have (or do) something; must; to become; to need |
| 肉 | ròu | meat |
| 肉丝 | ròusī | meat strips (*meat / matchstick-size strips*) |
| 鸡 | jī | chicken |
| 鸡丁 | jīdīng | cubed chicken without bones (*chicken / cube*) |
| ... 呢? | ne? | and ...? (interrogative particle, used at the end of a question) |

| | | |
|---|---|---|
| 喜欢 | xǐhuan | to like (*be happy / glad*) |
| 更 | gèng | more (and more); (even) more |
| 最 | zuì | syllable used to form the superlative |
| 怎么? | zěnme? | how? (*how / suffix*) |
| 做 | zuò | to make |
| 能 | néng | to be able; can |
| 筷子 | kuàizi | chopsticks (*chopsticks / suffix*); MW: shuāng 双 |
| 辣 | là | spicy |
| 还 | hái | still, yet |
| 对不起 | duìbuqǐ | excuse (*toward / not / rise up*) |
| 会 | huì | to be able; to have the skill for something, have learned something |
| 慢 | màn | slow |
| 快 | kuài | quick, fast |
| 可以 | kěyǐ | can; may (*can / by means of*) |
| 给 | gěi | to give; for |
| 打包 | dǎbāo | to pack, bag, box (*strike / wrap up*) |
| 谢谢 | xièxie | thank you; to thank (*thanks / thanks*) |

## Sample Sentences

### Topic 1: Orders/Requests with qǐng 请

请给我菜单！
Qǐng gěi wǒ càidān!
*Please / give / me / menu.*
Please bring me the menu.

If you want to ask a waiter or waitress to bring food and drink, start the sentence with qǐng lái 请来 and then add whatever it is you wish.

请来两瓶啤酒，三碗米饭！
Qǐng lái liǎngpíng píjiǔ, sānwǎn mǐfàn!
*Please / come / two MW / beer, / three MW / rice!*
Please bring me two bottles of beer and three small bowls of rice.

Your wish can be expanded on by adding attributes, here in the form of quantities.

### Topic 2: Sentences with Modal Verbs (see Grammar)

Modal verbs always precede the predicate of the sentence. The negation is always bù 不, placed before the modal verb.

#### Sentences with xiǎng 想

我想吃荤。
Wǒ xiǎng chī hūn.
*I / would like / eat / foods containing meat and fish.*
I would like to eat meat.

我想点菜！
Wǒ xiǎng diǎn cài!
*I / would like / choose / food.*
I would like to order.

Xiǎng 想 can be used to mean "would like" only in connection with another verb; otherwise it changes the meaning.

#### Sentences with yào 要 (less polite)

我要这个！
Wǒ yào zhège!
*I / want / this measure word.*
I want this.

Yào 要, unlike xiǎng 想, can also stand alone, without a verb after it.

#### Sentences with a Modal Verb and a Full Verb

我不想要那个！
Wǒ bù xiǎng yào nàge!
*I / not / would like / want / that MW.*
I would not like that.

Xiǎng 想 is a more polite modal verb than yào 要, and for this reason it is frequently used in negations. Simply to say bù 不 would be very rude.

The combination xiǎng yào 想要 works only in this sequence, not reversed.
我要喝绿茶。
Wǒ yào hē lǜchá.
*I / want / drink / green tea.*
I would like to drink green tea.

我想吃肉丝和鸡丁，你呢？
Wǒ xiǎng chī ròusī hé jīdīng, nǐ ne?
*I / would like / eat / meat strips / and / chicken cubes / you (sing.) / interrogative particle?*
I would like (to eat) meat strips and cubed chicken, and you?

## Writing Exercises

| | | | | |
|---|---|---|---|---|
| 菜 | 单 | 碗 | 米 | 想 |
| 荤 | 要 | 肉 | 丝 | 鸡 |
| 丁 | 呢 | 喜 | 欢 | 更 |
| 最 | 怎 | 做 | 能 | 筷 |
| 双 | 辣 | 对 | 起 | 会 |
| 慢 | 以 | 给 | 打 | 谢 |

The interrogative particle ne 呢 is translated as "and ...?" It can only be used, however, when the context is clear.

## Topic 3: Comparative and Superlative
(see Grammar)

### With Verbs
我很喜欢吃肉丝。
Wǒ hěn xǐhuan chī ròusī.
*I / very / like / eat / meat strips.*
I really enjoy eating meat strips.

我更喜欢吃鸡丁。
Wǒ gèng xǐhuan chī jīdīng.
*I / even more / like / eat / cubed chicken.*
I prefer to eat cubed chicken.

The comparative degree is formed by placing gèng 更 directly before the verb of comparison.

我最喜欢吃北京烤鸭。
Wǒ zuì xǐhuan chī Běijīng kǎoyā.
*I / most / like / eat / Peking duck.*
Most of all, I like to eat Peking duck.

The superlative is forming by placing zuì 最 directly before the verb.

### With Adjectives
花茶很好喝。
Huāchá hěn hǎohē.
*Flavored tea / very / delicious.*
Flavored tea tastes good.

啤酒更好喝。
Píjiǔ gèng hǎohē.
*Beer / even more / delicious.*
Beer tastes even better.

The comparative is formed by placing gèng 更 directly before the adjective being compared.

葡萄酒最好喝。
Pútaojiǔ zuì hǎohē.
*Wine / most / delicious.*
Wine tastes best.

The superlative is formed by placing zuì 最 directly before the adjective.

## Topic 4: The Waiter's Questions
怎么做?
Zěnme zuò?
*How / make?*
How do you want it prepared?

The waiter will ask you this short question if you state only that you want a certain kind of meat, fish, or vegetable to eat. In the conversation, it needs to be made clear what style of preparation and what flavor you want in the dish you're ordering.

你会不会用筷子吃饭?
Nǐ huì bú huì yòng kuàizi chī fàn?
*You (sing.) / can / not / can / use / chopsticks / eat / boiled rice?*
Can you eat with chopsticks?

In this positive-negative question using huì bú huì 会不会, yòng 用 is used to mean "with."

你能吃辣吗?
Nǐ néng chī là ma?
*You (sing.) / can / eat / spicy / interrogative particle?*
Can you eat spicy foods?

还要什么?
Hái yào shénme?
*Still / want / what?*
What else would you like?

# 6 Jiāngsū 江苏

## Topic: Apologies, Please, and Thanks

对不起，我不会说汉语。
Duìbuqǐ, wǒ bú huì shuō Hànyǔ.
*Sorry, / I / not / can / speak / Chinese.*
I'm sorry, I can't speak Chinese.

请你说慢一点！
Qǐng nǐ shuō màn yìdiǎn!
*Please / you / speak / slow / a little.*
Please speak a little slower.

请你快一点做！
Qǐng nǐ kuài yìdiǎn zuò!
*Please / you / fast / a little / do.*
Please hurry a little.

谢谢。
Xièxie.
*Thank / thank.*
Thank you.

## Topic 6: The Preposition gěi 给

你可以给我打包吗？
Nǐ kěyǐ gěi wǒ dǎbāo ma?
*You / can / for / me / wrap up / interrogative particle?*
Can you wrap it up/box it for me?

The preposition gěi 给 is always followed by mentioning the person who profits from an action. In English, this is most frequently accomplished by using a prepositional phrase.

## Semantic Fields

### Places of Interest

| | | |
|---|---|---|
| Nanjing (city) | Nánjīng | 南京 |
| Black Dragon Lake | Xuánwǔhú | 玄武湖 |
| Ming Dynasty city wall | Míngdài Chéngqiáng | 明代城墙 |
| Dr. Sun Yat-Sen's Mausoleum | Zhōngshān Líng | 中山陵 |
| Huai'an (city) | Huái'ān | 淮安 |
| Birthplace of Zhou Enlai | Zhōu Ēnlái Gùjū | 周恩来故居 |
| Suzhou (city) | Sūzhōu | 苏州 |
| Garden of the Master of the Nets | Wǎngshīyuán | 网师园 |
| Garden of the Humble Administrator | Zhuōzhèngyuán | 拙政园 |
| Tiger Hill | Hǔqiū | 虎丘 |
| Wuxi (city) | Wúxī | 无锡 |
| Taihu Lake | Tàihú | 太湖 |
| Zhenjiang (city) | Zhènjiāng | 镇江 |
| Gold Mountain | Jīnshān | 金山 |

### All about Meat

| | | |
|---|---|---|
| leg / hock | tuǐ | 腿 |
| slices of filet | piàn | 片 |
| steak | pái | 排 |
| strips (matchstick size) | sī | 丝 |
| pieces (with bone in) | kuài | 块 |
| cubes (boneless) | dīng | 丁 |

### Flavors

| | | |
|---|---|---|
| in oyster sauce | háoyóu | 蚝油 |
| bitter | kǔ | 苦 |

| | | |
|---|---|---|
| chili and peanuts | gōngbǎo | 宫保 |
| with three ingredients | sānxiān | 三鲜 |
| roasted (twice cooked) | huíguō | 回锅 |
| roasted (crispy) | xiāngsū | 香酥 |
| ginger, chili, garlic, vinegar | yúxiāng | 鱼香 |
| salty | xián | 咸 |
| sour | suān | 酸 |
| hot and sour | suānlà | 酸辣 |
| spicy (chili) | là | 辣 |
| spicy (Chinese pepper) | málà | 麻辣 |
| braised in soy sauce | hóngshāo | 红烧 |
| sautéed in soy sauce | jiàngbào | 酱爆 |
| sweet | tián | 甜 |
| sweet and sour | tángcù | 糖醋 |

| Table Setting | | |
|---|---|---|
| fork | chāzi | 叉子 |
| glass/cup/goblet | bēizi | 杯子 |
| pot | hú | 壶 |
| spoon | tiáogēng | 调羹 |
| knife | dāo | 刀 |
| small bowl | wǎn | 碗 |
| napkin | cānjīnzhǐ | 餐巾纸 |
| chopsticks | kuàizi | 筷子 |
| chopsticks (disposable) | wèishēng kuàizi | 卫生筷子 |
| plate | pánzi | 盘子 |

| Meat Dishes | | |
|---|---|---|
| pork | zhūròu | 猪肉 |
| spicy shredded pork | yúxiāng ròusī | 鱼香肉丝 |
| deep-fried filet of pork | yóuzhá lǐji | 油炸里脊 |

| | | |
|---|---|---|
| baked sweet-and-sour pork | gǔlǎoròu | 古老肉 |
| twice-cooked pork | huíguōròu | 回锅肉 |
| ground meat and chili sauce with glass noodles | máyǐ shàngshù | 蚂蚁上树 |
| beef | niúròu | 牛肉 |
| beef with onions and ginger | jiāngcōng niúròu | 姜葱牛肉 |
| spicy beef with carrots and onions | gānbiān niúròusī | 干煸牛肉丝 |
| spicy beef with black beans | dòuchǐ niúròu | 豆豉牛肉 |
| beef curry | gālí niúròu | 咖喱牛肉 |
| beef on a sizzling-hot iron plate | tiěbǎn niúròu | 铁板牛肉 |
| lamb | yángròu | 羊肉 |
| roasted lamb with coriander | xiāngcài kǎo yángròu | 香菜烤羊肉 |
| grilled lamb on a spit | kǎo yángròu chuàn | 烤羊肉串 |
| lamb hot pot | shuàn yángròu | 涮羊肉 |
| roasted leg of lamb | kǎo yángtuǐ | 烤羊腿 |
| poultry | | |
| duck with bananas and asparagus | bōluó lúsǔn yā | 菠萝芦笋鸭 |
| duck with mushrooms and bamboo shoots | shuāngdōng yā | 双冬鸭 |
| duck with cashew nuts | yāoguǒ yā | 腰果鸭 |
| roasted duck in spicy sauce | làzhī yā | 辣汁鸭 |

# 6 Jiāngsū 江苏

| spicy, crispy roasted chicken | xiāngsūjī | 香酥鸡 |
| chicken with chili and peanuts | gōngbǎo jīdīng | 宫保鸡丁 |
| very spicy chicken | làzi jīpiàn | 辣子鸡片 |
| Eight Jewel Chicken | bābǎo quánjī | 八宝全鸡 |
| spicy chicken wings | málà jīyì | 麻辣鸡翼 |

## Exercises

### Exercise 1

Practice the following sentences for a visit to a restaurant. Ask the waiter for:
1. the menu
2. a bottle of beer
3. two glasses of red wine
4. three bowls of rice

### Exercise 2

Which synonymous components do the following characters share:
吃，可，呢，哪，号，吗，喝？

### Exercise 3

Write different versions of the sample sentences, using the words from the vocabulary list.

### Exercise 4

Say the sample sentences aloud, using words from the semantic fields. Create sentences for this purpose by using the pyramid method.

Example:
xǐhuan
wǒmen xǐhuan
wǒmen zuì xǐhuan
wǒmen zuì xǐhuan zài
wǒmen zuì xǐhuan zài Zhōngguó
wǒmen zuì xǐhuan zài Zhōngguó chīfàn

### Exercise 5

Listen to the sample sentences on the audio CD, and then repeat them after the speaker.

### Exercise 6

First, write the following sentences in Pīnyīn, indicating the tones, and then translate them into English.

1. 我在这里可以不可以用人民币买菜。
2. 对不起，你能给我点啤酒和二两饺子吗？
3. 谢谢，我不喝酒。
4. 请你说普通话！
5. 我喜欢吃德国菜，更喜欢吃中国菜。

### Exercise 7

Find the meaning of the following words with the help of the Pīnyīn transcription in the (online) dictionary.

1. càipǔ 菜谱
2. càishì 菜市
3. fàntǒng 饭桶

Exercise 8

Translate the following sentences into Chinese:

1. Please bring me the English menu.

\_ \_ \_ \_ \_ \_ \_ \_ \_ \_ \_ \_ \_ \_ \_ \_ \_ \_ \_ \_

2. I'm fine. And you?

\_ \_ \_ \_ \_ \_ \_ \_ \_ \_ \_ \_ \_ \_ \_ \_ \_ \_ \_ \_

3. Please give me a little green tea.

\_ \_ \_ \_ \_ \_ \_ \_ \_ \_ \_ \_ \_ \_ \_ \_ \_ \_ \_ \_

4. I'm sorry, my Chinese is not very good.

\_ \_ \_ \_ \_ \_ \_ \_ \_ \_ \_ \_ \_ \_ \_ \_ \_ \_ \_ \_

5. Can you make it a little cheaper?

\_ \_ \_ \_ \_ \_ \_ \_ \_ \_ \_ \_ \_ \_ \_ \_ \_ \_ \_ \_

6. What kind of meat would you like to eat?

\_ \_ \_ \_ \_ \_ \_ \_ \_ \_ \_ \_ \_ \_ \_ \_ \_ \_ \_ \_

7. I can't eat spicy foods.

\_ \_ \_ \_ \_ \_ \_ \_ \_ \_ \_ \_ \_ \_ \_ \_ \_ \_ \_ \_

8. What would you like to eat this evening?

\_ \_ \_ \_ \_ \_ \_ \_ \_ \_ \_ \_ \_ \_ \_ \_ \_ \_ \_ \_

9. Where would you like to go out to eat this evening?

\_ \_ \_ \_ \_ \_ \_ \_ \_ \_ \_ \_ \_ \_ \_ \_ \_ \_ \_ \_

10. Most of all, I like to eat jiaozi and baozi.

\_ \_ \_ \_ \_ \_ \_ \_ \_ \_ \_ \_ \_ \_ \_ \_ \_ \_ \_ \_

Shànghǎi 上海

Abbreviation: Hù 沪

Directly subordinate to central government

1 county, 18 urban districts

Area: 2,448 square miles

Population: 16.74 million

Number of persons / square mile: 6,769

## Vocabulary

| 上海 | Shànghǎi | Shanghai (*above, on* / *ocean*) |
| 票 | piào | ticket; banknote, MW: zhāng 张 |
| 张 | zhāng | MW for flat things, such as tickets, maps, stamps, tables |
| 上海菜 | Shànghǎicài | Shanghai cuisine (*above, on* / *ocean* / *kitchen*) |
| 酸 | suān | sour |
| 汤 | tāng | soup |
| 喝汤 | hē tāng | to eat soup (*drink* / *soup*) |
| 酸辣汤 | suānlàtāng | hot-and-sour soup (*sour* / *spicy* / *soup*) |
| 小笼包 | xiǎolóngbāo | small, juicy baozi (*small* / *steamer* / *wrap up*) |
| 到 | dào | to arrive; to ...; as far as |
| 普通话 | Pǔtōnghuà | Standard Mandarin/Chinese (*general* / *usual* / *language*) |
| 地方 | dìfāng | place, locality (*earth* / *direction*) |
| 地方话 | dìfānghuà | dialect (*earth* / *direction* / *language*) |
| 上海话 | Shànghǎihuà | Shanghai dialect (*above, on* / *ocean* / *language*) |
| 但是 | dànshì | but, however (*but* / *be*) |
| 应该 | yīnggāi | should; must (*should* / *should*) |
| 汉字 | Hànzì | Chinese characters (*Han nationality* / *graphic characters*) |
| 拼音 | Pīnyīn | to spell, write in transcription; transcription (*combine* / *sound*) |
| 地址 | dìzhǐ | address (*earth* / *location*) |
| 本 | běn | measure word for bound writings, such as books |
| 词典 | cídiǎn | dictionary (*word* / *standard work*); measure word: běn 本 |
| 只 | zhǐ | only, merely |

| | | |
|---|---|---|
| 里面 | lǐmiàn | inside, within, inside of, in (*inside / suffix for position words*) |
| 银行 | yínháng | bank (*silver / business area*) |
| 茶馆 | cháguǎn | teahouse (*tea / business*), MW: jiā 家 |
| 右边 | yòubiān | (on the) right (*right / suffix for position words*) |
| 左边 | zuǒbiān | (on the) left (*left / suffix for position words*) |
| 对面 | duìmiàn | across from, opposite (*opposite / side, area*) |
| 再 | zài | again |
| 开 | kāi | issuing of receipts |
| 发票 | fāpiào | receipt (*send / card*), MW: zhāng 张 |
| 再见 | zàijiàn | goodbye (*again / see*) |

## Sample Sentences

Topic 1: Sentences with the Directional Verb qù 去

他去上海。
Tā qù Shànghǎi.
*He / go (there) / Shanghai*
He is going to Shanghai.

The verb qù 去 always expresses movement toward a goal.

他去买票。
Tā qù mǎi piào.
*He / go (there) / buy / ticket.*
He is going to buy the ticket(s).

The verb qù 去 can be linked with a verb-object combination.

他去上海买两张票。
Tā qù Shànghǎi mǎi liǎngzhāng piào.
*He / go (there) / Shanghai / buy / two MW / ticket.*
He is going to Shanghai to buy two tickets.

The verb qù 去 can also be separated from the second verb by a designation of place; that is, both verbs can have a complement.

我们去哪里吃饭？
Wǒmen qù nǎli chī fàn?
*We / go (there) / where / eat?*
Where are we going to eat?

我很想去上海喝酸辣汤，吃小笼包。
Wǒ hěn xiǎng qù Shànghǎi hē suānlàtāng, chī xiǎolóngbāo.
*I / very / would like / go (there) / Shanghai / drink / hot-and-sour soup, / eat / small baozi.*
I really would like to go to Shanghai and eat hot-and-sour soup and xiaolongbao.

The verb qù 去 can also be combined with modal verbs, which in this case precede qù 去.

### Info Box

A very widespread form of greeting among friends and acquaintances who meet by chance on the street is "Where are you going?" qù nǎli 去哪里? or qù nǎr 去哪儿?
To greet a guest (in business or privately), the Chinese say, "Very welcome!" hěn huānyíng! 很欢迎！

## Writing Exercises

| | | | | |
|---|---|---|---|---|
| 海 | 票 | 张 | 酸 | 汤 |
| 小 | 到 | 普 | 通 | 地 |
| 方 | 但 | 应 | 该 | 字 |
| 拼 | 音 | 址 | 本 | 词 |
| 典 | 只 | 银 | 行 | 右 |
| 边 | 左 | 再 | 发 | 见 |

**Topic 2: Adverbial Qualification of Place with Prepositions**

**Preposition** dào ... qù 到 ... 去
我们到上海去吃饭。
Wǒmen dào Shànghǎi qù chī fàn。
*We / to / Shanghai / go (there) / eat / boiled rice.*
We're going to Shanghai to eat.

Here, the preposition dào 到, in combination with the place designation Shànghǎi 上海, is the adverbial qualification of place. It always precedes the predicate of the sentence.

In terms of content, the sentence does not differ from 我们去上海吃饭. In colloquial Chinese, the shorter version is preferable.

**Preposition** cóng ... dào 从 ... 到
中国人从早到晚吃饭。
Zhōngguórén cóng zǎo dào wǎn chī fàn。
*Chinese / from / early / to / late / eat / boiled rice.*
The Chinese eat from morning to night.

他们从美国到中国去。
Tāmen cóng Měiguó dào Zhōngguó qù。
*You / from / United States / to / China / go (there).*
You are going from the United States to China.

The prepositions cóng 从 and dào 到, in combination with adverbs of time, indicate the beginning and ending time of an action; in combination with statements of place, they indicate the beginning and ending place of an action.

**Topic 3: Speaking and Writing**
你会说普通话吗?
Nǐ huì shuō Pǔtōnghuà ma?
*You / can / speak / Standard Mandarin?*
Can you speak Standard Mandarin?

The term Pǔtōnghuà 普通话 ("common speech") was introduced in the People's Republic of China in 1955. Thus the Beijing dialect—that is, the dialect of northern China—was defined as the standard for pronunciation.

我会说地方话,你呢?
Wǒ huì shuō dìfānghuà, nǐ ne?
*I / can / speak / dialect, / you / interrogative particle ...?*
I can speak dialect(s). And you ...?

---

### Info Box

**Dialects**
To the dismay of foreigners, the Chinese frequently speak only their own dialect (dìfānghuà 地方话) or Pǔtōnghuà 普通话, also heavily colored by their dialect.

China has seven main dialects: northern Chinese or Mandarin; the dialect of the provinces Jiangsu, Zhejiang, and Shanghai; the dialect of Fujian Province; the dialect of Jiangxi Province; the Hakka dialect in southern China; the dialect of Hunan Province; and Cantonese.

---

我会上海话,但是我应该说普通话。
Wǒ huì Shànghǎihuà, dànshì wǒ yīnggāi shuō Pǔtōnghuà。
*I / can / Shanghai dialect, / but / I / should / speak / Standard Mandarin.*
I know Shanghai dialect, but I (really) ought to speak Standard Mandarin.

To designate a dialect, the place (city, province, region) is combined with the syllable huà 话.

请你用汉字和拼音写你的地址！
Qǐng nǐ yòng Hànzì hé Pīnyīn xiě nǐde dìzhǐ！
*Request / you / use / Chinese characters / and / transcription / write / your / address.*
Please write your address down for me in Chinese characters and pinyin.

---

### Info Box

**Characters**
You can prevent misunderstandings by asking Chinese to write down important information in legible handwriting in Chinese characters. Unlike the spoken language, the characters are the same everywhere in the country.

---

你有汉德词典吗？
Nǐ yǒu Hàn-Dé cídiǎn ma？
*You / have / Chinese / German / dictionary / interrogative particle?*
Do you have a Chinese-German dictionary?

If all else fails, use the correct MW for books (běn 本) to ask for a dictionary. Chinese-English dictionaries Hàn-Yīng cídiǎn 汉英词典 are relatively easy to obtain in China.

我只有英汉词典。
Wǒ zhǐ yǒu Yīng-Hàn cídiǎn。
*I / only / have / English / Chinese / dictionary.*
I have only an English-Chinese dictionary.

Topic 4: Sentences with Position Words

**Sentences with** yǒu 有
包子里面有什么？
Bāozi lǐmiàn yǒu shénme？
*Baozi / inside / have / what?*
What is inside the baozi?

Here the position word follows a noun. If the larger unit (here: the dumpling is bigger than the filling) comes before the verb, usually at the beginning of the sentence, then the verb yǒu 有 is used.

里面有肉。
Lǐmiàn yǒu ròu。
*Inside / have / meat.*
There is meat inside.

The position word can also stand alone as a noun.

**Sentences with** zài 在
银行在哪里？
Yínháng zài nǎli？
*Bank / be located / where?*
Where is the bank?

银行在北京。
Yínháng zài Běijīng。
*Bank / be located / Beijing.*
The bank is in Beijing.

If, however, the smaller unit (here: a bank is smaller than a city) precedes the verb, then the verb zài 在 is used.

银行在茶馆的右边。
Yínháng zài cháguǎnde yòubiān。
*Bank / be located / teahouse / attributive particle / right side.*
The bank is on the right of the teahouse.

Position words can also be used with attributes (here: cháguǎn 茶馆). In this case, they are placed in front of the position word with de 的.

**Sentences with** shi 是
左边的银行是中国银行。
Zuǒbiānde yínháng shi Zhōngguó
Yínháng。
*Left side / attributive particle / bank / be /*
*China / Bank.*
The bank on the left is the Bank of China.

Position words can also be used adjectively.
Like attributes, they are joined to the word they
qualify (here: yínháng 银行) with de 的.

　　If a certain object is being identified, that is,
if you want to know or point out what is located
in a certain place, then the verb shi 是 is used.

对面的不是饭馆。
Duìmiànde bú shi fànguǎn。
*Opposite / attributive particle / not / be /*
*restaurant.*
The building opposite is not a restaurant.

The modified noun following de 的 can also
be omitted.

Topic 5: The Adverb of Time zài 再
请再来一瓶啤酒！
Qǐng zài lái yìpíng píjiǔ！
*Please / again / come / one MW / beer.*
Another bottle of beer, please.

Zài 再 is always used to refer to the future,
when an event has already occurred once and
will/should occur again.

请再给我开张发票！
Qǐng zài gěi wǒ kāi zhāng fāpiào！
*Please / again / give / me / make out / MW /*
*receipt.*
Please make out another receipt for me.

Frequently, zài 再 is used in both positive and
negative requests that refer to the repetition or
nonrepetition of an action in the future.

Topic 6: Saying Good-bye
再见。
Zàijiàn。
*Again / see.*
Good-bye.

The simplest way to say good-bye is to use the
words above, which mean "see you again."

今天晚上再见。
Jīntiān wǎnshang zàijiàn。
*Today / evening / see again.*
See you this evening.

This sentence can be supplemented with additional indications of time, which are placed at the
front. Prepositions are not necessary here.

## Semantic Fields

**Places of Interest**

| | | |
|---|---|---|
| Bund (riverfront promenade) | Wàitān | 外滩 |
| Yuyuan Garden | Yùyuán | 豫园 |
| Huxinting Teahouse | Húxīntíng | 湖心亭 |
| Peace Hotel | Hépíng Fàndiàn | 和平饭店 |
| Shanghai Museum | Shànghǎi Bówùguǎn | 上海博物馆 |
| Nanjing Road | Nánjīng Lù | 南京路 |
| Huaihai Road | Huáihǎi Lù | 淮海路 |
| Jade Buddha Temple | Yùfósì | 玉佛寺 |
| Longhua Temple | Lónghuásì | 龙华寺 |
| Pudong | Pǔdōng | 浦东 |

CD1 27

| | | |
|---|---|---|
| Jinmao Tower (420 m) | Jīnmào Dàshà | 金茂大厦 |
| Oriental Pearl TV Tower (468 m) | Dōngfāng Míngzhū Diànshìtǎ | 东方明珠电视塔 |

**Soups**

| | | |
|---|---|---|
| egg-drop soup with purple seaweed | zǐcài dànhuātāng | 紫菜蛋花汤 |
| egg-drop soup with tomatoes | fānqié dànhuātāng | 番茄蛋花汤 |
| soup with green vegetables | qīngcàitāng | 青菜汤 |
| seaweed soup with spareribs | hǎidài páigǔtāng | 海带排骨汤 |

**Position Words and Direction Words**

| | | |
|---|---|---|
| above | shàngbiān/ shàngmiàn | 上边/上面 |
| below | xiàbiān/ xiàmiàn | 下边/下面 |
| inside | lǐbiān/lǐmiàn | 里边/里面 |
| outside | wàibiān/ wàimiàn | 外边/外面 |
| in front | qiánbiān/ qiánmiàn | 前边/前面 |
| in back | hòubiān/ hòumiàn | 后边/后面 |
| (on the) left | zuǒbiān | 左边 |
| (on the) right | yòubiān | 右边 |
| opposite, across from | duìmiàn | 对面 |
| next to, beside | pángbiān | 旁边 |
| between | zhōngjiān | 中间 |
| door/house next door | gébì | 隔壁 |

**Points of the Compass**

| | | |
|---|---|---|
| east | dōngfāng | 东方 |
| west | xīfāng | 西方 |
| north | běifāng | 北方 |
| south | nánfāng | 南方 |
| southeast | dōngnán | 东南 |
| southwest | xī'nán | 西南 |
| northeast | dōngběi | 东北 |
| northwest | xīběi | 西北 |

**Names of Places**

| | | |
|---|---|---|
| antiques store | gǔdǒng shāngdiàn | 古董商店 |
| pharmacy | yàodiàn | 药店 |
| exhibition hall | zhǎnlǎnguǎn | 展览馆 |
| train station | huǒchēzhàn | 火车站 |
| bar | jiǔbā | 酒吧 |
| embassy | dàshǐguǎn | 大使馆 |
| bookstore | shūdiàn | 书店 |
| bus station | chángtú qìchēzhàn | 长途汽车站 |
| bus stop | qìchēzhàn | 汽车站 |
| women's rest room | nǚcè | 女厕 |
| disco | dísīkē wǔtīng | 迪斯科舞厅 |
| airport | fēijīchǎng | 飞机场 |
| hairdresser/ barber | lǐfàdiàn | 理发店 |
| gallery | huàláng | 画廊 |
| hotel | fàndiàn | 饭店 |
| hotel | bīnguǎn | 宾馆 |
| men's rest room | náncè | 男厕 |
| Internet café | wǎngbā | 网吧 |
| department store | bǎihuò shāngdiàn | 百货商店 |
| church | jiàotáng | 教堂 |
| art museum | měishùguǎn | 美术馆 |
| consulate | lǐngshìguǎn | 领事馆 |
| hospital | yīyuàn | 医院 |
| store | shāngdiàn | 商店 |
| market | shìchǎng | 市场 |
| massage parlor | ànmó zhōngxīn | 按摩中心 |
| mosque | qīngzhēnsì | 清真寺 |

| museum | bówùguǎn | 博物馆 |
| park | gōngyuán | 公园 |
| police station | gōng'ānjú | 公安局 |
| post office | yóujú | 邮局 |
| restaurant | fànguǎn | 饭馆 |
| restaurant | fàndiàn | 饭店 |
| gymnasium | tǐyùguǎn | 体育馆 |
| supermarket | chāojí shìchǎng | 超级市场 |
| gas station | jiāyóuzhàn | 加油站 |
| teahouse | cháguǎn | 茶馆 |
| temple | sìyuàn | 寺院 |
| theater | jùchǎng | 剧场 |
| ticket window/ counter | shòupiàochù | 售票处 |
| rest room (public) | gōnggòng cèsuǒ | 公共厕所 |
| subway stop | dìtiězhàn | 地铁站 |
| university | dàxué | 大学 |
| laundry | xǐyīdiàn | 洗衣店 |

## Exercises

### Exercise 1

Translate the following:
1. On the left.
2. The bank on the left.
3. On the left, next to the bank.
4. On the right.
5. The Chinese character on the right.
6. On the right, next to the Chinese character.

### Exercise 2

Which synonymous components do the following characters share:
没，酒，水，法，油，汤，海？

### Exercise 3

Write different versions of the sample sentences, using the words from the vocabulary list.

### Exercise 4

Say the sample sentences aloud, using words from the semantic fields. Create sentences by using the pyramid method.

Example:
cídiǎn
yòubiānde cídiǎn
yòubiānde cídiǎn shi
yòubiānde cídiǎn shi yìběn
yòubiānde cídiǎn shi yìběn Dé-Hàn
yòubiānde cídiǎn shi yìběn Dé-Hàn cídiǎn

### Exercise 5

Listen to the sample sentences on the audio CD, and then repeat them after the speaker.

### Exercise 6

First, write the following sentences in Pīnyīn, indicating the tones, and then translate them into English.

1. 上海的小笼包里面有肉，也有菜。
2. 请你再买一张票，我也要去。
3. 对面的饭馆没有好吃的菜。

## Exercise 7

Find the meaning of the following words by using the Pīnyīn transcription in the (online) dictionary.

1. Chángjiāng 长江
2. Huánghé 黄河
3. Zhūjiāng 珠江
4. Láncāngjiāng 澜沧江

## Exercise 8

Translate the following sentences into Chinese.

1. Where are we going to eat today?

_ _ _ _ _ _ _ _ _ _ _ _ _ _ _ _ _ _ _ _

2. The dictionary on the left is mine.

_ _ _ _ _ _ _ _ _ _ _ _ _ _ _ _ _ _ _ _

3. The teahouse is across from the bank.

_ _ _ _ _ _ _ _ _ _ _ _ _ _ _ _ _ _ _ _

4. Should I wrap it up for you?

_ _ _ _ _ _ _ _ _ _ _ _ _ _ _ _ _ _ _ _

5. Until 4:30 in the afternoon.

_ _ _ _ _ _ _ _ _ _ _ _ _ _ _ _ _ _ _ _

6. Please don't come back.

_ _ _ _ _ _ _ _ _ _ _ _ _ _ _ _ _ _ _ _

7. Can you speak English?

_ _ _ _ _ _ _ _ _ _ _ _ _ _ _ _ _ _ _ _

Province: Zhèjiāng 浙江

Abbreviation: Zhè 浙

Capital of province: Hāngzhōu 杭州

64 counties, 35 cities

Area: 39,305 square miles

Population: 46.77 million

Number of persons / square mile: 1,177

## Vocabulary

| | | |
|---|---|---|
| 菜市 | càishì | vegetable market (*vegetables; foods / market*) |
| 买菜 | mǎi cài | to shop for groceries (*buy / groceries*) |
| 吧 | ba | particle for indicating a request, agreement, or supposition |
| 走 | zǒu | to go (on foot), to walk |
| 休息 | xiūxi | to take a break (*rest / rest*) |
| 素菜 | sùcài | vegetarian dish(es) (*vegetarian / foods*) |
| 对 | duì | right, correct |
| 往 | wǎng | to; in the direction of |
| 前 | qián | in front |
| 一直 | yìzhí | straight ahead; uninterrupted, always (*one / straight*) |
| 就 | jiù | right away, soon, immediately |
| 拐 | guǎi | to turn, branch off |
| 得 | děi | must; need, require |
| 蔬菜 | shūcài | vegetables (*vegetables / vegetables*) |
| 豆腐 | dòufu | tofu (*bean / curd*) |
| 因为 | yīnwèi | because, since, as, on account of, owing to (*reason / preposition*) |

| | | |
|---|---|---|
| 客人 | kèrén | guest (*guest / human being*); MW: wèi 位 |
| 吃素 | chī sù | to eat vegetarian food (*eat / vegetarian*) |
| 都 | dōu | all (refers to preceding noun) |
| 一个人 | yígerén | alone (*one / MW / human being*) |
| 炒 | chǎo | to cook in a wok, stir-fry |
| 什锦 | shíjǐn | mixed (*different / multicolored*) |
| 素什锦 | sùshíjǐn | mixed vegetables (*vegetarian / different / multicolored*) |
| 鱼 | yú | fish; MW: tiáo 条 |
| 海味 | hǎiwèi | seafood (*sea / taste*) |
| 过敏 | guòmǐn | allergy (*go over / briskly*) |
| 对... 过敏 | duì... guòmǐn | to be allergic to ... (*across from ... / go over / briskly*) |
| 兴趣 | xìngqù | interest (*joy / interest*) |
| 对... 感兴趣 | duì ... gǎn xìngqù | to be interested in ... (*across from ... / feel / interest / interest*) |
| 抽烟 | chōuyān | to smoke (*suck in / smoke*) |
| 等 | děng | to wait |
| 一下 | yíxià | a bit, just for a second (*one / below*) |

## Writing Exercises

| | | | | |
|---|---|---|---|---|
| 市 | 吧 | 走 | 休 | 息 |
| 素 | 往 | 前 | 直 | 就 |
| 拐 | 得 | 蔬 | 豆 | 腐 |
| 因 | 为 | 客 | 都 | 炒 |
| 锦 | 鱼 | 味 | 敏 | 兴 |
| 趣 | 感 | 抽 | 烟 | 等 |

## Sample Sentences

### Topic 1: The Particle ba 吧

The particle ba 吧 always stands at the end of the sentence and cannot be used in combination with other interrogative particles.

**In Requests**

我们今天去菜市买菜，好吧？
Wǒmen jīntiān qù càishì mǎi cài, hǎo ba?
*We / today / go / vegetable market / buy / groceries, / good / particle?*
We'll go grocery shopping at the vegetable market today, all right?

很好，走吧！
Hěn hǎo, zǒu ba!
*Very / good, / go / particle!*
Fine, let's go!

不好，我们休息吧！
Bù hǎo, wǒmen xiūxi ba!
*Not / good; / we / take break / particle.*
Bad idea; let's rest instead.

**For Agreement**

好吧！
Hǎo ba!
*Good / particle.*
Okay.

**For Suppositions**

你喜欢吃素，对吧？
Nǐ xǐhuan chī sù, duì ba?
*You / like very much / eat / vegetarian, / right / particle?*
But you like to eat vegetarian foods, don't you?

The particle ba 吧 expresses a supposition or assumption on the part of the speaker.

### Topic 2: Finding the Way

到茶馆怎么走？
Dào cháguǎn zěnme zǒu?
*To / teahouse / how / go?*
How do you get to the teahouse?

To ask the way, use dào ... zěnme zǒu?
到 ... 怎么走？

往前走！
Wǎng qián zǒu!
*In direction of / in front / go!*
Up ahead!

The short answer usually begins with the preposition wǎng 往. It is followed by a position or direction word with the full verb of the sentence.

你一直往前走。
Nǐ yìzhí wǎng qián zǒu.
*You / always / in direction of / in front / go.*
Keep going straight ahead.

在中国银行往右拐。
Zài Zhōngguó Yínháng wǎng yòu guǎi.
*Be located / Bank of China / in direction of / right / turn.*
Turn right at the Bank of China.

### Topic 3: The Conjunction yīnwèi 因为

我还得买蔬菜和豆腐，因为我的客人吃素.
Wǒ hái děi mǎi shūcài hé dòufu, yīnwèi wǒde kèren chī sù.
*I / still / must / buy / vegetables / and / tofu / because / my / guests / eat / vegetarian.*
I still have to buy vegetables and tofu because my guests are vegetarians.

Yīnwèi 因为 introduces causal clauses.

## Topic 4: The Adverb dōu 都

你们都吃素吗？

Nǐmen dōu chī sù ma?

*You (pl.) / all / eat / vegetarian / interrogative particle?*

Are you all vegetarians?

The adverb dōu 都 is used for more than one person and placed right after the personal pronoun.

他们两个都吃荤，我一个人吃素。

Tāmen liǎngge dōu chī hūn, wǒ yíge rén chī sù.

*They / both / all / eat / meat-containing; / I / alone / eat / vegetarian.*

The other two eat meat; I'm the only vegetarian.

我们都喜欢炒素菜，在饭馆也常常吃素什锦。

Wǒmen dōu xǐhuan chǎo sùcài, zài fànguǎn yě chángcháng chī sùshíjǐn.

*We / all / like / fried / vegetarian / foods, / in / restaurant / also / often / eat / vegetarian / mixture.*

We all like stir-fried vegetables, and in a restaurant I also often eat mixed vegetables.

他们都吃荤。肉、鱼和海味都可以。

Tāmen dōu chī hūn. Ròu, yú hé hǎiwèi dōu kěyǐ.

*They / all eat / meat-containing. / Meat, / fish, / and / seafood / everything / can; may.*

They all are nonvegetarians and eat all kinds of meat, fish, and seafood.

The adverb dōu 都 is used not only with persons but also with animals and things.

## Topic 5: The Preposition duì 对

你对我很好。

Nǐ duì wǒ hěn hǎo.

*You / across from / me / very / good.*

You are very good to me.

对不起，但是我不能吃鱼，我对鱼过敏。

Duìbuqǐ, dànshi wǒ bù néng chī yú, wǒ duì yú guòmǐn.

*Sorry, / but / I / not / can / eat / fish; / I / across from / fish / allergy.*

I'm sorry, but I can't eat fish; I'm allergic to fish.

我对中国茶很感兴趣。

Wǒ duì Zhōngguó chá hěn gǎn xìngqù.

*I / across from / China / tea leaves / very / feel / interest.*

I'm very interested in Chinese tea.

## Topic 6: The Doubling of Adjectives

我休息一下抽烟，你们慢慢吃！

Wǒ xiūxi yíxià chōuyān, nǐmen mànmàn chī!

*I / take break / a bit / smoke, / you / slow / eat!*

I'll take a break and have a quick smoke; you go ahead and eat in peace.

The doubling of the adjective conveys intensification. In this case, the stress falls on the second syllable.

## Topic 7: The Measure Word for Verbs yíxià 一下

请你等一下！

Qǐng nǐ děng yíxià!

*Ask / you (sing.) / wait / a bit!*

Please, wait just a second.

你休息一下吧！
Nǐ xiūxi yíxià ba!
*You (sing.) rest / a bit / particle!*
Just rest a little!

Yíxià 一下 (a bit, just quickly, just for a second) is used to count activities that are of short duration. There are other MWs for verbs, a few of which you will find in the Grammar section. They are always used in combination with a number, usually yī 一.

## Semantic Fields

**Places of Interest**

| | | |
|---|---|---|
| Hangzhou (city) | Hāngzhōu | 杭州 |
| West Lake | Xīhú | 西湖 |
| Dragon Well | Lóngjǐng | 龙井 |
| Shaoxing (city) | Shàoxīng | 绍兴 |
| Birthplace of Lu Xun | Lǔ Xùn Gùjū | 鲁迅故居 |
| Ningbo (city) | Níngbō | 宁波 |
| Mount Putuo, Putuoshan | Pǔtuóshān | 普陀山 |

**Fish**

| | | |
|---|---|---|
| eel | shànyú | 鳝鱼 |
| trout | zūnyú | 鳟鱼 |
| grass carp | cǎoyú | 草鱼 |
| carp | lǐyú | 鲤鱼 |
| salmon | guīyú | 鲑鱼 |
| tuna | jīnqiāngyú | 金枪鱼 |
| squid | mòyú | 墨鱼 |
| squid (calamari) | yóuyú | 鱿鱼 |

**Seafood**

| | | |
|---|---|---|
| abalone | bàoyú | 鲍鱼 |
| crayfish | héxiè | 河蟹 |
| shrimp | dàxiā | 大虾 |
| shrimp meat | xiārén | 虾仁 |
| lobster | lóngxiā | 龙虾 |
| scallop | shànbèi | 扇贝 |
| crabs | xiā | 虾 |
| crab | pángxiè | 螃蟹 |
| spiny lobster | lóngxiā | 龙虾 |
| mussel | hǎibèi | 海贝 |

**Vegetables**

| | | |
|---|---|---|
| eggplant | qiézi | 茄子 |
| bamboo sprouts | zhúsǔn | 竹笋 |
| bitter melon (bitter gourd) | kǔguā | 苦瓜 |
| leafy greens | qīngcài | 青菜 |
| leafy vegetables (hearts) | càixīn | 菜心 |
| cauliflower | huācài | 花菜 |
| beans | càidòu | 菜豆 |
| beans (white) | sìjìdòu | 四季豆 |
| bean sprouts | dòuyá | 豆芽 |
| broccoli | xīlánhuā | 西兰花 |
| button mushrooms (Chinese) | xiānggū | 香菇 |
| chili pods | làjiāo | 辣椒 |
| Chinese cabbage | dàbáicài | 大白菜 |
| peas | wāndòu | 豌豆 |
| peanut | huāshēng | 花生 |
| green onions, scallions | dàcōng | 大葱 |
| cucumber | huángguā | 黄瓜 |
| hyacinth beans (lablab beans) | biǎndòu | 扁豆 |
| carrots | húluóbo | 胡萝卜 |
| potatoes | tǔdòu | 土豆 |
| kohlrabi | piělán | 苤蓝 |
| pumpkin | nánguā | 南瓜 |
| leek | qīngsuàn | 青蒜 |
| lotus root | lián'ǒu | 莲藕 |
| corn | yùmǐ | 玉米 |

| | | |
|---|---|---|
| mung beans | lǜdòu | 绿豆 |
| mung bean sprouts | lǜdòuyá | 绿豆芽 |
| bok choy (cabbage) | xiǎo báicài | 小白菜 |
| pepper (green) | qīngjiāo | 青椒 |
| pepper (hot) | làjiāo | 辣椒 |
| peppermint | bòhe | 薄荷 |
| button mushrooms (fresh) | mógu | 蘑菇 |
| mushrooms | xiānggū | 香菇 |
| mushrooms (dried) | dōnggū | 冬菇 |
| radishes | xiǎo luóbo | 小萝卜 |
| lettuce | luóbo | 萝卜 |
| chives | shēngcài / shālā | 生菜 / 沙拉 |
| hot pickled mustard tuber | jiǔcài | 韭菜 |
| arugula | zhàcài | 榨菜 |
| mustard, fresh | gānlán | 甘蓝 |
| soybeans | huángdòu | 黄豆 |
| soybean sprouts | dòuyá | 豆芽 |
| asparagus | lúsǔn | 芦笋 |
| spinach | bōcài | 菠菜 |
| celery stalks | qíncài | 芹菜 |
| sweet potato | gānshǔ | 甘薯 |
| tomatoes | fānqié / xīhóngshì | 番茄 / 西红柿 |
| water chestnut | mǎtí | 马蹄 |
| white cabbage | yángbáicài | 洋白菜 |
| winter melon | dōngguā | 冬瓜 |
| sugar snaps | hélándòu | 荷兰豆 |
| onions | yángcōng | 洋葱 |

## Exercises

### Exercise 1

Form sentences with words for foods and drinks to which you are allergic.
Form sentences with places of interest in China that you would like to visit.

### Exercise 2

Which synonymous components do the following characters share:
等，笼，笋，筷，算，笔 ?

### Exercise 3

Write different versions of the sample sentences, using the words from the vocabulary list.

### Exercise 4

Say the sample sentences aloud, using words from the semantic fields. Form sentences by using the pyramid method.

Example:
pí jiǔ
Déguó pí jiǔ
duì Déguó pí jiǔ
duì Déguó pí jiǔ guòmǐn
Wáng nǚshì duì Déguó pí jiǔ guòmǐn

### Exercise 5

Listen to the sample sentences on the audio CD, and repeat them after the speaker.

**Exercise 6**

First, write the following sentences in Pīnyīn, indicating the tones, and then translate them into English.

1. 马先生对李小姐很感兴趣。
2. 我们常常去菜市买蔬菜，豆腐和面条。
3. 到饭馆你要往前走！

**Exercise 7**

Find the meaning of the following words by using the Pīnyīn transcription in the (online) dictionary.

1. zhàoxiàngjī 照相机
2. shǒujī 手机
3. jìsuànjī 计算机

**Exercise 8**

Translate the following sentences into Chinese.

1. Let's go eat!

– – – – – – – – – – – – – – – – – – – – –

2. Please go north (in a northerly direction).

– – – – – – – – – – – – – – – – – – – – –

3. I am interested in China.

– – – – – – – – – – – – – – – – – – – – –

4. I am allergic to alcohol.

– – – – – – – – – – – – – – – – – – – – –

5. I can't smoke (for health-related reasons).

– – – – – – – – – – – – – – – – – – – – –

6. Please, just write it down quickly.

– – – – – – – – – – – – – – – – – – – – –

7. What is that across the way?

– – – – – – – – – – – – – – – – – – – – –

# 9  Fújiàn 福建

Province: Fújiàn 福建
Abbreviation: Mǐn 闽
Capital of province: Fúzhōu 福州
60 counties, 23 cities
Area: 46,873 square miles
Population: 34.71 million
Number of persons / square mile: 733

## Vocabulary

| 馒头 | mántou | unflavored yeast dumpling (yeast dumpling / head) |
| 花钱 | huā qián | to spend money (spend / money) |
| 左右 | zuǒyòu | approximately (left / right) |
| 时间 | shíjiān | time (time / space) |
| 花时间 | huā shíjiān | to spend time on something (spend / time / space) |
| 朋友 | péngyou | friend (friend / friend) |
| 家 | jiā | family, home |
| 叫 | jiào | (used with full name or only first name) to be named; to call |
| 名字 | míngzi | name (name / character) |
| 姓 | xìng | to be named (used only with last name) |
| 介绍 | jièshào | to introduce (oneself); to explain (between / continue) |
| 认识 | rènshi | to become acquainted (recognize / know) |
| 高兴 | gāoxìng | happy, cheerful; with pleasure (high / joy) |
| 工作 | gōngzuò | to work (work / do) |

| 在 | zài | to be in progress (be located) |
| 男朋友 | nánpéngyou | boyfriend (male / friend / friend) |
| 女朋友 | nǚpéngyou | girlfriend (female / friend / friend) |
| 咖啡 | kāfēi | coffee |
| 粥 | zhōu | (thick) porridge made of rice/millet and water |
| 油条 | yóutiáo | long, salted, deep-fried strip of dough (oil / stalk) |
| 鸡蛋 | jīdàn | hen's egg (chicken / egg) |
| 咖啡馆 | kāfēiguǎn | coffeehouse, café (coffee / shop) |
| 一般 | yìbān | normally, usually, generally (one / way, manner) |
| 一起 | yìqǐ | all/everything together (one / stand up) |
| 看 | kàn | to look (at); to read; to visit |
| 看朋友 | kàn péngyou | to visit friends (look at / friend) |
| 跟 | gēn | with; to follow someone |
| 上 | shàng | to serve |
| 买单 | mǎidān | check, bill, tab (buy / list) |
| 一共 | yígòng | altogether, in total (one / same, general) |
| 算 | suàn | to calculate |

| | | |
|---|---|---|
| 付钱 | fù qián | to pay (*pay / money*) |
| 可能 | kěnéng | can, be possible; probably, perhaps (*can / can*) |
| 错 | cuò | wrong; erroneous; accidental |
| 了 | le | aspect particle |
| 听 | tīng | to hear; to listen (to) |
| 一定 | yídìng | absolutely; in any event (*one / determine*) |

## Sample Sentences

### Topic 1: The Verb huā 花

买一个馒头要花多少钱？

Mǎi yíge mántou yào huā duōshǎo qián?

*Buy / one MW / yeast dumpling / must / pay out / how much / money?*

How much (money) do you have to pay for a mantou?

买一个馒头要花五毛钱左右。

Mǎi yíge mántou yào huā wǔ máo qián zuǒyòu.

*Buy / one MW / yeast dumpling / must / pay out / five Mao / money / approximately.*

For one mantou, you have to pay approximately 0.50 RMB.

去银行要花多少时间？

Qù yínháng yào huā duōshǎo shíjiān?

*Go (there) / bank / must / spend / how much / time?*

How much time does it take to get to the bank?

去银行要花十分钟左右。

Qù yínháng yào huā shífēn zhōng zuǒyòu。

*Go (there) / bank / must / spend / ten minutes / time measured in hours / approximately*

It takes approximately ten minutes to get to the bank.

### Topic 2: People in Statements of Place (zài 在 and person)

If persons are to be used in statements of place, the designation of the person(s) must be followed by a place word such as zhèli 这里, zhèr 这儿, nàli 那里, nàr 那儿, or jiā 家.

我在我朋友那儿吃早饭。

Wǒ zài wǒ péngyou nàr chī zǎofàn。

*I / be located / my / friends / there / eat / breakfast.*

I'm having breakfast at my friends' (place).

你在王先生家休息。

Nǐ zài Wáng xiānsheng jiā xiūxi。

*You / be located / Wang / Mr. / at home / rest.*

You are taking a rest at Mr. Wang's (home).

### Topic 3: Introducing Yourself and Others

#### Asking for the Full Name or First Name
你叫什么名字？

Nǐ jiào shénme míngzi?

*You / be called / what kind of / name?*

What is your name?

#### Asking for the Last Name
你姓什么？

Nǐ xìng shénme?

*You / be called (by surname) / what?*

What is your last name?

## Writing Exercises

| | | | | |
|---|---|---|---|---|
| 馒 | 头 | 时 | 间 | 朋 |
| 友 | 家 | 叫 | 名 | 姓 |
| 介 | 绍 | 认 | 识 | 高 |
| 工 | 作 | 男 | 咖 | 啡 |
| 粥 | 油 | 蛋 | 般 | 看 |
| 跟 | 共 | 算 | 付 | 错 |
| 了 | 听 | 定 | | |

## Making Introductions

我介绍一下：这是我的朋友。

Wǒ jièshào yíxià: zhè shì wǒde péngyou.

*I / introduce / just quickly: / this / be / my / friend.*

May I introduce you: This is my friend.

我的朋友姓 …

Wǒde péngyou xìng …

*My / friend / (by surname) be called …*

My friend's last name is …

我的朋友叫 …

Wǒde péngyou jiào …

*My / friend / be called by full name or only first name …*

My friend's name is …

认识你，我很高兴。

Rènshi nǐ, wǒ hěn gāoxìng.

*Get acquainted / you, / I / very / happy.*

I'm glad to meet you.

## Asking about Work

你在哪里工作？

Nǐ zài nǎli gōngzuò?

*You / be located / where / work?*

Where do you work?

我在上海工作。

Wǒ zài Shànghǎi gōngzuò.

*I / be located / Shanghai / work.*

I work in Shanghai.

## Topic 4: The Progressive Aspect

我男朋友在喝咖啡，不在喝粥。

Wǒ nánpéngyou zài hē kāfēi, bú zài hē zhōu.

*My / boyfriend / right now / drink / coffee, / not / right now / drink / rice porridge.*

My boyfriend is drinking coffee at the moment and not eating rice porridge.

---

### Info Box

**English First Names**

| | | |
|---|---|---|
| Anna | Ānnà | 安娜 |
| Anthony | Āndōngní | 安东尼 |
| Ellen | Āilín | 埃琳 |
| Frank | Fólánkè | 弗兰克 |
| John | Yuēhàn | 约翰 |
| Kathleen | Kǎisīlín | 凯思琳 |
| Margaret | Mǎgélìtè | 玛格丽特 |
| Mary | Mǎlì | 玛丽 |
| Michael | Màikèér | 迈克尔 |
| Richard | Lǐchádé | 理查德 |
| Steven | Shǐdìwén | 史蒂文 |

**English Last Names**

| | | |
|---|---|---|
| Arnold | Ānuòdé | 阿诺德 |
| Brown | Bùlǎng | 布朗 |
| Douglas | Dàogélāsī | 道格拉斯 |
| Edwards | Àidéhuázī | 爱德华兹 |
| Green | Gélín | 格林 |
| Hawkins | Huòjīnsī | 霍金斯 |
| Jackson | Jiékèxùn | 杰克逊 |
| Lawrence | Láolúnsī | 劳伦斯 |
| Morgan | Mógēn | 摩根 |
| Olson | Àoěrsēn | 奥尔森 |
| Roberts | Luóbócí | 罗伯茨 |
| Spencer | Sībīnsè | 斯宾塞 |
| Taylor | Tàilè | 泰勒 |
| Williams | Wēiliánsī | 威廉斯 |
| Young | Yáng | 杨 |

我女朋友在吃油条和鸡蛋。
Wǒ nǚpéngyou zài chī yóutiao hé jīdàn.
*My / girlfriend / right now / eat / deep-fat-fried dough strips / and / eggs.*
My girlfriend is eating dough strips fried in deep fat and hen's eggs right now.

我先生现在没有时间，他在工作。
Wǒ xiānsheng xiànzài méi yǒu shíjiān, tā zài gōngzuò.
*My / husband / now / not have / time, / he / right now / work.*
My husband doesn't have time now, he's working at the moment.

The progressive aspect indicates that an action is in progress and has not yet been concluded.

By placing zhèngzài 正在 or zài 在 in front of the verbal predicate, you make it clear that you are using the progressive aspect, not stating a location.

## Topic 5: Eating Breakfast
我能不能请你到咖啡馆来吃英国早饭？
Wǒ néng bù néng qǐng nǐ dào kāfēiguǎn lái chī Yīnguó zǎofàn.
*I / can / not / can / invite / you / still / café / eat / English / breakfast.*
May I invite you to a café for an English breakfast?

英国早饭最好吃。
Yīnguó zǎofàn zuì hǎochī.
*English / breakfast / most / delicious.*
The English breakfast is the best.

早上中国人一般喝粥，不喝茶。
Zǎoshàng Zhōngguórén yìbān hē zhōu, bù hē chá.
*In the morning / Chinese / usually / drink / rice porridge, / not drink / tea.*
In the morning, the Chinese usually eat thin rice porridge and don't drink tea.

早饭我们在我家吃，晚饭去你那儿吃。
Zǎofàn wǒmen zài wǒ jiā chī, wǎnfàn qù nǐ nàr chī.
*Breakfast / we / be located / my / home / eat, / dinner / go (there) / you / there / eat / boiled rice.*
We'll eat breakfast at my house, and for dinner we'll go to your place.

## Topic 6: The Adverb yìqǐ 一起
The adverb yìqǐ 一起 can stand alone following the subject of the sentence.

我们一起去看朋友。
Wǒmen yìqǐ qù kàn péngyou.
*We / together / go (there) / visit / friends.*
We're going together to visit friends.

Or it can appear in the fixed combination
... gēn ... yìqǐ ... 跟 ... 一起

请米饭跟菜一起上！
Qǐng mǐfàn gēn cài yìqǐ shàng!
*Please / rice / with / main dishes / together / serve!*
Please serve the rice along with the main dishes.

我跟你一起去吃饭。
Wǒ gēn nǐ yìqǐ qù chī fàn.
*I / with / you / together / go (there) / eat / boiled rice.*
I'm going along with you to eat.

## Topic 7: Paying the Check
请买单！
Qǐng mǎidān!
*Please / bill!*
The check, please.

一共多少钱？
Yígòng duōshǎo qián?
*Together / how much / money?*
How much is all that together?

请你算一下我要付多少钱！
Qǐng nǐ suàn yíxià, wǒ yào fù
duōshǎo qián!
*Please / you / calculate / a bit / I / must / pay /
how much / money!*
Please, just figure out quickly what I need
to pay.

## Topic 8: Making a Mistake
(see Grammar)

The complement cuò 错 and the particle
le 了 are attached directly to the verb, in
order to express an incorrect or mistaken
action. Objects may follow.

你可能算错了。
Nǐ kěnéng suàncuòle.
*You / possibly / calculate / incorrectly / particle.*
You probably miscalculated.

对不起，我可能听错了。
Duìbuqǐ, wǒ kěnéng tīngcuòle.
*Sorry, / I / possibly / hear / incorrectly / particle.*
Excuse me, I probably misheard.

## Topic 9: Saying Goodbye at a Restaurant
The guest uses the following sentence when
leaving:

我一定再来！
Wǒ yídìng zài lái!
*I / definitely / again / come!*
I'm definitely coming back!

The waiter and/or the person staying behind says:

慢走。
Mànzǒu。
*Slow / go.*
Goodbye!

## Semantic Fields  (CD2 3)
### Places of Interest

| | | |
|---|---|---|
| Fuzhou (city) | Fúzhōu | 福州 |
| Mt. Wuyi | Wǔyí Shān | 武夷山 |
| Xiamen/Amoy (city) | Xiàmén | 厦门 |
| South Putuo Temple | Nánpǔtuó Sì | 南普陀寺 |
| Drum Wave Island | Gǔlàng Yǔ | 鼓浪屿 |
| Quanzhou (city) | Quánzhōu | 泉州 |
| Mosque of Peace and Clarity | Qīngjìng Sì | 清静寺 |
| Temple of the Beginning of the New Age | Kāiyuán Sì | 开元寺 |
| Museum of the History of Foreign Trade | Hǎiwài Jiāotōngshǐ Bówùguǎn | 海外交通史博物馆 |

### Breakfast (Western and Chinese)

| | | |
|---|---|---|
| porridge made of rice and water, very thin | xīfàn | 稀饭 |
| bread | miànbāo | 面包 |
| roll | xiǎomiànbāo | 小面包 |
| butter | huángyóu | 黄油 |
| vegetables, pickled | pàocài | 泡菜 |
| yeast roll ("flower roll") | huājuǎn | 花卷 |
| honey | fēngmì | 蜂蜜 |
| yogurt | suānnǎi | 酸奶 |

| cheese | nǎilào | 奶酪 |
|---|---|---|
| crackers | bǐnggān | 饼干 |
| sticky rice dumplings in bamboo leaves | zòngzi | 粽子 |
| margarine | zhíwùyóu | 植物油 |
| jam | guǒjiàng | 果酱 |
| milk tea (Mongolian, Caucasian) | nǎichá | 奶茶 |
| pancake, filled | xiànbǐng | 馅饼 |
| ham | huǒtuǐ | 火腿 |
| soy milk | dòujiāng | 豆浆 |
| sausages | xiāngcháng | 香肠 |
| yak butter tea (Tibetan) | sūyóuchá | 酥油茶 |
| sugar | táng | 糖 |

## Sweets (Western and Chinese)

| apple, candied | básī píngguǒ | 拔丝苹果 |
|---|---|---|
| ice cream on a stick | bīnggùn | 冰棍 |
| ice cream | bīngqílín | 冰淇淋 |
| candied fruits on a stick | bīngtáng húlu | 冰糖葫芦 |
| cookies | bǐnggān | 饼干 |
| sticky rice dumplings with sesame-seed filling | zhīma tāngyuán | 芝麻汤圆 |
| sticky rice dumplings with brandy | báijiǔ zhēnzhū tāngyuán | 白酒珍珠汤圆 |
| cake | dàngāo | 蛋糕 |
| cream | nǎiyóu | 奶油 |
| toffees | nǎitáng | 奶糖 |
| chocolate | qiǎokèlì | 巧克力 |
| white morel soup with Chinese rock sugar | bīngtáng yín'ěr | 冰糖银耳 |

## Quantities (in containers)

| cup, mug, tub | yì bēi | 一杯 |
|---|---|---|
| bag | yí dài | 一袋 |
| steamer | yì lóng | 一笼 |
| can | yì guǎn | 一管 |
| bottle | yì píng | 一瓶 |
| glass (jar) | yì bēi | 一杯 |
| cardboard box | yì hé | 一盒 |
| package, pack | yì bāo | 一包 |
| roll | yì juǎn | 一卷 |
| box, carton | yì hé | 一盒 |
| bowl | yì wǎn | 一碗 |
| slice | yí piàn | 一片 |
| skewer | yí chuàn | 一串 |
| piece | yí kuài | 一块 |
| slab | yì bǎn | 一板 |
| cup | yì bēi | 一杯 |
| plate | yì pán | 一盘 |
| tube | yì guǎn | 一管 |
| sack | yí dài | 一袋 |

## Family Members

| parents | fùmǔ | 父母 |
|---|---|---|
| father | fùqin | 父亲 |
| mother | mǔqin | 母亲 |
| papa | bàba | 爸爸 |
| mama | māma | 妈妈 |
| husband | xiānsheng | 先生 |
| wife | tàitai | 太太 |
| siblings, brothers and sisters | xiōngdì jiěmèi | 兄弟姐妹 |
| brothers | xiōngdì | 兄弟 |
| sisters | jiěmèi | 姐妹 |
| child | háizi | 孩子 |
| son | érzi | 儿子 |
| daughter | nǚ'ér | 女儿 |
| grandson | sūnzi | 孙子 |
| granddaughter | sūn'nǚ | 孙女 |

# Fújiàn 福建  9

## Exercises

### Exercise 1

Introduce yourself, your best male friend, and your best female friend, giving first and last names.

### Exercise 2

Which synonymous components do the following characters share:
她，好，妹，安，姐，妈，奶，姓？

### Exercise 3

Write different versions of the sample sentences, using the words from the vocabulary list.

### Exercise 4

Say the sample sentences aloud, using words from the semantic fields. Create sentences by using the pyramid method.

Example:
wǒ
wǒ gēn
wǒ gēn tāmen
wǒ gēn tāmen yìqǐ
wǒ gēn tāmen yìqǐ qù
wǒ gēn tāmen yìqǐ qù kàn
wǒ gēn tāmen yìqǐ qù kàn wǒmende
wǒ gēn tāmen yìqǐ qù kàn wǒmende
péngyou

### Exercise 5

Listen to the sample sentences on the audio CD, and repeat them after the speaker.

### Exercise 6

First, write the following sentences in Pīnyīn, indicating the tones, and then translate them into English.

1. 早上美国人一般喝咖啡，不喝啤酒。
2. 李女士在休息，马小姐在抽烟。
3. 咖啡官里面没有北京烤鸭。你看错了！

### Exercise 7

Find the meaning of the following words by using the Pīnyīn transcription in the (online) dictionary.

1. pīngpāngqiú 乒乓球
2. Wǎngqiú 网球
3. Lánqiú 篮球

### Exercise 8

Translate the following sentences into Chinese:

1. Just take a quick look!

_____

2. Just wait a minute! I'm still eating breakfast.

_____

3. Do you want to celebrate your girlfriend's birthday with her this evening?

_____

4. You absolutely must introduce your Chinese friends to me!

_____

5. I'm sorry. I misspoke.

_____

6. How long does it take to get from your place to my place?

_____

# 10 Guǎngdōng 广东

Province: Guǎngdōng 广东
Abbreviation: Yuè 粤
Capital of province: Guǎngzhōu 广州
79 counties, 54 cities
Area: 68,726 square miles
Population: 86.42 million
Numbers of persons / square mile: 1,246

## Vocabulary

| | | |
|---|---|---|
| 谁 | shéi | who? |
| 南方人 | nánfāngrén | South Chinese (*south / direction / human being*) |
| 动物 | dòngwù | animal (*move / thing*) |
| 时候 | shíhou | point in time, moment (*time / time*) |
| 什么时候 | shénme shíhou | when? (*various / suffix / time / time*) |
| 除了… 以外 | chúle… yǐwài | except, besides (*exclude / particle … / by means of / outside*) |
| 点心 | diǎnxīn | dim sum; light snack; pastries and cake (*little thing / heart*) |
| 别的 | biéde | something else/other |
| 特餐 | tècān | specialty (*special / food*) |
| 唱歌 | chànggē | to sing (*sing / song*) |
| 踢 | tí | to kick; to step; to play |
| 足球 | zúqiú | soccer (*foot / ball*) |
| 得 | de | for forming the complement of degree (CoD) |
| 马马虎虎 | mǎmahūhū | so-so (*horse / horse / tiger / tiger*) |

| | | |
|---|---|---|
| 打 | dǎ | with card games and mahjong: to play |
| 麻将 | májiàng | mahjong/mah-jongg (*hemp / general*) |
| 真 | zhēn | real; genuine; true |
| 唱卡拉OK | chàng KǎlāOK | to sing karaoke (*sing / karaoke*) |
| 非常 | fēicháng | extreme; exceptional (*not be / usual*) |
| 不错 | búcuò | not bad (*not / incorrect*) |
| 北方人 | běifāngrén | North Chinese (*north / direction / human being*) |
| 下 | xià | with board games: to play; to position |
| 象棋 | xiàngqí | chess (*elephant / board game*) |
| 懂 | dǒng | to understand |
| 预订 | yùdìng | to reserve (*in advance / order*) |
| 房间 | fángjiān | room (*room / space*); MW: jiān 间 |
| 打电话 | dǎ diànhuà | to telephone (*hit / electricity / speech*) |
| 住 | zhù | to live, reside |

| | | |
|---|---|---|
| 楼 | lóu | floor, story; multistory building |
| 钥匙 | yàoshi | key (key/spoon); MW: bǎ 把 |
| 过 | guo | aspect particle |
| 别 | bié | must not, to be not supposed to (imperative negation of "must") |
| 忘 | wàng | to forget |

## Sample Sentences

**Topic 1: Question Word and dōu 都**

谁什么都吃？
Shéi shénme dōu chī?
*Who / what / all / eat?*
Who eats everything?

南方人什么都吃。
Nánfāngrén shénme dōu chī。
*South Chinese / what / all / eat*
The South Chinese eat everything.

南方人什么动物都吃。
Nánfāngrén shénme dòngwù dōu chī。
*South Chinese / what kind of / animals / all /eat.*
The South Chinese eat all animals.

中国人什么时候都能吃。
Zhōngguórén shénme shíhou dōu néng chī。
*Chinese / what / point in time / all / can / eat.*
The Chinese can eat all the time.

谁都不喜欢他。
Shéi dōu bù xǐhuan tā。
*Who / all / not / like / him.*
Nobody likes him at all.

他怎么都不想走。
Tā zěnme dōu bù xiǎng zǒu。
*He / as / all / not / want to / go.*
He doesn't want to leave at all.

这里什么都没有。
Zhèli shénme dōu méi yǒu。
*Here / what / all / not (have) / have.*
Here there is nothing at all.

Dōu 都 can be used both in affirmative and in negative sentences. It always conveys intensification.

**Topic 2: The Preposition chúle ... yǐwài 除了 ... 以外**

除了点心以外，我还要吃别的特餐。
Chúle diǎnxīn yǐwài, wǒ hái yào chī biéde tècān。
*Excluded / dim sum / besides, / I / still / want / eat / other / specialties.*
Besides dim sum, I want to eat other specialties, too.

除了我以外他们都会唱歌。
Chúle wǒ yǐwài, tāmen dōu huì chànggē。
*Excluded / I / besides, / they / all / can / sing / songs.*
Aside from me, they all can sing.

**Topic 3: Sentences with the Complement of Degree (CoD)**
**(see Grammar)**

Adverbs are formed with the complement of degree. By means of the particle de 得, verbs are linked with an adjective, and then they generally express the past tense or a habit. In this case, the particles le 了 and guo 过 may **not** be used.

## Writing Exercises

| | | | | |
|---|---|---|---|---|
| 南 | 谁 | 动 | 物 | 候 |
| 除 | 外 | 心 | 别 | 特 |
| 餐 | 唱 | 歌 | 踢 | 足 |
| 球 | 虎 | 麻 | 将 | 真 |
| 卡 | 拉 | 非 | 象 | 棋 |
| 懂 | 预 | 订 | 房 | 钥 |
| 匙 | 住 | 楼 | 忘 | |

## Verbs with No Object

他吃得快。
Tā chīde kuài。
*He / eat / CoD / quickly.*
He eats quickly. / He ate quickly.

## Negation

她喝得不慢。
Tā hēde bú màn。
*She / drink / CoD / not / slowly.*
She doesn't drink slowly. / She didn't drink
slowly.

The negation always precedes the adjective.

## Verbs with an Object

If the verb has an object, the verb must be
repeated because de 得 can be attached only
to a verb, never to a noun.

他吃饭吃得快。
Tā chī fàn chīde kuài。
*He / eat / boiled rice / eat / CoD / quickly.*
He eats quickly. / He ate quickly.

德国人踢足球踢得马马虎虎。
Déguórén tí zúqiú tíde mǎmahūhu。
*Germans / kick / soccer / kick / CoD / so-so.*
The Germans are so-so soccer players.

广东人打麻将打得真好。
Guǎngdōngrén dǎ májiàng dǎde zhēn
hǎo。
*Cantonese / play / mahjong / play / CoD /
really / well.*
The Cantonese play mahjong really well.

上海人唱卡拉OK唱得非常不错。
Shànghǎirén chàng KǎlāOK chàngde
fēicháng búcuò。
*Shanghainese / sing / karaoke / sing / CoD /
extremely / not bad.*

The Shanghainese don't sing karaoke badly
at all.

Additional adverbs such as hěn 很, fēicháng
非常, and others can appear as complements
of an adjective.

北方人下象棋下得还可以。
Běifāngrén xià xiàngqí xiàde hái
kěyǐ。
*North Chinese / play / chess / play / CoD /
still / can.*
The North Chinese play chess very well.

南方人说汉语说得我不能懂。
Nánfāngrén shuō Hànyǔ shuōde wǒ bù
néng dǒng。
*South Chinese / speak / Chinese / speak / CoD /
I / not / in a position / understand.*
The South Chinese speak Chinese in a way that
I can't understand.

The complement can also consist of complete
clauses, which in English would require a
construction such as "in a way that."

Topic 4: In a Hotel
我想预定房间。
Wǒ xiǎng yùdìng fángjiān。
*I / would like / reserve / rooms.*
I would like to reserve rooms.

我给你打电话预订了八月二十号的一个
房间。
Wǒ gěi nǐ dǎ diànhuà yùdìngle bāyuè
èrshíhào de yìge fángjiān。
*I / give / you / telephone / reserve / aspect
particle / August / twenty-number / attributive
article / "one" measure word / room.*
I phoned to make a reservation for August 20.

我住十六楼一六二七号房间。
Wǒ zhù shíliù lóu yāo liù èr qī hào
fángjiān
*I / live / sixteen-floor / one six two seven
number / room.*
I'm staying on the 16th floor, Room 1627.

请给我五一三号房间的钥匙！
Qǐng gěi wǒ wǔ yāo sān hào
fángjiānde yàoshi!
*Please / give / me / five one three number /
room / attributive particle / key.*
Please give me the key for Room 513.

### Topic 5: The Aspect Particle guo 过
(see Grammar)

你来过中国吗？
Nǐ láiguo Zhōngguó ma?
*You / come / aspect particle / China /
interrogative particle?*
Have you ever been in China?

你吃过北京烤鸭吗？
Nǐ chīguo Běijīng kǎoyā ma?
*You / eat / aspect particle / Peking duck /
interrogative particle?*
Have you ever eaten Peking duck?

The particle guo 过 is attached to the verb,
and it refers to an experience in an indefinite
past time. In English, this often is rendered
as "ever."

我去过中国，但是没有吃过北京烤鸭。
Wǒ qùguo Zhōngguó, dànshì méi yǒu
chīguo Běijīng kǎoyā。
*I / go / aspect particle / China, / but / not (have) /
have / eat / aspect particle / Peking duck.*
I've been to China, but I've never eaten
Peking duck.

### Info Box

**Difference between** le 了 **and** guo 过
Le 了 often is connected with a definite time,
and it describes a concluded action in a neutral
way.

Guo 过 often is connected with an indefinite
time, and it refers to a particular experience.

### Topic 6: Imperative with bié 别

别忘了！
Bié wàng le!
*Must not / forget / aspect particle!*
Don't forget it!

Bié 别 directly precedes the verb and expresses
a negated exclamation. In this case, the
command-like imperative is slightly softened
by the particle le 了.

### Semantic Fields
Places of Interest

| | | |
|---|---|---|
| Guangzhou/ Canton (city) | Guǎngzhōu | 广州 |
| Ancestral Temple of the Chen Family | Chénjiā Cí | 陈家祠 |
| Temple of the Six Banyan Trees | Liùróng Sì | 六榕寺 |
| Birthplace of Sun Yat-sen | Zhōngshān Gùjū | 中山故居 |
| White Clouds Mountain | Báiyúnshān | 白云山 |
| Foshan (city) | Fóshān | 佛山 |
| Ancestors' Temple | Fóshān Zǔmiào | 佛山祖庙 |

| | | | | |
|---|---|---|---|---|
| Animals | ZEW | | dòngwù | 动物 |
| abalone | zhī | 只 | bàoyú | 鲍鱼 |
| monkey | zhī | 只 | hóuzi | 猴子 |
| ant | zhī | 只 | mǎyǐ | 蚂蚁 |

| bear | zhī | 只 | xióng | 熊 |
| bee | zhī | 只 | mìfēng | 蜜蜂 |
| dragon | zhī | 只 | lóng | 龙 |
| elephant | tóu | 头 | dàxiàng | 大象 |
| duck | zhī | 只 | yāzi | 鸭子 |
| donkey | pǐ | 匹 | lúzi | 驴子 |
| fish | tiáo | 条 | yú | 鱼 |
| bat | zhī | 只 | biānfú | 蝙蝠 |
| flea | zhī | 只 | tiàozǎo | 跳蚤 |
| frog | zhī | 只 | qīngwā | 青蛙 |
| fox | zhī | 只 | húli | 狐狸 |
| goose | zhī | 只 | é | 鹅 |
| shark | tiáo | 条 | shāyú | 鲨鱼 |
| hare | zhī | 只 | tùzi | 兔子 |
| grasshopper | zhī | 只 | huángchóng | 蝗虫 |
| chicken | zhī | 只 | jī | 鸡 |
| dog | zhī | 只 | gǒu | 狗 |
| cockroach | zhī | 只 | zhāngláng | 蟑螂 |
| camel | tóu | 头 | luòtuo | 骆驼 |
| cat | zhī | 只 | māo | 猫 |
| crocodile | zhī | 只 | èyú | 鳄鱼 |
| mouse | zhī | 只 | lǎoshǔ | 老鼠 |
| seagull | zhī | 只 | hǎi'ōu | 海鸥 |
| mosquito | zhī | 只 | wénzi | 蚊子 |
| panda | zhī | 只 | xióngmāo | 熊猫 |
| horse | pǐ | 匹 | mǎ | 马 |
| cattle | tóu | 头 | niú | 牛 |
| sheep | zhī | 只 | miányáng | 绵羊 |
| tortoise, turtle | zhī | 只 | guī | 龟 |
| snake | tiáo | 条 | shé | 蛇 |
| butterfly | zhī | 只 | húdié | 蝴蝶 |
| pig | zhī | 只 | zhū | 猪 |
| scorpion | zhī | 只 | xiēzi | 蝎子 |
| tiger | zhī | 只 | lǎohǔ | 老虎 |
| turkey | zhī | 只 | huǒjī | 火鸡 |
| bedbug | zhī | 只 | chòuchóng | 臭虫 |
| water buffalo | tóu | 头 | shuǐniú | 水牛 |

| soft-shelled tortoise | zhī | 只 | jiǎyú | 甲鱼 |
| yak | tóu | 头 | máoniú | 牦牛 |
| goat | zhī | 只 | shānyáng | 山羊 |
| cicada | zhī | 只 | chán | 蝉 |

**Exotic Dishes**

| fish stomach, fermented | bǎihuā niàng yúdù | 百花酿鱼肚 |
| frogs' legs, stir fried | chǎo tiánjītuǐ | 炒田鸡腿 |
| live "drunken" shrimp | zuìxiā | 醉虾 |
| shark fin soup | yúchì tāng | 鱼翅汤 |
| chicken feet | jīzhuǎ | 鸡爪 |
| dog meat | gǒuròu/ xiāngròu | 狗肉/香肉 |
| bullfrog steeped in oil | yóupào niúwā | 油泡牛蛙 |
| jellyfish in sesame oil | xiāngyóu zhépí | 香油蛰皮 |
| beef tripe, pan fried | niú bǎiyè | 牛百叶 |
| snake with mushrooms and bamboo | shuāngdōng shéduàn | 双冬蛇段 |
| swallow's nest soup | yànwō tāng | 燕窝汤 |
| pig's ears | zhū ěrduo | 猪耳朵 |
| sea cucumber | hǎishēn | 海参 |
| scorpion on a skewer | xiēzichuàn | 蝎子串 |
| pigeon eggs with bird's stomach | zhēnqiú cuān gēdàn | 胗球氽鸽蛋 |
| thousand-year-old eggs | pídàn | 皮蛋 |
| water cockroaches, deep fried | zhá shuǐ zhāngláng | 炸水蟑螂 |

| soft-shelled tortoise with mushrooms | mógu jiǎyú | 蘑菇甲鱼 |
|---|---|---|

| Games | | |
|---|---|---|
| backgammon | xī yáng shuānglùqí | 西洋 双路棋 |
| checkers | xī yángqí | 西洋棋 |
| Go | wéiqí | 围棋 |
| cards | pūkèpái | 扑克牌 |
| chess (international) | guójì xiàngqí | 国际象棋 |
| chess (Chinese) | Zhōngguó xiàngqí | 中国象棋 |

## Exercises

### Exercise 1

According to the ancient Chinese calendar, the years are named for a series of twelve animals. After each character, write the English meaning of each of the twelve Chinese signs of the zodiac.

| | | | | |
|---|---|---|---|---|
| 1. shǔ | 鼠 | | 7. mǎ | 马 |
| 2. niú | 牛 | | 8. yáng | 羊 |
| 3. hǔ | 虎 | | 9. hóu | 猴 |
| 4. tù | 兔 | | 10. jī | 鸡 |
| 5. lóng | 龙 | | 11. gǒu | 狗 |
| 6. shé | 蛇 | | 12. zhū | 猪 |

### Exercise 2

Which synonymous components do the following characters share:
快，慢，怎，息，感，忘？

### Exercise 3

Write different versions of the sample sentences, using the words from the vocabulary list.

### Exercise 4

Say the sample sentences aloud, using words from the semantic fields. Create sentences by using the pyramid method.

Example:
zhōngguórén
zhōngguórén chī
zhōngguórén chī yú
zhōngguórén chī yú chīde
zhōngguórén chī yú chīde hěn
zhōngguórén chī yú chīde hěn duō

### Exercise 5

Listen to the sample sentences on the audio CD, and repeat them after the speaker.

### Exercise 6

First, write the following sentences in Pīnyīn, indicating the tones, and then translate them into English.

1. 我要买两张到上海的火车票！
2. 我们在哪里上车？
3. 他们坐飞机去中国，我坐火车去。

## Exercise 7

Find the meaning of the following words by using the Pīnyīn transcription in the (online) dictionary.

1. diànshì 电视
2. zhuōzi 桌子
3. chuáng 床
4. kōngtiáo 空调

## Exercise 8

Translate the following sentences into Chinese.

1. You mustn't speak any more English with me.

— — — — — — — — — — — — — — — — — — — —

2. Besides English, I can also speak Chinese.

— — — — — — — — — — — — — — — — — — — —

3. The Chinese speak Chinese very rapidly.

— — — — — — — — — — — — — — — — — — — —

4. Do you have an even cheaper room?

— — — — — — — — — — — — — — — — — — — —

5. I would like to stay in this room from March 15 to 20.

— — — — — — — — — — — — — — — — — — — —

6. We paid too much money.

— — — — — — — — — — — — — — — — — — — —

7. I'll telephone you.

— — — — — — — — — — — — — — — — — — — —

# 11 Nèi Měnggǔ 内蒙古

Autonomous region: Nèi Měnggǔ 内蒙古
(Inner Mongolia)

Abbreviation: Měng 蒙

Capital: Hohhot (Hūhéhàotè) 呼和浩特

84 counties, 20 cities

Area: 456,759 square miles

Population: 23.76 million

Number of persons / square mile: 51

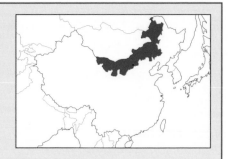

CD2 7

## Vocabulary

| | | |
|---|---|---|
| 万 | wàn | ten thousand |
| 万岁 | wànsuì | long live ... (*ten thousand / years*) |
| 干杯 | gānbēi | cheers, to your health (*dry / cup*) |
| 为 ... | wèi | to ...; for ... |
| 健康 | jiànkāng | health (*healthy, strong / health*) |
| 火锅 | huǒguō | hot pot (*fire / pot*) |
| 离 | lí | distant; far from; away from; as far as |
| 远 | yuǎn | far |
| 近 | jìn | near |
| 多远 | duōyuǎn | how far? (*much / far*) |
| 公里 | gōnglǐ | kilometer (*metric / lǐ*) |
| 多少公里 | duōshǎo gōnglǐ | how many kilometers? (*much / little / metric / lǐ*) |
| 步行 | bùxíng | on foot (*step / go*) |
| 小时 | xiǎoshi | hour (*small / time*) |
| 火车 | huǒchē | train (*fire / vehicle*) MW: liè 列 |
| 火车站 | huǒchēzhàn | train station (*fire / vehicle / stop*) |
| 坐 ... | zuò | to travel with; to travel by ...; to go by ... |
| 车 | chē | vehicle; MW: liàng 辆 |
| 出租汽车 | chūzū qìchē | taxi; rental car (*out of / rent / steam / vehicle*); MW: liàng 辆 |
| 飞机 | fēijī | airplane (*fly / machine*); MW: tài 台 |
| 飞机场 | fēijīchǎng | airport (*fly / machine / place*) |
| 知道 | zhīdao | to know (*know / way*) |
| 马路 | mǎlù | street, road (*horse / street*); MW: tiáo 条 |
| 上车 | shàng chē | to get in/on, board (*get in / vehicle*) |
| 下车 | xià chē | to get out/off, disembark (*get off / vehicle*) |
| 饭店 | fàndiàn | hotel, restaurant (*boiled rice / shop*); MW: jiā 家 |
| 多少时间 | duōshǎo shíjiān | how long? how much time? (*much / little / time / space*) |
| 需要 | xūyào | to need, require (*need / demand*) |
| 差不多 | chàbuduō | approximately (*lack / not / much*) |
| 带 | dài | to take with, bring along |

| | | |
|---|---|---|
| 零钱 | língqián | change, small/loose change (*zero / money*) |
| 开 | kāi | to steer; to put in gear; to drive off |
| 排队 | páiduì | to get in line; to stand in line (*arrange / persons in rank and file*) |
| 车票 | chēpiào | ticket (for transportation) (*vehicle / card*) MW: zhāng 张 |
| 座位 | zuòwèi | seat; place (*sit; seat / place*) |
| 明天 | míngtiān | tomorrow (*clear / day*) |
| 硬卧 | yìngwò | "hard sleeper," sleeping car compartment with nonpadded beds (*hard / lie*) |
| 行李 | xíngli | baggage, luggage; travel paraphernalia (*move along, trip / plum*) |
| 退 | tuì | to give back; to bring back |
| 所以 | suǒyǐ | therefore (*place / by means of*) |
| 骑 | qí | to ride (a horse); to ride a bike; to ride a motorcycle |
| 马 | mǎ | horse; MW: pǐ 匹 |
| 自行车 | zìxíngchē | bicycle (*self / move along / vehicle*); MW: liàng 辆 |

## Sample Sentences

### Topic 1: Drinking Toasts

祝你万岁，干杯！
Zhù nǐ wànsuì, gānbēi!
*Wish / you / ten thousand years . / Cheers!*
I wish you a long life. Cheers!

为你的健康，干杯！
Wèi nǐde jiànkāng, gānbēi!
*For / your / health. / Cheers!*
To your health. Cheers!

Even without a toast, you can say gānbēi 干杯 to someone in China to mean "bottoms up."

### Topic 2: Stating Distances with lí 离

吃火锅的地方离这里远吗？
Chī huǒguōde dìfang lí zhèli yuǎn ma?
*Eat / hot pot / attributive particle / place / distant from / here / far / interrogative particle?*
Is the place where you can eat hot pot far from here?

离这里不远，很近。
Lí zhèli bù yuǎn, hěn jìn.
*Distant from / here / not / far / very / near.*
It's not far from here but very near.

Lí 离 is always followed by a designation of place and then by the distance.

多远？
Duōyuǎn?
*How far?*
How far?

三公里远，步行半个小时。
Sān gōnglǐ yuǎn, bùxíng bànge xiǎoshí.
*Three kilometers / far, / on foot / half MW / hour.*
It is 3 km away, half an hour on foot.

## Writing Exercises

| | | | | |
|---|---|---|---|---|
| 万 | 干 | 健 | 康 | 火 |
| 锅 | 离 | 远 | 近 | 公 |
| 步 | 车 | 站 | 租 | 汽 |
| 飞 | 机 | 场 | 知 | 道 |
| 路 | 店 | 需 | 带 | 排 |
| 队 | 座 | 位 | 明 | 硬 |
| 卧 | 退 | 所 | 骑 | 自 |

## Topic 3: Taking a Taxi

When you travel in a vehicle without driving it yourself, zuò 坐 directly precedes the means of transportation.

坐出租汽车到火车站多少钱？
Zuò chūzū qìchē dào huǒchēzhàn duōshǎo qián?
*Sit / taxi / to train station / how much / money?*
How much does a taxi to the train station cost?

请给我叫一辆到飞机场的出租汽车！
Qǐng gěi wǒ jiào yíliàng dào fēijīchǎngde chūzūqìchē!
*Please / give / me / call / one MW / to / airport / attributive particle / taxi!*
Please call me a taxi to go to the airport!

你得过马路上车。
Nǐ děi guò mǎlù shàng chē.
*You / must / cross / street / get in / car.*
You have to cross the street to get in.

去飞机场！
Qù fēijīchǎng!
*Go (there) / airport!*
To the airport!

你知道怎么去飞机场吗？
Nǐ zhīdao zěnme qù fēijīchǎng ma?
*You / know / how / go / airport / interrogative particle?*
Do you know how to get to the airport?

请你快一点开车！
Qǐng nǐ kuài yìdiǎn kāichē!
*Please / you / fast / a little / drive!*
Please drive faster!

你能不能等我十分种？
Nǐ néng bù néng děng wǒ shí fēnzhōng?

*You / can / not / can / wait / me / ten minutes?*
Can you wait ten minutes for me?

九点能到吗？
Jiǔdiǎn néng dào ma?
*Nine o'clock / can / arrive / interrogative particle?*
Can we get there by 9 o'clock?

### Info Box

Tips (xiǎofèi 小费) are not expected by Chinese taxi drivers, or, by the way, by servers in restaurants or hairdressers either. As a rule, a receipt is printed out in the taxi, and you pay the charge without rounding it up. Tour guides and baggage porters are an exception.

到我们的饭店需要多少时间？
Dào wǒmende fàndiàn xūyào duōshǎo shíjiān?
*To / our / hotel / need / how much / time?*
How long does it take to get to our hotel ?

差不多四十分钟。
Chàbuduō sìshí fēnzhōng.
*Approximately / forty minutes.*
Approximately forty minutes.

到了，下车吧！
Dàole, xiàchē ba!
*Arrive / aspect particle, / get out / particle!*
Here we are. All out, please!

对不起，我没带零钱。
Duìbuqǐ, wǒ méi dài língqián.
*Sorry; / I / not (have) / bring with / loose change.*
I'm sorry; I don't have any change on me.

## Topic 4: Driving Yourself

If you drive a car yourself, zuò 坐 is not used.

开车要五分钟，走路要半个小时。
Kāi chē yào wǔ fēnzhōng, zǒu lù yào
bànge xiǎoshí。
*Drive / car / need / five minutes; / go / street /
need / half MW / hour.*
By car, it's five minutes; on foot, half an hour.

The measure word ge 个 must also be used
after the statement of quantity bàn 半.

我开错了。
Wǒ kāi cuòle。
*I / drive / wrong / aspect particle.*
I took the wrong road.

## Topic 5: Taking the Train

请你排队买车票！
Qǐng nǐ páiduì mǎi chēpiào！
*Please / you / line up / buy / ticket!*
Please stand in line to purchase a ticket.

还有没有座位？
Hái yǒu méi yǒu zuòwèi？
*Still / have / not (have) / have / place?*
Are any seats still available?

我想买一张明天去北京的硬卧票。
Wǒ xiǎng mǎi yìzhāng míngtiān qù
Běijīngde yìngwòpiào。
*I / would like / buy / one MW / tomorrow /
go (there) / Beijing / attributive particle /
hard sleeper ticket.*
I would like to buy a "hard sleeper" ticket to
Beijing for tomorrow.

火车几点开？
Huǒchē jǐdiǎn kāi？
*Train / how much hour / depart?*
When does the train leave?

## Topic 6: Flying

坐飞机可以带多少行李？
Zuò fēijī kěyǐ dài duōshǎo xíngli？
*Sit / airplane / may / take along / how much /
baggage?*
How much baggage can you take on the plane?

我想退飞机票。
Wǒ xiǎng tuì fēijīpiào。
*I / would like / give back / airline ticket.*
I would like to return the airline ticket.

---

### Info Box

The four classes on Chinese trains:

| | | |
|---|---|---|
| 硬座 | yìngzuò | "Hard seater": compartment with nonpadded seats (*hard / seat*) |
| 软座 | ruǎnzuò | "Soft seater": compartment with padded seats (*soft / seat*) |
| 硬卧 | yìngwò | "Hard sleeper": sleeping car compartment with nonpadded beds (*hard / lie*) |
| 软卧 | ruǎnwò | "Soft sleeper"; sleeping car compartment with padded beds (*soft / lie*) |

---

## Topic 7: Riding a Bike and Horseback Riding

In the case of vehicles that require you to sit
astride, as if on horseback, the verb qí 骑
is used.

今天没有车票了，所以我们骑马，再骑自
行车。
Jīntiān méi yǒu chēpiàole, suǒyǐ
wǒmen qí mǎ, zài qí zìxíngchē。
*Today / not (have) / have / ticket / aspect
particle, / therefore / we / ride / horse, /
again / ride / bicycle.*
Today there are no more tickets left; therefore
we'll go horseback riding and biking.

## Topic 8: Events in the Near Future

我们快要到了。

Wǒmen kuài yào dàole.

*We / fast / will / arrive / aspect particle.*

We'll be there soon.

To express the near future, the Chinese use the formula kuài yào ... le 快要 ... 了. The particle le 了 is then placed at the end of the sentence.

## Topic 9: Recommendations

你可以给我介绍一个好饭店吗？

Nǐ kěyǐ gěi wǒ jièshào yíge hǎo fàndiàn ma?

*You / can / me / introduce / one MW / good / hotel / interrogative particle?*

Can you recommend a good hotel to me?

**(CD2 9)**

## Semantic Fields

### Places of Interest

| | | |
|---|---|---|
| Hohhot (city) | Hūhéhàotè | 呼和浩特 |
| Five-Pagoda Temple | Wǔtǎ Sì | 五塔寺 |
| Great Mosque | Qīngzhēn Sì | 清真寺 |
| Lama Temple | Lǎma Sì | 喇嘛寺 |
| White Pagoda | Báitǎ | 白塔 |
| Baotou (city) | Bāotóu | 包头 |
| Willow Tree Monastery | Wǔdāng Zhào | 五当召 |

### Means of Transportation

| | | |
|---|---|---|
| car | qìchē | 汽车 |
| slow train | mànchē | 慢车 |
| donkey | lǘzi | 驴子 |
| bicycle | zìxíngchē | 自行车 |
| airplane | fēijī | 飞机 |
| camel | luòtuo | 骆驼 |
| regular (intercity) bus | gōnggòng qìchē | 公共汽车 |
| maglev (magnetic levitation) train | cíxuánfú lièchē | 磁悬浮列车 |
| motorcycle | mótuōchē | 摩托车 |
| horse | mǎ | 马 |
| horse-drawn carriage | mǎchē | 马车 |
| touring bus | lǚxíngchē | 旅行车 |
| ship | chuán | 船 |
| fast train | kuàichē | 快车 |
| taxi | chūzūqìchē | 出租汽车 |
| subway | dìtiě | 地铁 |
| overland bus | chángtúchē | 长途车 |
| train | huǒchē | 火车 |

### Measures of Length

| | | |
|---|---|---|
| millimeter | háomǐ | 毫米 |
| centimeter | límǐ | 厘米 |
| meter | mǐ | 米 |
| kilometer | gōnglǐ | 公里 |
| li (trad. Chinese mile: 0.5 km) | lǐ | 里 |

### Toasts

| | | |
|---|---|---|
| To German-Chinese friendship! | Wèi Zhōng-Dé yǒuyì, gānbēi! | 为中德友谊干杯！ |
| To your health! | Wèi nǐ de jiànkāng, gānbēi! | 为你的健康干杯！ |
| To our success! | Wèi wǒmen néng chénggōng, gānbēi! | 为我们能成功干杯！ |
| To our collaboration! | Wèi wǒmende hézuò, gānbēi! | 为我们的合作干杯 |

## Exercises

### Exercise 1

Imagine a conversation with your Chinese taxi driver.
Tell him the following:
1. What your name is and where you're from.
2. Where you're staying in China and where you live in the United States.
3. Where you work.
4. How old you are.
5. What your sign of the zodiac is.
6. Information about your family.
7. What kind of car you drive.
8. What you think about soccer.
9. What you find interesting about China.

### Exercise 2

Which synonymous components do the following characters share:
远，近，进，这，道，过？

### Exercise 3

Write different versions of the sample sentences, using the words from the vocabulary list.

### Exercise 4

Say the sample sentences aloud, using words from the semantic fields. Create sentences by using the pyramid method.

Example:
huǒchēzhàn
dào huǒchēzhàn
zuò chē dào huǒchēzhàn
wǒmen zuò chē dào huǒchēzhàn
wǒmen jīntiān zuò chē dào huǒchēzhàn

### Exercise 5

Listen to the sample sentences on the audio CD, and repeat them after the speaker.

### Exercise 6

First, write the following sentences in Pīnyīn, indicating the tones, and then translate them into English.

1. 我要买两张到上海的火车票！
2. 我们在哪里上车？
3. 他们坐飞机去中国，我坐火车去。

### Exercise 7

Find the meaning of the following words by using the Pīnyīn transcription in the (online) dictionary.

1. lǚxíngbāo 旅行包
2. lǚxíngshè 旅行社
3. lǚxíngtuán 旅行团
4. lǚxíng zhǐnán 旅行指南

### Exercise 8

Translate the following sentences into Chinese.

1. How far is it from the train station to the airport?

_____

2. I've lost my way.

_____

3. Please drive a little slower!

_____

4. I can't wait here for you.

_____

5. I need a receipt.

_____

Autonomous region: Xīnjiāng 新疆
Abbreviation: Jiāng 疆
Capital: Ürümqi (Wūlǔmùqí) 乌鲁木齐
85 counties, 19 cities
Area: 640,930 square miles
Population: 19.25 million
Number of persons / square mile: 31

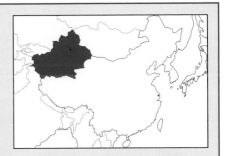

## Vocabulary

| | | |
|---|---|---|
| 给 | gěi | to give |
| 面子 | miànzi | face (face / suffix) |
| 道理 | dàoli | basis; principle; reason, argument (way / reason) |
| 完全 | wánquán | complete; full |
| 流利 | liúlì | flowing, fluent; dashing (flow / favorable) |
| 丢 | diū | to lose |
| …的时候 | de shíhou | at the time when / when … |
| 清真 | qīngzhēn | Islamic, Muslim (clear / true) |
| 寺 | sì | temple |
| 清真寺 | qīngzhēnsì | mosque (clear / true / temple) |
| 清真菜 | qīngzhēncài | Muslim cuisine (clear / true / kitchen) |
| 办法 | bànfǎ | method; ways and means (take care of / law) |
| 猪肉 | zhūròu | pork (pig / meat) |
| 戴 | dài | wearing of caps, eyeglasses, gloves |
| 手 | shǒu | hand |

| | | |
|---|---|---|
| 沙漠 | shāmò | desert (sand / desert) |
| 帽子 | màozi | head covering (head covering / suffix) |
| 太阳镜 | tàiyángjìng | sunglasses (highest / sun / optical glass) |
| 西部 | xībù | western part (west / part) |
| 绿洲 | lùzhōu | oasis (green / small island in a river) |
| 羊肉 | yángròu | lamb (meat) (sheep; goat / meat) |
| 山 | shān | mountain |
| 背 | bēi | to carry/wear something on one's back |
| 背包 | bēibāo | backpack (back / pocket) |
| 面包 | miànbāo | bread (flour / enclose) |
| 提 | tí | to carry something (in your hand/s) |
| 拿 | ná | to take, seize, hold, grasp |

## Sample Sentences

Topic 1: Giving Face gěi miànzi 给面子

The Chinese love to praise things and give compliments. You can try it sometime, too.

## Writing Exercises

理 完 全 流 利
丢 清 寺 办 法
猪 戴 手 沙 漠
帽 阳 镜 西 部
洲 羊 山 背 提
拿

你的话很有道理。
Nǐde huà hěn yǒu dàoli.
*Your / speech / very / have / reason.*
What you said is very convincing.

你说得完全对。
Nǐ shuōde wánquán duì.
*You / speak / CoD / completely / correct.*
What you said is completely correct.

你说英语说得很流利。
Nǐ shuō Yīngyǔ shuōde hěn liúlì.
*You / speak / English / speak / CoD / very / fluent.*
You speak English fluently.

Topic 2: Losing Face diū miànzi 丢面子

If you are dissatisfied and want to express criticism, you can use the following sentences.

你的话没有道理。
Nǐde huà méi yǒu dàoli.
*Your / speech / not (have) / have / reason.*
What you said is nonsense.

你说得完全不对。
Nǐ shuōde wánquán bú duì.
*You / speak / CoD / completely / not / correct.*
What you said is completely wrong.

你说英语说得不流利。
Nǐ shuō Yīngyǔ shuōde bù liúlì.
*You / speak / English / speak / CoD / not / fluent.*
You speak broken English.

Topic 3: Temporal Clauses with . . .
de shíhou . . . 的时候

Clauses that begin in English with "when," "whenever," or "while" end in Chinese with . . . de shíhou . . . 的时候 ("at the point in time when . . .").

Info Box

Chinese has no single, universally applicable word for "to wear." Different verbs are used, depending on which body part is wearing something.

进清真寺的时候，得戴帽子。
Jìn qīngzhēnsìde shíhou, děi dài màozi.
*Enter / mosque / attributive particle / point in time, / must / wear / head covering.*
When you enter a mosque, you have to wear a head covering.

吃清真菜的时候, 没有办法吃猪肉, 喝酒。
Chī qīngzhēncàide shíhou, méi yǒu bànfǎ chī zhūròu, hē jiǔ.
*Eat / Muslim cuisine / attributive particle / point in time / not (have) / have / possibility / eat / pork, / drink / alcohol.*
In Muslim cuisine, there is no opportunity to eat pork and drink alcohol.

在清真饭馆里面吃饭的时候，不应该用左手吃饭。
Zài qīngzhēn fànguǎn lǐmiàn chī fànde shíhou, bù yīnggāi yòng zuǒshǒu chī fàn.
*Be located / Muslim / restaurant / inside / eat / boiled rice / attributive particle / point in time / not / should / use / left hand / eat / boiled rice.*
When you eat in Muslim restaurants, you should not use your left hand for eating.

去沙漠的时候，一定要戴帽子和太阳镜。
Qù shāmòde shíhou, yídìng yào dài màozi hé tàiyángjìng.

*Go (there) / desert / attributive particle, / absolutely / must / wear / head covering / and / sunglasses.*

When you go into the desert, you absolutely must wear a head covering and sunglasses.

你去中国西部的绿洲的时候，能吃烤羊肉。

Nǐ qù Zhōngguó xībù de lǜzhōude shíhou, néng chī kǎoyángròu.

*You / go (there) / China / western part / attributive particle / oasis / attributive particle / point in time, / can / eat / grilled lamb.*

When you go to the oases of western China, you can eat grilled lamb.

上山的时候，要背背包，带面包和点心。

Shàng shānde shíhou, yào bēi bēibāo, dài miànbāo hé diǎnxīn.

*Go up / mountain / attributive particle / point in time, / must / carry on back / backpack / take along / bread / and / snacks.*

When you climb a mountain, you have to take along a backpack, bread, and snacks.

提行李的时候，别忘拿钥匙！

Tí xínglide shíhou, bié wàng ná yàoshi!

*Carry / baggage / attributive particle / point in time, / must not / forget / take / key!*

Don't forget the key when you take the baggage!

## Semantic Fields

### Places of Interest

| | | |
|---|---|---|
| Kashgar (city) | Kāshí | 喀什 |
| Idkah Mosque | Àitígǎ'ér Qīngzhēnsì | 艾提尕儿清真寺 |
| Sunday market | Xīngqītiān Shìchǎng | 星期天市场 |

| | | |
|---|---|---|
| Turfan/Turpan (city) | Tùlǔfān | 吐鲁番 |
| Emin Mosque | Sūgōng Tǎ | 苏公塔 |
| Ancient City of Jiaohe | Jiāohé Yízhǐ | 交河遗址 |
| Ancient City of Gaochang | Gāochāng Yízhǐ | 高昌遗址 |
| Bezeklik Thousand Buddha Caves | Bǎizīkèlìkè Qiānfódòng | 柏孜克里克千佛洞 |
| Flaming Mountains | Huǒyàn Shān | 火焰山 |
| Astana Tombs | Āsītǎnà Gǔmùqū | 阿斯塔那古墓区 |
| Ürümqi (city) | Wūlǔmùqí | 乌鲁木齐 |
| Red Mountain | Hóngshān | 红山 |
| Heavenly Lake | Tiānchí | 天池 |
| Heavenly Mountain | Tiānshān | 天山 |

### Landscapes

| | | |
|---|---|---|
| mountain | shān | 山 |
| river | héliú | 河流 |
| mountain range | shānmài | 山脉 |
| grassland, steppe | cǎoyuán | 草原 |
| oasis | lǜzhōu | 绿洲 |
| woods, forest | sēnlín | 森林 |
| desert | shāmò | 沙漠 |

### Religions and Schools of Thought

| | | |
|---|---|---|
| Taoism/Daoism (religion) | Dàojiào | 道教 |
| Taoism/Daoism (philosophy) | Dàojiā | 道家 |
| Buddhism | Fójiào | 佛教 |
| Confucianism | Rújiā | 儒家 |
| Islam | Yīsīlánjiào | 伊斯兰教 |
| Christianity | Jīdūjiào | 基督教 |

Seasonings

| | | |
|---|---|---|
| oyster sauce | háoyóu | 蚝油 |
| bean paste (red, sweetened) | dòushā | 豆沙 |
| chili (fresh) | làjiāo | 辣椒 |
| chili powder | làzi | 辣子 |
| chili oil | làjiàngyóu | 辣酱油 |
| chili paste | làjiàng | 辣酱 |
| curry powder | gālífěn | 咖喱粉 |
| vinegar | cù | 醋 |
| MSG | wèijīng | 味精 |
| hoisin sauce | hǎixiānjiàng | 海鲜酱 |
| ginger | jiāng | 姜 |
| garlic | dàsuàn | 大蒜 |
| coriander | xiāngcài | 香菜 |
| oil | yóu | 油 |
| pepper (black) | hújiāo | 胡椒 |
| plum sauce | Běijīng yājiàng | 北京鸭酱 |
| salt | yán | 盐 |
| sesame oil | xiāngyóu | 香油 |
| Chinese rice wine | huángjiǔ | 黄酒 |
| shrimp sauce | xiāyóu | 虾油 |
| Szechuan pepper (anise pepper) | huājiāo | 花椒 |
| soy sauce (spicy) | làjiàngyóu | 辣酱油 |
| tomato paste | fānqiéjiàng | 番茄酱 |
| sugar | táng | 糖 |

---

## Info Box

**Swearwords**

| | | |
|---|---|---|
| 糟糕 | zāogāo | Crap! (*mess / cake*) |
| 傻瓜 | shǎguā | imbecile, jackass (*dumb / cucumber; pumpkin*) |
| 笨蛋 | bèndàn | imbecile, jackass (*dumb / egg*) |
| 混蛋 | húndàn | idiot, jerk (*muddled / egg*) |

---

## Info Box

**Idiomatic Expressions**

| | | |
|---|---|---|
| 帮帮忙 | bāngbāng-máng | to have lost one's marbles (*help / help / urgent*); used only in Shanghai |
| 等半天 | děng bàntiān | to wait a long time for someone/something (*wait / half / day*) |
| 炒鱿鱼 | chǎo yóuyú | to fire someone (*fry / squid*) |
| 吃苦 | chī kǔ | bitterness; to suffer hardship (*eat / bitterness*) |
| 吃醋 | chī cù | to be jealous (*eat / vinegar*) |
| 吃错药了 | chī cuò yào le | to be crazy; to have a screw loose (*eat / wrong / medications / aspect particle!*) |
| 二奶 | èrnǎi | mistress, concubine (*two / breasts, milk*) |
| 小秘 | xiǎomì | "little secretary" (*little / secret, secretary*), term used publicly for the mistress of a married businessman |
| 酒肉朋友 | jiǔròu péngyou | fair-weather friend (*alcohol / meat / friends*) |
| 够朋友 | gòu péngyou | true friend (*actually / friends*) |

# 12 Xīnjiāng 新疆

## Exercises

### Exercise 1

Look for pictures in travel catalogs, and try to describe what you see in them.

### Exercise 2

Which synonymous components do the following characters share:
提，打，拉，拿，拐，抽，排？

### Exercise 3

Write different versions of the sample sentences, using the words from the vocabulary list.

### Exercise 4

Say the sample sentences aloud, using words from the semantic fields. Create sentences by using the pyramid method.

Example:
qù
qù Zhōngguó
qù Zhōngguó xībùde
qù Zhōngguó xībùde shíhou,
qù Zhōngguó xībùde shíhou, néng
qù Zhōngguó xībùde shíhou, néng kàn

### Exercise 5

Listen to the sample sentences on the audio CD, and repeat them after the speaker.

### Exercise 6

First, write the following sentences in Pīnyīn, indicating the tones, and then translate them into English.

1. 你朋友的汉语说得很不错。
2. 我们不吃猪肉，也不喝啤酒。
3. 他们星期五去清真寺。

### Exercise 7

Find the meaning of the following words by using the Pīnyīn transcription in the (online) dictionary.

1. bàngōngshì 办公室
2. bàn shǒuxù 办手续
3. bànshì 办事

### Exercise 8

Translate the following sentences into Chinese.

1. You speak Chinese fluently.

_ _ _ _ _ _ _ _ _ _ _ _ _ _ _ _ _ _ _ _ _

2. In western China, you can eat grilled baozi.

_ _ _ _ _ _ _ _ _ _ _ _ _ _ _ _ _ _ _ _ _

3. What time are we going to the mosque tomorrow?

_ _ _ _ _ _ _ _ _ _ _ _ _ _ _ _ _ _ _ _ _

4. When will you buy me a backpack?

_ _ _ _ _ _ _ _ _ _ _ _ _ _ _ _ _ _ _ _ _

5. Excuse me, is it possible to go into the mosque without a head covering?

_ _ _ _ _ _ _ _ _ _ _ _ _ _ _ _ _ _ _ _ _

6. I would like to eat Muslim food together with my girlfriend.

_ _ _ _ _ _ _ _ _ _ _ _ _ _ _ _ _ _ _ _ _

Province: Sìchuān 四川
Abbreviation: Chuān 川
Capital of province: Chéngdū 成都
144 counties, 31 cities
Area: 188,418 square miles
Population: 83.29 million
Number of persons / square mile: 438

## Vocabulary

| | | |
|---|---|---|
| 肚子 | dùzi | belly, stomach (*belly / suffix*) |
| 饿 | è | to be hungry |
| 肚子饿 | dùzi è | to be hungry (*belly / suffix / hungry*) |
| 口 | kǒu | mouth |
| 渴 | kě | to be thirsty |
| 口渴 | kǒukě | to be thirsty (*mouth / thirsty*) |
| 不舒服 | bù shūfu | unpleasant; to feel unwell (*not / stretch / settle in*) |
| 厕所 | cèsuǒ | toilet (*toilet / place*) |
| 吐 | tù | to throw up |
| 好象 | hǎoxiàng | to seem; apparently (*good / look, as if*) |
| 感冒 | gǎnmào | to have caught a cold (*feel / rise*) |
| 牙 | yá | tooth |
| 疼 | téng | to hurt, be painful |
| 头 | tóu | head |
| 发烧 | fāshāo | to have a fever (*feel / have fever*) |
| 眼睛 | yǎnjing | eyes (*eye / eyeball*) |
| 发炎 | fāyán | to be inflamed (*feel / inflammation*) |
| 眼镜 | yǎnjìng | (eye)glasses (*eye / optical glass*) |

| | | |
|---|---|---|
| 坏了 | huàile | broken; to have spoiled (*broken / aspect particle*) |
| 修 | xiū | to repair |
| 胃 | wèi | stomach |
| 川菜 | Chuāncài | Szechuan cuisine (*river / cooking*) |
| 以后 | yǐhòu | after that; later; afterward; after (*by means of / through*) |
| 拉肚子 | lā dùzi | to have diarrhea (*pull / belly / suffix*) |
| 昨天 | zuótiān | yesterday (*yesterday / day*) |
| 按摩 | ànmó | to massage; massage (*press / rub*) |
| 以前 | yǐqián | previous; former; before |
| 腿 | tuǐ | leg |
| 自己 | zìjǐ | self, -self (*self / self*) |
| 带来 | dàilái | to bring (*take with / come*) |
| 药 | yào | medications; medicine |
| 西药 | Xīyào | Western medications (*west / medications*) |
| 中药 | Zhōngyào | traditional Chinese medications (*China / medications*) |
| 大夫 | dàifu | physician, doctor (*big / man*) |
| 过来 | guòlái | to come over/across (*cross / come*) |

| | | |
|---|---|---|
| 打针 | dǎzhēn | to give an injection / a shot (hit / needle) |
| 随便 | suíbiàn | at will, at one's discretion (at will / comfortable, informal) |
| 医院 | yīyuàn | hospital (medicine / public institution); MW: suǒ 所 |
| 西医 | Xīyī | Western medicine (west / medicine) |
| 中医 | Zhōngyī | traditional Chinese medicine (China / medicine) |
| 病 | bìng | to be ill; illness, mistake; lack; defect |
| 看病 | kànbìng | to go to the doctor; to treat the sick (look at / illness) |

## Sample Sentences

Topic 1: Feeling Unwell/III
(see Grammar)

**The Particle** le 了
The particle le 了 expresses a completed action, the near future, and a change in a state or condition.

   This new situation can arise and visibly affect everyone, or it can also represent a situation that appears altered only from the speaker's point of view.

我肚子饿了，口渴了，吃得太多，所以我现在不舒服。
Wǒ dùzi è le, kǒu kě le, chīde tài duō, suǒyǐ wǒ xiànzài bù shūfu.
*My / belly / hungry / aspect particle, / mouth / thirsty / aspect particle, / eat / CoD / too / much, / therefore / I / now / not / feel well.*
Because I was hungry and thirsty, I ate too much, and now I don't feel well.

厕所在哪里，我快要吐了。
Cèsuǒ zài nǎli, wǒ kuài yào tùle.
*Toilet / be located / where, / I / soon / must / throw up / aspect particle.*
Where is the toilet? I have to throw up right away.

我好像感冒了。
Wǒ hǎoxiàng gǎnmàole.
*I / seem / afflicted with a cold / aspect particle.*
I seem to have caught a cold.

我牙疼，头不疼了。
Wǒ yá téng, tóu bù téngle.
*My / teeth / hurt, / head / not / hurt / aspect particle.*
My teeth ache, (but) my head doesn't hurt anymore.

我发烧了。
Wǒ fāshāole.
*I / have fever / aspect particle.*
I've developed a fever.

我眼睛发炎了。
Wǒ yǎnjing fāyánle.
*My / eyes / inflamed / aspect particle.*
My eyes are inflamed.

我的眼镜坏了，你能修吗？
Wǒde yǎnjìng huàile, nǐ néng xiū ma?
*My / glasses / broken / aspect particle, / you / can / repair / interrogative particle?*
My glasses are broken. Can you repair them?

我吃坏了胃。
Wǒ chīhuàile wèi.
*I / eat / broken / aspect particle / stomach.*
I have an upset stomach.

Writing Exercises

| 肚 | 饿 | 渴 | 舒 | 服 |
| 厕 | 吐 | 冒 | 牙 | 疼 |
| 烧 | 眼 | 睛 | 炎 | 坏 |
| 修 | 胃 | 川 | 后 | 昨 |
| 按 | 摩 | 腿 | 已 | 药 |
| 夫 | 针 | 随 | 医 | 院 |
| 病 | | | | |

## Topic 2: Sentences with yǐhou 以后 and yǐqián 以前

Clauses that are introduced in English with the words "before" and "after" end in Chinese with yǐqián 以前 and yǐhou 以后.

我吃了川菜以后，就拉肚子了。
Wǒ chīle Chuāncài yǐhou, jiù lā dùzile。
*I / eat / aspect particle / Szechuan kitchen / after, / then / pull / belly / aspect particle.*
After I ate Szechuan-style food, I got diarrhea.

昨天按摩以前，我腿还没有疼。
Zuótiān ànmó yǐqián, wǒ tuǐ hái méi yǒu téng。
*Yesterday / massage / before, / my / legs / yet / not (have) / hurt.*
Before the massage yesterday, my legs weren't hurting yet.

## Topic 3: Directional Complements

The directional complements qu 去 and lai 来 complete the verb by indicating movement toward or away from the speaker. They are attached to the verb as suffixes and in this case are pronounced as unstressed.

我自己从美国带来了药。
Wǒ zìjǐ cóng Měiguó dàilaile yào。
*I / self / from / United States / bring with / aspect particle / medications.*
I brought along medications from the United States myself.

你可以进去。
Nǐ kěyǐ jìnqu。
*You / be allowed to / go in.*
You can go in.

请进来！
Qǐng jìnlai!
*Please / come in!*
Please come in.

请大夫过来看一下。
Qǐng dàifu guòlai kàn yíxià。
*Ask / doctor / come over here / look at / just a moment.*
Get a doctor to have just a quick look.

## Topic 4: Indirect Discourse

Sentences with indirect discourse contain a main clause and a subordinate clause. The main clause contains a verb of saying or asking as an introduction to the indirect discourse. In Chinese, the subordinate clause needs no special introductory conjunction such as "that" or "whether." It contains the speech or thought that is being reported.

### Declarative Sentences

大夫说，他要给我打针。
Dàifu shuō, tā yào gěi wǒ dǎzhēn。
*Doctor / say, / he / want / give / me / shot / give.*
The doctor says (that) he wants to give me a shot.

大夫说，这里有开水，渴了请我随便喝。
Dàifu shuō, zhèli yǒu kāishuǐ, kěle qǐng wǒ suíbiàn hē。
*Doctor / say, / here / have / boiled water, / thirsty / aspect particle / please / I / at will / drink.*
The doctor says there is boiled water here, and I should drink some whenever I'm thirsty.

大夫说，我只要吃一点药，就可以了。
Dàifu shuō, wǒ zhǐ yào chī yìdiǎn yào, jiù kěyǐle。

*Doctor / say, / I / only / must / eat / a little / medications, / then / can / sentence-final particle.*
The doctor says I have to take a little medicine; then it will be all right again.

### Interrogative Sentences

In interrogative sentences, ma 吗 cannot be used in the indirect discourse.

大夫问我，吃西药还是吃中药。
Dàifu wèn wǒ, chī xīyào háishi chī zhōngyào。
*Doctor / ask / me, / eat / Western medications / or / eat / Chinese medications.*
The doctor is asking me whether I want to take Western or Chinese medicines.

大夫问我，去西医院还是去中医院看病。
Dàifu wèn wǒ, qù xīyīyuàn háishi qù zhōngyīyuàn kànbìng。
*Doctor / ask / me, / go (there) / Western hospital / or / go (there) / Chinese hospital / treat.*
The doctor is asking me whether I want to go to a Western or a Chinese hospital for treatment.

## Semantic Fields

### Places of Interest

| | | |
|---|---|---|
| Chengdu (city) | Chéngdū | 成都 |
| Thatched Cottage of Du Fu | Dù Fǔ Cǎotáng | 杜甫草堂 |
| Manjushri Temple | Wénshū Yuàn | 文书院 |
| Dujiangyan irrigation system | Dūjiāngyàn | 都江堰 |
| Wolong Panda Reserve | Wòlóng Gōu | 卧龙沟 |
| Leshan Giant Buddha | Lèshān Dàfó | 乐山大佛 |
| Mt. Emei Shan | Éméishān | 峨眉山 |
| Juzhaigou National Park | Jiǔzhàigōu | 九寨沟 |

### Parts of the Body

| | | |
|---|---|---|
| arms | gēbo | 胳膊 |
| eyes | yǎnjing | 眼睛 |
| belly, abdomen, stomach | dùzi | 肚子 |
| legs | tuǐ | 腿 |
| bladder | pángguāng | 膀胱 |
| appendix | mángcháng | 盲肠 |
| breast | rǔfáng | 乳房 |
| intestine | cháng | 肠 |
| finger | shǒuzhǐ | 手指 |
| fingernail | zhǐjia | 指甲 |
| feet | jiǎo | 脚 |
| joint | guānjié | 关节 |
| bottom, derriere | pìgu | 屁股 |
| face | liǎn | 脸 |
| gallbladder | dǎnnáng | 胆囊 |
| neck | bózi | 脖子 |
| hand | shǒu | 手 |
| skin | pífū | 皮肤 |
| heart | xīnzàng | 心脏 |
| jaw | xiàba | 下巴 |
| knee | xīgài | 膝盖 |
| bone | gǔtou | 骨头 |
| head | tóu | 头 |
| liver | gānzàng | 肝脏 |
| lips | chún | 唇 |
| lung | fèi | 肺 |
| stomach | wèi | 胃 |
| tonsils | biǎntáotǐ | 扁桃体 |
| spleen | pí | 脾 |
| mouth | zuǐ | 嘴 |
| muscle | jīròu | 肌肉 |

| nape, back of the neck | hòujǐng | 后颈 |
|---|---|---|
| nose | bízi | 鼻子 |
| kidney | shēn | 肾 |
| thigh | dàtuǐ | 大腿 |
| ears | ěrduo | 耳朵 |
| pharynx, throat | sǎngzi | 嗓子 |
| ribs | lèigǔ | 肋骨 |
| back | bèi | 背 |
| shoulder | jiānbǎng | 肩膀 |
| tooth | yá | 牙 |
| toe | jiǎozhǐ | 脚指 |
| toenail | jiǎozhǐjiǎ | 脚指甲 |
| tongue | shétou | 舌头 |

| Health Problems | | |
|---|---|---|
| AIDS | àizībìng | 艾滋病 |
| asthma | xiāochuǎn | 哮喘 |
| diabetes | tángniàobìng | 糖尿病 |
| encephalitis | nǎomóyán | 脑膜炎 |
| yellow fever | huángrèbìng | 黄热病 |
| jaundice | huángdǎn | 黄疸 |
| cough | késou | 咳嗽 |
| infection | chuánrǎn | 传染 |
| infectious disease | chuánrǎnbìng | 传染病 |
| pneumonia | fèiyán | 肺炎 |
| SARS (severe acute respiratory syndrome) | fēidiǎn | 非典 |
| malaria | nüèji | 疟疾 |
| dizziness | tóuyùn | 头晕 |
| sunburn | shàishāng | 晒伤 |
| constipation | biànbì | 便秘 |

## Exercises

### Exercise 1

Make some cards of the kind used in memory or concentration games—pairs of cards with the same body part shown on them—and play a game, using the standard rules for such games, by uncovering a card and naming the body part in Chinese.

### Exercise 2

Which synonymous components do the following characters share:
病，疼，疸，痛，瘦？

### Exercise 3

Write different versions of the sample sentences, using the words from the vocabulary list.

### Exercise 4

Say the sample sentences aloud, using words from the semantic fields. Create sentences by using the pyramid method.

Example:
kànbìng
kànbìng yǐhou
kànbìng yǐhou wǒ
kànbìng yǐhou wǒ dùzi
kànbìng yǐhou wǒ dùzi bù téngle

### Exercise 5

Listen to the sample sentences on the audio CD, and repeat them after the speaker.

## Exercise 6

First, write the following sentences in Pīnyīn, indicating the tones, and then translate them into English.

1. 请别给我打针！
2. 我要吃西药，不吃中药！
3. 我昨天不舒服，现在好了。

## Exercise 7

Find the meaning of the following words by using the Pīnyīn transcription in the (online) dictionary.

1. zhēnjiǔ 针灸
2. mázuì 麻醉
3. kàngjūnsù 抗菌素
4. tuīná 推拿

## Exercise 8

Translate the following sentences into Chinese.

1. It hurts here.

_ _ _ _ _ _ _ _ _ _ _ _ _ _ _ _ _ _ _ _

2. I would like to talk to a doctor.

_ _ _ _ _ _ _ _ _ _ _ _ _ _ _ _ _ _ _ _

3. I'm allergic to eggs.

_ _ _ _ _ _ _ _ _ _ _ _ _ _ _ _ _ _ _ _

4. After the massage, I went out to eat.

_ _ _ _ _ _ _ _ _ _ _ _ _ _ _ _ _ _ _ _

5. When I have a headache, I don't go to the doctor right away.

_ _ _ _ _ _ _ _ _ _ _ _ _ _ _ _ _ _ _ _

6. When I was little, I often had a stomachache.

_ _ _ _ _ _ _ _ _ _ _ _ _ _ _ _ _ _ _ _

7. When can I see the doctor?

_ _ _ _ _ _ _ _ _ _ _ _ _ _ _ _ _ _ _ _

# 14 Yúnnán 云南

Province: Yúnnán 云南
Abbreviation: Diān 滇
Capital of province: Kūnmíng 昆明
121 counties, 15 cities
Area: 152,124 square miles
Population: 42.88 million
Number of persons / square mile: 279

## Vocabulary

| | | |
|---|---|---|
| 衣服 | yīfu | clothes; clothier (*clothing / clothing*); MW: jiàn 件 |
| 条 | tiáo | MW for elongated things like pants and skirts |
| 裤子 | kùzi | pants (*pants / suffix*), MW: tiáo 条 |
| 合适 | héshì | to fit (*correspond / be suitable*) |
| 件 | jiàn | MW for tops like sweaters and T-shirts |
| 毛衣 | máoyī | wool sweater (*hair, wool / clothing*); MW: jiàn 件 |
| 短 | duǎn | short |
| 长 | cháng | long |
| 紧 | jǐn | tight, taut |
| 大号 | dàhào | for clothing: large size |
| 穿 | chuān | to wear |
| 用...付 | yòng ... | to pay in ... |
| 钱 | fùqián | (*use ... / pay / money*) |
| 信用卡 | xìnyòngkǎ | credit card (*trust / use / card*) |
| 甜 | tián | sweet |
| 玩笑 | wánxiào | joke, jest (*play / laugh*) |

| | | |
|---|---|---|
| 开玩笑 | kāi wánxiào | to make jokes, to make fun of someone (*lead / play / laugh*) |
| 西瓜 | xīguā | melon (*west / pumpkin; cucumber; melon*) |
| 苹果 | píngguǒ | apple (*apple / fruit*) |
| 些 | xiē | MW for an indefinite number of things in the plural |
| 这些 | zhèxiē | these (*this / MW for the indefinite plural*) |
| 那些 | nàxiē | those (over ) there (*those / MW for the indefinite plural*) |
| 旅行 | lǚxíng | to travel (*travel / go*) |
| 东西 | dōngxi | things (*east / west*) |
| 买东西 | mǎi dōngxi | to shop (*buy / east / west*) |
| 手工 | shǒugōng | handicraft, handwork |
| 照相机 | zhàoxiàngjī | (still) camera (*expose / picture / device*) |
| 比 | bǐ | to compare |
| 好看 | hǎokàn | good looking (*good / look at*) |
| 斤 | jīn | pound |
| 水果 | shuǐguǒ | fruit (*water / fruit*) |
| 市场 | shìchǎng | market (*market, town / place*) |

| 超市 | chāoshì | supermarket (*pass, overtake; super / market*) |
| 手机 | shǒujī | cell phone (*hand / device*) |
| 质量 | zhìliàng | quality (*quality / measure*) |
| 跟... | gēn... | to be on a par with ... |
| 一样 | yíyàng | (*with ... / one / kind*) |
| 礼物 | lǐwù | gift (*gift / object*) |
| 手提包 | shǒutíbāo | purse, handbag (*hand / carry / bag*) |
| 外面 | wàimiàn | outside (*outside / side*) |
| 冷 | lěng | cold |
| 暖和 | nuǎnhuo | warm (*warm / mix*) |

## Sample Sentences

Topic 1: Buying from a Clothier

这条裤子不合适。
Zhètiáo kùzi bù héshì。
*This MW / pants / not / fit.*
These pants don't fit.

这件毛衣太短。
Zhèjiàn máoyī tài duǎn。
*This MW / sweater / too / short.*
This sweater is too short.

请给我一件长一点的!
Qǐng gěi wǒ yíjiàn cháng yìdiǎnde。
*Please / give / me / one MW / long / a little / attributive particle.*
Please give me a longer one (sweater).

这件太紧。有没有大号的?
Zhèjiàn tài jǐn。 Yǒu méi yǒu dàhàode?
*This MW / too / tight. Have / not (have) / have / large size / attributive particle?*

This one (sweater) is too tight. Do you have a larger size?

对不起,只有你穿的。
Duìbuqǐ, zhǐ yǒu nǐ chuānde。
*Sorry, / only / have / you / wear / attributive particle.*
I'm sorry, but we only have the one you're wearing.

可以不可以用信用卡付钱?
Kěyǐ bù kěyǐ yòng xìnyòngkǎ fùqián?
*Can / not / can / use / credit card / pay money?*
Can I pay with a credit card?

你开玩笑吗?
Nǐ kāi wánxiào ma?
*You / lead / jokes / interrogative particle?*
Are you joking?

Topic 2: Shi ... de 是 ... 的 Construction

The clause delineated by the shi ... de 是 ... 的 construction can be given special emphasis in this way.

这个西瓜是最甜的。
Zhège xīguā shi zuì tiánde。
*This MW / melon / be / sweetest / attributive particle.*
This melon is the sweetest.

这些苹果是我的, 那些是你的。
Zhèxiē píngguǒ shi wǒde, nàxiē shi nǐde。
*These MW / apples / be / mine, / those MW / be / yours.*
These apples are mine; those (over there) are yours.

## Writing Exercises

| | | | | |
|---|---|---|---|---|
| 衣 | 裤 | 合 | 适 | 件 |
| 短 | 长 | 紧 | 穿 | 信 |
| 甜 | 玩 | 笑 | 瓜 | 苹 |
| 果 | 些 | 旅 | 东 | 照 |
| 相 | 比 | 斤 | 超 | 质 |
| 量 | 样 | 礼 | 外 | 冷 |
| 暖 | | | | |

我是来旅行的。
Wǒ shi lái lǚxíngde。
*I / be / come / travel / attributive particle.*
I'm a tourist.

这个东西是手工作的吗？
Zhège dōngxi shi shǒugōng zuòde ma?
*This MW / thing / be / handicraft / make / attributive particle / interrogative particle?*
Is this thing made by hand?

## Topic 3: Comparative with bǐ 比
(see Grammar)

Comparative sentences with bǐ 比 are based on this formula: A compared with B with regard to C. A 比 B C

他的照相机比我的好看。
Tāde zhàoxiàngjī bǐ wǒde hǎokàn。
*His / (still) camera / compare / mine / good looking.*
His camera is nicer than mine.

这条裤子比那条紧。
Zhètiáo kùzi bǐ nàtiáo jǐn。
*This MW / pants / compare / that MW / tight.*
These pants are tighter than those (over there).

一斤水果比一斤蔬菜贵。
Yì jīn shuǐguǒ bǐ yì jīn shūcài guì。
*One pound / fruit / compare / one pound / vegetables / expensive.*
A pound of fruit is more expensive than a pound of vegetables.

在市场买东西比在超市买东西便宜。
Zài shìchǎng mǎi dōngxi bǐ zài chāoshì mǎi dōngxi piányi。
*Be located / market / buy / things / compare / be located / supermarket / buy / things / cheap.*
It's cheaper to buy things at the market than in the supermarket.

## Topic 4: Comparative with méi yǒu 没有
(see Grammar)

Comparative sentences with méi yǒu 没有 are based on this formula: A is not on a par with B with regard to C. A 没有 B C

我的中文没有你的好。
Wǒde Zhōngwén méi yǒu nǐde hǎo。
*My / Chinese / not (have) / have / yours / good.*
My Chinese is not as good as yours.

我的手机的质量没有你的好。
Wǒde shǒujīde zhìliàng méi yǒu nǐde hǎo。
*My / cell phone / attributive particle / quality / not (have) / have / yours / good.*
The quality of my cell phone is not as good as yours.

美国人踢足球踢得没有以前好。
Měiguórén tí zúqiú tíde méi yǒu yǐqián hǎo。
*Americans / kick / soccer ball / kick / CoD / not (have) / have / previous / good.*
The Americans don't play soccer as well as they did previously.

## Topic 5: Comparative Sentences (Equative Sentences) with gēn ... yíyàng 跟 ... 一样

Comparative sentences with gēn ... yíyàng 跟 ... 一样 are based on this formula: A is on a par with B. A 跟 B 一样

我的礼物跟你的一样。
Wǒde lǐwù gēn nǐde yíyàng。
*My / gift / with / yours / same.*
I have the same gift as you.

If another adjective follows, the comparison refers to its quality: A is on a par with B with regard to C. A 跟 B 一样 C.

我的衣服跟你的一样紧。
Wǒde yīfu gēn nǐde yíyàng jǐn.
*My / clothing / with / yours / same / tight.*
My clothes are just as tight as yours.

To negate the statement, use bù 不, followed by yíyàng 一样.

我的手提包跟你的不一样。
Wǒde shǒutíbāo gēn nǐde bù yíyàng.
*My / purse / with / yours / not / same.*
My purse is not like yours.

## Topic 6: Yǒu yìdiǎn 有一点

When yǒu yìdiǎn 有一点 precedes adjectives, it is translated as "somewhat, slightly" and used to modify the sentence.

外面有一点冷。
Wàimiàn yǒu yídiǎn lěng.
*Outside / have / a little / cold.*
It is somewhat cold outside.

我有一点冷。
Wǒ yǒu yídiǎn lěng.
*I / have / a little / cold.*
I'm slightly cold.

After adjectives, only yìdiǎn 一点 is used (without yǒu 有), and in the comparative sense it designates a lesser degree of the property or quality in question.

你最好穿暖和一点。
Nǐ zuìhǎo chuān nuǎnhuo yìdiǎn.
*You / best / put on / warm / a little.*
You'd best dress a little more warmly.

## Semantic Fields

CD2 18

### Places of Interest

| | | |
|---|---|---|
| Kunming (city) | Kūnmíng | 昆明 |
| Stone Forest | Shílín | 石林 |
| Temple of Perfection and Success | Yuántōng Sì | 圆通寺 |
| Western Hills | Xīshān | 西山 |
| Black Dragon Pool | Hēilóngtán | 黑龙潭 |
| Dali (city) | Dàlǐ | 大理 |
| Old City | Gǔchéng | 古城 |
| Erhai Lake | Ěrhǎi Hú | 洱海湖 |
| Three Pagoda Temple | Sāntǎ Sì | 三塔寺 |
| Cangshan Mountains | Cāngshān | 苍山 |
| Lijiang (city) | Lìjiāng | 丽江 |
| Tiger Leaping Gorge | Hǔtiàoxiá | 虎跳峡 |
| Black Dragon Pool | Hēilóngtán | 黑龙潭 |
| Zhongdian/ Shangri-La (city) | Zhōngdiàn/ Xiānggélǐlā | 中甸 / 香格里拉 |
| Jinghong (city) | Jǐnghóng | 景洪 |
| Xishuang Banna Tropical Forest | Xīshuāngbǎnnà Zìrán Bǎohùqū | 西双版纳 自然保护 区 |
| White Pagoda of Damenglong | Dàménglóng Báitǎ | 大蒙龙白 塔 |

### Fruit

| | | |
|---|---|---|
| apple | píngguǒ | 苹果 |
| pineapple | bōluó | 菠萝 |
| banana | xiāngjiāo | 香蕉 |
| pear | lí | 梨 |
| red date (jujube) | zǎo | 枣 |
| durian | liúlián | 榴莲 |

| | | |
|---|---|---|
| longyan/ dragon's eye | lóngyǎn | 龙眼 |
| strawberry | cǎoméi | 草莓 |
| fig | wúhuāguǒ | 无花果 |
| pomegranate | shíliu | 石榴 |
| grapefruit/ pomelo | yòuzi | 柚子 |
| hazelnut | bǎnlì | 板栗 |
| honeydew melon | Hāmì guā | 哈密瓜 |
| persimmon/kaki/ Chinese fig | shìzi | 柿子 |
| cactus fig | huǒlóngguǒ | 火龙果 |
| chestnuts (soft) | lìzi | 栗子 |
| cherries | yīngtáo | 樱桃 |
| kiwi fruit | míhóutáo | 猕猴桃 |
| coconut | yēzi | 椰子 |
| lychee | lìzhī | 荔枝 |
| tangerine | júzi | 橘子 |
| mango | mángguǒ | 芒果 |
| mulberry | sāngshèn | 桑葚 |

| | | |
|---|---|---|
| orange | chéngzi | 橙子 |
| papaya | mùguā | 木瓜 |
| passion fruit | xīfānlián | 西番莲 |
| peach | táozi | 桃子 |
| plum | lǐzi | 李子 |
| rambutan fruit | hóngmáodān | 红毛丹 |
| star fruit/ carambola | yángtáo | 杨桃 |
| grapes | pútao | 葡萄 |
| walnut | hétao | 核桃 |
| watermelon | xīguā | 西瓜 |
| lemon | níngméng | 柠檬 |
| sugar melon | mìguā | 蜜瓜 |

| Weights | | |
|---|---|---|
| gram | kè | 克 |
| half a pound | bànjīn | 半斤 |
| pound | jīn | 斤 |
| half a kilo | bàn gōngjīn | 半公斤 |
| kilogram | gōngjīn | 公斤 |

| Clothing | MW | | | fúzhuāng | | 服装 |
|---|---|---|---|---|---|---|
| suit (Western) | yítào | 一套 | | xīfú | | 西服 |
| bathing suit | yítào | 一套 | | yóuyǒngyī | | 游泳衣 |
| bathing trunks | yìtiáo | 一条 | | yóuyǒngkù | | 游泳裤 |
| bra | yíjiàn | 一件 | | xiōngzhào | | 胸罩 |
| bikini | yítào | 一套 | | bǐjīní | | 比基尼 |
| blouse | yíjiàn | 一件 | | nǚchènshān | | 女衬衫 |
| flip-flops | yìshuāng | 一双 | | rénzì tuōxié | | 人字拖鞋 |
| belt | yìtiáo | 一条 | | pídài | | 皮带 |
| purse/handbag | yíge | 一个 | | shǒutíbāo | | 手提包 |
| shirt | yíjiàn | 一件 | | chènshān | | 衬衫 |
| pants | yìtiáo | 一条 | | kùzi | | 裤子 |
| hat | yìdǐng | 一顶 | | màozi | | 帽子 |
| jacket (padded) | yíjiàn | 一件 | | jiákè | | 夹克 |
| jacket (long) | yíjiàn | 一件 | | wàitào | | 外套 |
| jacket | yíjiàn | 一件 | | wàiyī | | 外衣 |
| jeans | yìtiáo | 一条 | | niúzǎikù | | 牛仔裤 |
| dress | yítào | 一套 | | liányīqún | | 连衣裙 |

| tie | yì tiáo | 一条 | lǐngdài | 领带 |
|---|---|---|---|---|
| leggings | yì tiáo | 一条 | bǎngtuǐ | 绑腿 |
| coat | yí jiàn | 一件 | dàyī | 大衣 |
| cap | yì dǐng | 一顶 | màozi | 帽子 |
| sweater (wool) | yí jiàn | 一件 | máoyī | 毛衣 |
| pajamas | yí jiàn | 一件 | shuìyī | 睡衣 |
| qipao/cheongsam (Chinese dress) | yí jiàn | 一件 | qípáo | 旗袍 |
| rain gear | yí jiàn | 一件 | yǔyī | 雨衣 |
| skirt | yì tiáo | 一条 | qúnzi | 裙子 |
| sandals (pair) | yì shuāng | 一双 | liángxié | 凉鞋 |
| shawl; scarf | yì tiáo | 一条 | wéijīn | 围巾 |
| shoes (pair) | yì shuāng | 一双 | xiézi | 鞋子 |
| shoes (athletic) | yì shuāng | 一双 | yùndòngxié | 运动鞋 |
| shorts | yì tiáo | 一条 | duǎnkù | 短裤 |
| socks (pair) | yì shuāng | 一双 | wàzi | 袜子 |
| boots (pair) | yì shuāng | 一双 | xuēzi | 靴子 |
| stockings (pair) | yì shuāng | 一双 | chángtǒngwà | 长筒袜 |
| sweatshirt | yí jiàn | 一件 | miánmáoshān | 棉毛衫 |
| T-Shirt | yí jiàn | 一件 | T-xùshān | T-恤衫 |
| underpants, panties | yì tiáo | 一条 | nèikù | 内裤 |

## Crafts and Souvenirs

| antiquities | gǔdǒng | 古董 |
|---|---|---|
| scroll painting | huàjuǎn | 画卷 |
| cloisonné | jǐngtàilán | 景泰蓝 |
| fan | gōngyìshān | 工艺扇 |
| jade | yùshí | 玉石 |
| calligraphy | shūfǎ | 书法 |
| calligraphy set | wénfáng sìbǎo | 文房四宝 |
| painting | huìhuà | 绘画 |
| porcelain and ceramics | táocí | 陶瓷 |
| jewelry | shǒushi | 首饰 |
| silk | sīchóu | 丝绸 |
| seal, stamp | túzhāng | 图章 |
| tea | cháyè | 茶叶 |
| vases | huāpíng | 花瓶 |

### Info Box

**Tips for Tailoring**

| with long sleeves | chángxiù | 长袖 |
|---|---|---|
| with short sleeves | duǎnxiù | 短袖 |
| with a V neck | V-xíng lǐng | V-型领 |
| with a round collar | yuánlǐng | 圆领 |

## Exercises

### Exercise 1

Make a shopping list, including your favorite fruits and the appropriate weights.

## Exercise 2

Which synonymous components do the following characters share:
裤，衣，衬，衫，裙，袍，袜?

## Exercise 3

Write different versions of the sample sentences, using the words from the vocabulary list.

## Exercise 4

Say the sample sentences aloud, using words from the semantic fields. Create sentences by using the pyramid method.

Example:
máoyī
liǎng jiàn máoyī
liǎng jiàn máoyī méi yǒu
liǎng jiàn máoyī méi yǒu sì jiàn
liǎng jiàn máoyī méi yǒu sì jiàn guì

## Exercise 5

Listen to the sample sentences on the audio CD, and repeat them after the speaker.

## Exercise 6

First, write the following sentences in Pīnyīn, indicating the tones, and then translate them into English.

1. 德国的照相机是最好的。
2. 我们要多穿一些衣服去旅行。
3. 英国的白酒比中国的辣。

## Exercise 7

Find the meaning of the following words by using the Pīnyīn transcription in the (online) dictionary.

1. xī fāng 西方
2. xī zhuāng 西装
3. xī hóngshì 西红柿

## Exercise 8

Translate into Chinese:

1. Do you have anything better?

_____

2. I like these pants.

_____

3. This camera is just as expensive as that one (over there).

_____

4. Does that also come in black?

_____

5. That is too expensive! I don't want it anymore.

_____

6. It is somewhat too small and doesn't fit.

_____

# 15 Húnán 湖南

Province: Húnán 湖南
Abbreviation: Xiāng 湘
Capital of province: Chángshā 长沙
88 counties, 29 cities
Area: 81,738 square miles
Population: 64.40 million
Number of persons / square mile: 779

## Vocabulary

| | | |
|---|---|---|
| 麻烦 | máfan | anger, annoyance (*uneven / annoyed*) |
| 一些 | yìxiē | some, several (*one / MW for the indefinite plural*) |
| 问题 | wèntí | question, problem (*ask / topic*) |
| 帮助 | bāngzhù | help (*help / help*) |
| 事 | shì | matter, thing; MW: jiàn 件 |
| 公安局 | gōng'ānjú | police station (*public / security / office*) |
| 延长 | yáncháng | to extend (*extend / long*) |
| 签证 | qiānzhèng | visa (*sign / pass, certificate*) |
| 空 | kòng | free time |
| 有空 | yǒu kòng | to have (free) time (*free time / have*) |
| 关系 | guānxi | connection, relation (*concern / concern*) |
| 没关系 | méi guānxi | it doesn't matter; never mind (*not have / concern / concern*) |
| 明白 | míngbái | clear; open; to understand; to comprehend (*clear / white*) |
| 意思 | yìsi | meaning (*meaning / thought*) |
| 过期 | guòqī | to run out; to be over-due (*exceed / deadline*) |
| 还是 | háishi | it would be better; rather (*still / be*) |
| 老板 | lǎobǎn | boss; proprietor, shopkeeper (*old / board*) |
| 讲 | jiǎng | to speak; to tell |
| 讲道理 | jiǎng dàoli | to present arguments; to "talk turkey" (*talk / way / reason*) |
| 找 | zhǎo | to seek; to seek out; to contact |
| 听 | tīng | to hear |
| 得 ... | de | for forming the complement of possibility (CoP) |
| ... 到 | dào | for forming the complement of result (CoR) and the CoP |
| ... 见 | jiàn | for forming the CoR and the CoP |
| ... 懂 | dǒng | for forming the CoR and the CoP |
| ... 了 | liao | for forming the CoP |
| ... 动 | dòng | for forming the CoR and the CoP |

| 护照 | hùzhào | passport (*protect / license*) |
| 警察 | jǐngchá | police officer (*alert / investigate*) |
| 职业 | zhíyè | profession, career (*profession / trade*) |
| 公司 | gōngsī | firm, company (*concerted, joint / lead*) |

## Sample Sentences

**CD2 20**

### Topic 1: Having Problems and Expressing Lack of Understanding

麻烦你，我有一些问题，请你帮助我！
Máfan nǐ, wǒ yǒu yìxiē wèntí, qǐng nǐ bāngzhù wǒ!
*Annoyance / you, / I / have / some / problems / issues. / request / you / help / me!*
I'm sorry to bother you, (but) I have a few problems. Please help me!

没有问题，你有什么事？
Méi yǒu wèntí, nǐ yǒu shénme shì?
*Not (have) / have / problem. / you / have / what kind of / matter?*
It's not a problem. What's the matter?

我需要去公安局延长我的签证。
Wǒ xūyào qù gōng'ānjú yáncháng wǒde qiānzhèng.
*I / need / go (there) / police station / extend / my / visa.*
I have to go to the police station to extend my visa.

你什么时候有空帮助我？
Nǐ shénme shíhou yǒu kòng bāngzhù wǒ?
*You / what kind of / point in time / have / free time / help / me?*
When do you have time to help me?

对不起，我现在没有时间，明天再说吧！
Duìbuqǐ, wǒ xiànzài méi yǒu shíjiān, míngtiān zài shuō ba!
*Sorry, / I / now / not (have) / have / time. / tomorrow / again / speak / particle!*
I'm sorry, I don't have time now. Let's talk about it again tomorrow!

没关系。
Méi guānxi.
*Not (have) / connection.*
It doesn't matter.

我不明白你的意思！
Wǒ bù míngbái nǐde yìsi!
*I / not / clear / your / meaning.*
I don't understand what you mean.

这个问题你明白不明白？
Zhège wèntí nǐ míngbái bù míngbái?
*This MW / problem / you / clear / not / clear?*
Is the problem clear to you?

我还是跟老板讲道理好！
Wǒ háishi gēn lǎobǎn jiǎng dàolǐ hǎo!
*I / rather / with / boss / speak / principle / aspect particle / good!*
I'd rather talk turkey with the boss!

谢谢你的帮助。
Xièxie nǐde bāngzhù.
*Thanks / your / help.*
Thanks for your help.

### Topic 2: Sentences with the Complement of Result (CoR)
(see Grammar)

The complement of result points to the result of an action (kāicuòle 开错了 to have taken the wrong road, gone the wrong way). Verbs or

## Writing Exercises

烦　题　帮　助　事

安　局　延　签　证

空　关　系　意　思

老　板　讲　找　护

警　察　职　业　司

adjectives are directly attached to the verb of the sentence as complements.

找到了吗？
Zhǎodàole ma?
*Seek / arrive / aspect particle / interrogative particle?*
Have you found it ?

---

听到了吗？
Tīngdàole ma?
*Hear / arrive / aspect particle / interrogative particle?*
Did you hear it ?

**Negated CoR**
Generally, méi yǒu 没有 is used in a negation.

我没有看到，我的签证过期了。
Wǒ méi yǒu kàndào, wǒde qiānzhèng guòqīle.
*I / not (have) / have / see / arrive, / my / visa / expire / aspect particle.*
I didn't notice that my visa has expired.

我没有找到我的护照。
Wǒ méi yǒu zhǎodào wǒde hùzhào.
*I / not (have) / have / seek / arrive / my / passport.*
I haven't found my passport.

Topic 3: Sentences with the Complement of Possibility (CoP)
(see Grammar)

The complement of possibility, in its affirmative form, seems exactly like the complement of degree but is translated as "can ..." De 得 is inserted between the verb and its complement, and only the context determines the meaning. The formula "verb + de 得 + complement" could also be replaced with "néng 能 + verb + complement," but according to Chinese custom, preference is given to the complement of possibility.

我找得到。
Wǒ zhǎo de dào.
*I / seek / CoP / arrive.*
I can find it.

我听得见。
Wǒ tīng de jiàn.
*I / hear / CoP / see.*
I can hear it.

**Negated CoP**
In the negation, de 得 is replaced by bù 不.

**Important U.S. States**

| Alaska | Ālāsjiā | 阿拉斯加 |
|---|---|---|
| California | Jiālìfúníyà | 加利福尼亚 |
| Florida | Fóluólǐdá | 佛罗里达 |
| Illinois | Yīlìnuòyī | 伊利诺伊 |
| Massachusetts | Mǎsāzhūsè | 马萨诸塞 |
| Michigan | Mìxīgēn | 密西根 |
| Missouri | Mìsūlǐ | 密苏里 |
| New Jersey | Xīnzéxī | 新泽西 |
| New York | Niǔyuē | 纽约 |
| North Carolina | Běi Kǎluóláinà | 北卡罗来纳 |
| Ohio | Éhàié | 俄亥俄 |
| Oregon | Élègāng | 俄勒冈 |
| Pennsylvania | Bīngxìfǎníyà | 宾夕法尼亚 |
| South Carolina | Nán Kǎluóláinà | 南卡罗来纳 |
| Texas | Dékèsāsī | 得克萨斯 |
| Washington | Huáshèngdùn | 华盛顿 |

我找不到我的护照。
Wǒ zhǎo bú dào wǒde hùzhào.
*I / seek / not / arrive / my / passport.*
I can't find my passport.

我一辆出租汽车都看不见。
Wǒ yíliàng chūzū qìchē dōu kàn bú jiàn.
*I / one MW / taxi / all / see / not / see.*
I can't see a single taxi.

我听不懂警察的汉语。
Wǒ tīng bú dǒng jǐngcháde Hànyǔ.
*I / hear / not / understand / police officer / attributive particle / Chinese.*
I can't understand the police officer's Chinese.

我忘不了你。
Wǒ wàng bù liǎo nǐ.
*I / forget / not / can / you.*
I can't forget you.

**Names of American Companies**

| American Express | Měiguó Yùntōng | 美国运通 |
|---|---|---|
| Apple Computer | Píngguǒ Diànnǎo | 苹果电脑 |
| Boeing | Bōyīn | 波音 |
| Caterpillar | Kǎtèbǐlè | 卡特彼勒 |
| Colgate-Palmolive | Gāolùjié Zōnglǎn | 高露洁．棕榄 |
| Exxon-Mobil | Āikèsēn Měifú | 埃克森．美孚 |
| Delta Airlines | Dáměi Hángkōng | 达美航空 |
| Ford | Fútè | 福特 |
| General Motors | Tōngyòng Qìchē | 通用汽车 |
| Microsoft | Wēiruǎn | 微软 |
| Wal-Mart | Wòěrmǎ | 沃尔玛 |
| Westing-house | Xīwū | 西屋 |

我拿不动我的背包。
Wǒ ná bú dòng wǒde bēibāo.
*I / take / not / move / my / backpack.*
I can't move (lift) my backpack.

Topic 5: Asking about Someone's
Occupation/Job

你的职业是什么？
Nǐde zhíyè shi shénme?
*Your / profession / be / what?*
What do you do (for a living)?

你在什么公司工作？
Nǐ zài shénme gōngsī gōngzuò?
*You / be located / what kind of / company / work?*
What company do you work for?

我在北京住，在上海工作。
Wǒ zài Běijīng zhù, zài Shànghǎi
gōngzuò.
*I / be located / Beijing / live, / be located /
Shanghai / work.*
I live in Beijing and work in Shanghai.

CD2
21

## Semantic Fields

### Places of Interest

| | | |
|---|---|---|
| Changsha (city) | Chángshā | 长沙 |
| Hunan Provincial Museum | Húnán shěng Bówùguǎn | 湖南省 博物馆 |
| Heavenly Heart Pavilion | Tiānxīn Gé | 天心阁 |
| Lei Feng Memorial Museum | Léi Fēng Jìniànguǎn | 雷锋 纪念馆 |
| Shaoshan (city) | Sháoshān | 韶山 |
| Mao Zedong's Birthplace | Máo Zédōng Gùjū | 毛泽东 故居 |
| Hengyang (city) | Héngyáng | 衡阳 |
| Hengshan Mountain | Héngshān | 衡山 |

### Snack Foods

| | | |
|---|---|---|
| cashew nuts | yāoguǒ | 腰果 |
| dried shredded meat | ròusōng | 肉松 |
| peanuts | huāsheng | 花生 |
| dried tofu | dòufugān | 豆腐干 |
| pumpkin seeds | guāzǐ | 瓜子 |
| crispy beef strips with curry | niúròugān | 牛肉干 |
| soybeans | máodòu | 毛豆 |
| sunflower seeds | guāzǐ | 瓜子 |
| stinky tofu | chòudòufu | 臭豆腐 |
| tea eggs | cháyèdàn | 茶叶蛋 |
| walnuts | hétao | 核桃 |

### Job Titles

| | | |
|---|---|---|
| employee | zhíyuán | 职员 |
| worker | gōngrén | 工人 |
| doctor, physician | dàifu | 大夫 |
| farmer | nóngmín | 农民 |
| official, civil servant | gōngwùyuán | 公务员 |
| ambassador | dàshǐ | 大使 |
| interpreter | fānyì | 翻译 |
| driver | sījī | 司机 |
| flight attendant | chéngwùyuán | 乘务员 |
| engineer | gōngchéngshī | 工程师 |
| journalist | jìzhě | 记者 |
| cook | chúshī | 厨师 |
| consul | lǐngshì | 领事 |
| nurse | hùshì | 护士 |
| artist | yìshùjiā | 艺术家 |
| teacher | lǎoshī | 老师 |
| manager | jīnglǐ | 经理 |
| politician | zhèngzhìjiā | 政治家 |
| police officer | jǐngchá | 警察 |
| lawyer, attorney | lǜshī | 律师 |
| tour guide | dǎoyóu | 导游 |

# 15 Húnán 湖南

| ship captain | chuánzhǎng | 船长 |
| secretary (f.) | mìshū | 秘书 |
| salesperson | shòuhuòyuán | 售货员 |

1. 有问题，来找我.
2. 我办得了.
3. 有关系就可以延长签证.

## Exercises

### Exercise 1

Describe yourself and your friends, stating your occupation, origin, and/or current place of residence (country, state, city).

### Exercise 2

Which synonymous components do the following characters share:
明，是，意，得，早，时，星，晚？

### Exercise 3

Write different versions of the sample sentences, using the words from the vocabulary list.

### Exercise 4

Say the sample sentences aloud, using words from the semantic fields. Create sentences by using the pyramid method.

Example:
wǒ
wǒ zài
wǒ zài dàzhòng
wǒ zài dàzhòng gōngsī
wǒ zài dàzhòng gōngsī gōngzuò

### Exercise 5

Listen to the sample sentences on the audio CD, and repeat them after the speaker.

### Exercise 6

First, write the sample sentences in Pīnyīn, indicating the tones, and then translate them into English.

### Exercise 7

Find the meaning of the following words by using the Pīnyīn transcription in the (online) dictionary.

1. gōngzuòzhèng 工作证
2. xǔkězhèng 许可证
3. shēnfenzhèng 身份证

### Exercise 8

Translate the following sentences into Chinese.

1. The police officer over there says that my visa has expired.

_ _ _ _ _ _ _ _ _ _ _ _ _ _ _ _ _ _ _ _ _

2. I'm sorry to bother you just for a second. Could you help me extend the visa?

_ _ _ _ _ _ _ _ _ _ _ _ _ _ _ _ _ _ _ _ _

3. I don't have time now to talk to my boss.

_ _ _ _ _ _ _ _ _ _ _ _ _ _ _ _ _ _ _ _ _

4. I can't find my camera.

_ _ _ _ _ _ _ _ _ _ _ _ _ _ _ _ _ _ _ _ _

5. Did you hear what I said?

_ _ _ _ _ _ _ _ _ _ _ _ _ _ _ _ _ _ _ _ _

## Short Grammar

### Aspects

**The Aspect Particle** le 了
In general, the aspect particle le 了 is used to express the past, present, and future.

In particular, it is used:
1. To express the near future
火车快到了。
Huǒchē kuài dàole。
The train is about to arrive.

2. At the end of imperative sentences to convey intensification
太贵了。
Tài guìle。
Too expensive!

3. To express a new, altered situation in the present
咖啡没有了。
Kāfēi méi yǒu le
There's no coffee left.

4. To express the past
他去了。
Tā qùle。
He went there.

5. Usually combined with a definite time
他昨天来了。
Tā zuótiān láile。
He came yesterday.

6. For neutral description (in comparison with the aspect particle guo 过)
我吃了。
Wǒ chīle。
I ate/have eaten.

7. To express anteriority and posteriority
你明天来了，我们就去买东西。
Nǐ míngtiān láile，wǒmen jiù qù mǎi dōngxi。
Tomorrow, if you have come, we'll go shopping.

The negation of le 了 is méi yǒu 没有.
In the negated sentence, le 了 is omitted.

我没有买。
Wǒ méi yǒu mǎi。
I didn't buy.

我没有去。
Wǒ méi yǒu qù。
I didn't go there.

The particle le 了 is not used
1. with zài 在 and shì 是
2. with the complement of degree
3. with the complement of possibility
4. with repeated or habitual actions

The particle le 了 is rarely used
1. with modal verbs
2. with verbs of feeling and emotion
3. with verbs of knowing
4. a relative clause

### Info Box

The past tense can also be expressed without le 了, by using adverbs of time such as "yesterday" or "last year.".

**The Aspect Particle** guò 过
The particle guò 过 is attached to the verb as a suffix and thus expresses a particular occurrence in the indefinite past. In English, it often is translated as "already" or "before."

# Grammar

我吃过北京烤鸭。
Wǒ chīguo Běijīng kǎoyā。
I've eaten Peking duck before.

The negation of guò 过 is méi yǒu 没有.
In the negated sentence, guò 过 remains;
unlike le 了, it is not omitted.

我没有吃过北京烤鸭。
Wǒ méi yǒu chīguo Běijīng kǎoyā。
I've never eaten Peking duck (before).

Guò 过 and le 了 can also be used together
in short sentences.

我吃过了。
Wǒ chīguole。
I've already eaten.

## The progressive Aspect
It is formed by placing zài 在 before the verb,
and it can be used in the past, present, and
future. The negation is méi yǒu 没有; in this
case, zài 在 is omitted.

我在打电话。
Wǒ zài dǎ diànhuà。
I'm making a phone call.

我没有打电话，我在吃饭。
Wǒ méi yǒu dǎ diànhuà, wǒ zài chī
fàn。
I wasn't making a phone call; I'm eating.

我在喝茶.
Wǒ zài hē chá.
I'm drinking tea.

## Attributive Particle

The attributive particle de 的 is used to form a
possessive and to link adjectives to nouns.

de 的 with Pronouns
我的啤酒。
Wǒde píjiǔ。
My beer.

## Info Box

Exceptions: de 的 usually is not used
– with hěnduō 很多 and hěnshǎo 很少.
– with one-syllable adjectives, unless they are
  heavily stressed.
– if there is a close relationship or a relationship
  of kinship between pronoun and noun.

de 的 with Nouns
王先生的电话号码。
Wáng xiānshengde diànhuà hàomǎ。
Mr. Wang's telephone number.

de 的 with One-Syllable or Doubled
Adjectives, or with Adjectives Modified
by an Adverb
好喝的茶。
Hǎohēde chá。
The delicious tea.

de 的 with Relative Clauses/Attributive
Clauses
我今天买的鱼。
Wǒ jīntiān mǎide yú。
The fish that I bought today.

## Info Box

Note the difference:
北京烤鸭　　　　　北京的烤鸭
Běijīng kǎoyā　　　Běijīngde kǎoyā
Peking duck　　　　Peking's roasted ducks

## Declarative Sentences

### with a Noun (Nominal) Predicate
我是美国人。
Wǒ shì Měiguórén.
I am an American.

### with a Verb (Verbal) Predicate
美国人喝啤酒。
Měiguórén hē píjiǔ.
Americans drink beer.

### with an Adjective (Verbal) Predicate
我很好。
Wǒ hěn hǎo.
I'm fine.

## Demonstrative Pronouns

| | | |
|---|---|---|
| this | zhè | 这 |
| this | zhège | 这个 |
| these (plural) | zhèxiē | 这些 |
| here | zhèr | 这儿 |
| here | zhèli | 这里 |
| this side, here | zhèbiān | 这边 |
| that | nà | 那 |
| that | nàge | 那个 |
| those (plural) | nàxiē | 那些 |
| there | nàr | 那儿 |
| there | nàli | 那里 |
| that side, there | nàbian | 那边 |

## Types of Interrogative Sentences

With a few exceptions, the interrogative sentence has the same structure as the expected reply.

### with Interrogative Particles
In yes-no questions, the particle ma 吗 is added at the end of the sentence.

你是上海人吗?
Nǐ shì Shànghǎirén ma?
Are you from Shanghai?

The particle ne 呢 is used only if the context makes it clear what is intended; it is translated as "and ...?"

我是美国人。你呢?
Wǒ shi Měiguórén. Nǐ ne?
I'm an American. And you ...?

### with a Positive-Negative Question
The affirmative and negated forms of the predicate together constitute the question.

你是不是上海人?
Nǐ shì bú shì Shànghǎirén?
Are you from Shanghai?

你有没有钱?
Nǐ yǒu méi yǒu qián?
Do you have money?

你喝不喝啤酒?
Nǐ hē bù hē píjiǔ?
Do you drink beer?

### with Question Words

| | | |
|---|---|---|
| what? | shénme? | 什么? |
| when? | shénme shíhou? | 什么时候? |
| how ...? (in combination with an adjective) | duō ...? | 多...? |
| how much? | duōshǎo? | 多少? |
| how long? | duōshǎo shíjiān? | 多少时间? |
| how many? | jǐge? | 几个? |
| what day of the month? | jǐhào? | 记号? |

# Grammar

| | | |
|---|---|---|
| what day of the week? | xīngqī jǐ? | 星期几? |
| how? | zěnme? | 怎么? |
| who? | shéi? | 谁? |
| which? | nǎ...? | 哪...? |
| where? | zài nǎr?/ zài nǎli? | 在哪儿?/ 在哪里? |
| where (to)? | qù nǎr?/ qù nǎli? | 去哪儿?/ 去哪里? |
| why? | wèishénme? | 为什么? |
| how come/how so? (colloquial) | gànmá? | 干吗? |

## Info Box

The difference between jǐ 几 and duōshǎo 多少:
duōshǎo 多少 is used to ask about all numbers. The measure word usually is omitted. jǐ 几 asks about numbers from 1 to 10. The measure word must be retained.

## Complement of Degree (CoD)

The complement of degree is used to form adjectives. Verbs are linked by means of the particle de 得 with an adjective, adverb, or verb construction, and then they usually express the past tense or a habit. In this case, the particles le 了 and guo 过 cannot be used.

### Verbs with No Object

她唱得不好听。
Tā chàngde bù hǎotīng.
She doesn't sing well. / She didn't sing well.

The negation always precedes the adjective.

### Verbs with an Object

If the verb has an object, the verb must be repeated because de 得 can be attached only to a verb, never to a noun.

我们买衣服买得很多。
Wǒmen mǎi yīfu mǎide hěn duō.
We bought many dresses.

Additional adverbs, such as hěn 很, fēichǎng 非常, and others, can be used as complements for an adjective.

他说汉语说得我听不懂。
Tā shuō Hànyǔ shuōde wǒ tīng bù dǒng.
He speaks Chinese in such a way (so) that I can't understand it.

The complement can also consist of complete clauses, which often are translated into English with a "so that" construction.

## Complement of Result (CoR)

The complement of result is formed with verbs and adjectives, which are attached to the main verb of the sentence. Negation is accomplished by placing méi yǒu 没有 before the main verb.

| Complement | Main Verb + Complement | Negation | Translation |
|---|---|---|---|
| ...dào 到 | mǎidào 买到 | 没有买到 méi yǒu mǎidào | (not) bought |
| ...dǒng 懂 | tīngdǒng 听懂 | 没有听懂 méi yǒu tīngdǒng | (not) understood |
| ...hǎo 好 | chīhǎo 吃好 | 没有吃好 méi yǒu chīhǎo | (not) eaten up |
| ...duì 对 | shuōduì 说对 | 没有说对 méi yǒu shuōduì | (not) correctly said |

## Complement of Possibility (CoP)

The CoP is formed with de 得 or in the negated form with bu 不.

| | | | |
|---|---|---|---|
| …dào 到 | mǎidedào 买得到 | mǎibudào 买不到 | can (not) buy |
| …dǒng 懂 | kàndedǒng 看得懂 | kànbudǒng 看不懂 | can (not) understand |
| …dòng 动 | nádedòng 拿得动 | nábudòng 拿不动 | can (not) hold |
| …jiàn 见 | tīngdejiàn 听得见 | tīngbujiàn 听不见 | can (not) hear |
| …liǎo 了 | hēdeliǎo 喝得了 | hēbuliǎo 喝不了 | can (not) drink |
| …hǎo 好 | chīdehǎo 吃得好 | chībuhǎo 吃不好 | can (not) eat up |

## Conjunctions

Chinese uses conjunctions less frequently than English. Once the sense is clear from the context, the conjunction can be dispensed with.

| | | |
|---|---|---|
| but | dànshì | 但是 |
| therefore | suǒyǐ | 所以 |
| or | háishi | 还是 |
| because | yīnwèi | 因为 |

## Modal Verbs

**can** kěyǐ 可以

In the sense of "may," "it's allowed," or "possible." Frequently used to ask for permission or express prohibitions.

这里可以不可以抽烟？
Zhèli kěyǐ bù kěyǐ chōuyān?
Is smoking allowed here?

**can** huì 会

In the sense of "to know how to do something," "to have a good command of something" because it has been learned. Huì 会 expresses expertise or expert knowledge, and it can be used as a full verb.

他会说汉语。
Tā huì shuō Hànyǔ.
He has a good command of Chinese.

**can** néng 能

In the sense of "to be able," "to have a natural ability." Because of health or external circumstances (such as weather), one has a limited ability to do something. Néng 能 cannot be used as a full verb.

我今天不能踢足球。
Wǒ jīntiān bù néng tí zúqiú.
I'm not able to play soccer today.

**want (to)** yào 要

To express a strongly emphasized wish.

我什么都不要买！
Wǒ shénme dōu bú yào mǎi!
I don't want to buy anything.

**would like** xiǎng 想

To express a polite wish or to decline.

我不想去。
Wǒ bù xiǎng qù.
I wouldn't like (don't want) to go there.

**must** děi 得

In the sense of "need," "require," "have to," "necessary."

# Grammar

天晚了，我得走了。
Tiān wǎnle, wǒ děi zǒule.
It's gotten late; I have to go.

**should** yīnggāi 应该
To express a moral obligation.

我应该学汉语。
Wǒ yīnggāi xué Hànyǔ.
I (really) should learn Chinese.

**must** bìxū 必须
To express a duty imposed from outside.

我必须工作。
Wǒ bìxū gōngzuò.
I must work.

## Prepositions

Many Chinese prepositions were originally verbs, such as gěi 给 "for" (give).

**for** gěi 给
我给你买礼物
wǒ gěi nǐ mǎi lǐwù.
I'm buying presents for you.

**to** duì 对
我对你说 …
Wǒ duì nǐ shuō, …
I'm saying to (telling) you, …

**with** gēn 跟, often combined with yìqǐ 一起
我跟你一起去喝茶。
Wǒ gēn nǐ yìqǐ qù hē chá.
I'm going with you to drink tea.

**with** hé 和
我和你说汉语。
Wǒ hé nǐ shuō Hànyǔ.
I speak Chinese with you.

## Verbs to Introduce Clauses

| | | |
|---|---|---|
| I believe that … | wǒ juéde … | 我觉得 … |
| I hold the opinion that … | wǒ rènwéi … | 我认为 … |
| I assume that … | wǒ yǐwéi … | 我以为 … |
| I think that … | wǒ xiǎng … | 我想 … |
| I estimate that … | wǒ gūjì … | 我估计 … |
| I fear that … | wǒ kǒngpà … | 我恐怕 … |
| I've heard that … | wǒ tīngshuō … | 我听说 … |
| I know that … | wǒ zhīdào … | 我知道 … |
| I'm convinced that … | wǒ xiāngxìn … | 我相信 … |
| In my view, … | wǒ kàn … | 我看 … |
| As for me, … | duì wǒ láishuō … | 对我来说 … |
| I suggest that … | wǒ jiànyì … | 我建议 … |
| I'm telling you that … | wǒ gàosu nǐ … | 我告诉你 … |
| I doubt that … | wǒ huáiyí … | 我怀疑 … |

## Comparisons

### Comparative and Superlative

Comparative: gèng
Superlative: zuì

1. with adjectives
面条好吃，包子更好吃，饺子最好吃。
Miàntiáo hǎochī, bāozi gèng hǎochī, jiǎozi zuì hǎochī.
Noodles taste good, baozi taste better, and jiaozo taste best.

2. with verbs
我喜欢红茶, 更喜欢花茶, 最喜欢绿茶。
Wǒ xǐhuan hóngchá, gèng xǐhuan huāchá, zuì xǐhuan lǜchá.
I like black tea, I prefer jasmine tea, and I like green tea best.

**"Just like"** gēn … yíyàng 跟 …一样
Formula: A gēn B yíyàng.

我的裤子跟你的一样。
Wǒde kùzi gēn nǐde yíyàng.
My pants are just like yours.

In the negation, bù 不 is used. Generally it precedes yíyàng一样.

我的毛衣跟你的不一样。
Wǒde máoyī gēn nǐde bù yíyàng.
My sweater is not just like yours.

**"Compare"** bǐ 比
It compares A with B in a certain area.
Formula: A bǐ B adjective

北京烤鸭比饺子贵。
Běijīng kǎoyā bǐ jiǎozi guì。
Peking ducks are more expensive than jiaozi.

The negation usually involves the use of:
A méi yǒu 没有 B …

**"A is not as ... as B"** A méi yǒu 没有 B …
Formula: A méi yǒu B adjective

北京烤鸭没有饺子便宜。
Běijīng kǎoyā méi yǒu jiǎozi piányi。
Peking ducks are not as cheap as jiaozi.

**"A little"** yìdiǎn 一点

请你慢一点说!
Qǐng nǐ màn yìdiǎn shuō!
Please speak a little slower!

In a sentence with an adjectival predicate (see Declarative Sentences), the adjective can be followed by yìdiǎn 一点.

## Negation
**Negation with** bù 不
1. With verbs in the present and future
我们今天不工作, 明天也不工作。
Wǒmen jīntiān bù gōngzuò, míngtiān yě bù gōngzuò.
Today we're not working, and tomorrow we're not working either.

2. In all tenses before adjectives and adverbs
这条裤子不长, 也不短。
Zhètiáo kùzi bù cháng, yě bù duǎn.
These pants are (were) not long and not short either.

3. In all tenses with shì 是 and zài 在
昨天他还不在这里。
Zuótiān tā hái bú zài zhèli.
Yesterday he was not here yet

4. In all tenses with all modal verbs, verbs of feeling/emotion, and verbs of knowing
一个月以前他还不知道他今天去中国。
Yíge yuè yǐqián tā hái bù zhīdào tā jīntiān qù Zhōngguó.
One month ago he did not know yet that he would travel to China today.

# Grammar

5. In the past tense, with frequently repeated actions

小的时候他常常不吃蔬菜。

Xiǎode shíhou tā chángcháng bù chī shūcài.

When he was young, he often would not eat vegetables.

6. with the complement of degree

他走得不远。

Tā zǒude bù yuǎn.

He didn't walk far.

7. with the complement of possibility

他走不动。

Tā zǒu bu dòng.

He can't walk.

**Negation with** méi 没

Méi 没 is used in all tenses for the negation of yǒu 有.

我没有手机。

Wǒ méi yǒu shǒujī.

I have/had no cell phone.

Generally, it is used for negation of the past tense.

我没有买手机。

Wǒ méi yǒu mǎi shǒujī.

I didn't buy a cell phone.

## Measure Words for Nouns

| bǎ | 把 | things that can be grasped (knife, scissors, key, chairs, umbrellas) |
| bāo | 包 | packages or bundles (cigarettes, cookies) |
| bēi | 杯 | cups, glasses, goblets |
| běn | 本 | books, magazines, dictionaries (not newspapers) |
| bǐ | 笔 | sums of money |
| dài | 袋 | sacks, bags |
| diǎn | 点 | dot, hour (designates the full hour) |
| duàn | 段 | interval of time or length |
| dùn | 顿 | meals |
| fēn | 分 | part, minute, cent |
| fèn | 份 | portion (serving of food); newspapers; magazines; jobs |
| fēng | 封 | sealed communications (letters) |
| gè | 个 | generic, catch-all measure word (MW) |
| hú | 壶 | can, jug |
| jiā | 家 | businesses, firms, banks |
| jià | 架 | airplanes, helicopters |
| jiān | 间 | rooms |
| jiàn | 件 | outer garments (tops), gifts, matters/affairs |
| jiǎo | 角 | money unit of 10 cents |
| jù | 句 | sentences |
| juǎn | 卷 | rolls (spring rolls; toilet paper; rolls of film) |
| kè | 刻 | time unit of 15 minutes |
| kuài | 块 | piece, largest unit of money (for all currencies, in colloquial speech) |
| liè | 列 | trains |
| lóng | 笼 | round bamboo container in various sizes, used as a steamer |
| máo | 毛 | money unit of 10 cents (colloquial term) |
| pán | 盘 | plates |
| píng | 瓶 | bottle |
| shǒu | 首 | songs |
| shuāng | 双 | paired things (hands, eyes, shoes, socks, gloves) |
| tào | 套 | sets, apartments (tea service, multiroom residence, suit, multivolume books) |

| | | |
|---|---|---|
| tiáo | 条 | long, narrow objects (bamboo, streets, fish, snakes, pants, skirts, ties, belts) |
| tǒng | 桶 | tubular objects (bucket, barrel, vat) |
| tóu | 头 | certain animals (elephants, cattle) |
| wǎn | 碗 | bowl, small bowl |
| wèi | 位 | classifier for people (very polite) |
| yè | 页 | pages (of paper) |
| yuán | 元 | largest unit of money for all currencies |
| zhāng | 张 | flat objects (tickets, tables, beds, photos, faces, maps) |
| zhī | 只 | hands, suitcases, small boats, certain animals |
| zhī | 支 | long, straight things (pens, roses) |
| zuò | 座 | large structures (mountains, cities, bridges, monuments) |

## Measure Words for Verbs

Activities are counted with these measure words.

**"time"** cì 次
他打了三次电话。
Tā dǎle sāncì diànhuà.
He has called three times.

**"just for a second"** xià 下
你休息一下吧。
Nǐ xiūxi yíxià ba!
Rest for just a bit!

## Time Designations/Adverbs of Time

The time designation usually is the second element in the sentence, preceding the verb. That is, it directly follows the subject, unless there is some reason to give it special emphasis. In that case, it is the first element in the sentence.

**Examples of adverbs of time that can either precede or follow the subject:**

Past:

| | | |
|---|---|---|
| a long time ago | cóngqián | 从前 |
| previously | yǐqián | 以前 |
| formerly | guòqù | 过去 |
| at that time | dāngshí | 当时 |
| last year | qùnián | 去年 |
| last month | shànggeyuè | 上个月 |
| thus far | jìnlái | 近来 |
| recently | zuìjìn | 最近 |

Present:

| | | |
|---|---|---|
| now | xiànzài | 现在 |
| instantly | dāngqián | 当前 |
| presently | mùqián | 目前 |
| sometimes | yǒu shíhou | 有时候 |

Future:

| | | |
|---|---|---|
| in (the) future | jiānglái | 将来 |

**Examples of adverbs of time that must always follow the subject:**

| | | |
|---|---|---|
| already (past) | yǐjīng | 已经 |
| always (colloquial) | lǎo | 老 |
| always | zǒngshì | 总是 |
| frequently, often | chángcháng | 常常 |
| immediately | mǎshàng | 马上 |

**Day, week, month, year**

| | | |
|---|---|---|
| yesterday | zuótiān | 昨天 |
| today | jīntiān | 今天 |
| tomorrow | míngtiān | 明天 |
| last week | shàng(ge)xīngqī | 上个星期 |
| this week | zhè(ge)xīngqī | 这个星期 |
| next week | xià(ge)xīngqī | 下个星期 |
| last month | shàngge yuè | 上个月 |
| this month | zhège yuè | 这个月 |
| next month | xiàge yuè | 下个月 |
| last year | qùnián | 去年 |
| this year | jīnnián | 今年 |
| next year | míngnián | 明年 |

# Answers

## Answers

### Lesson 1

**Exercise 2:** Grass  艹

**Exercise 6:** 1. Zhèr yǒu lǜchá ma? Is there green tea here? 2. Zhèli méi yǒu kěkǒu kělè. There is no Coca-Cola here. 3. Zhōngguó yǒu méi yǒu huāchá? Is there flavored tea in China? 4. Méi yǒu píjiǔ, yě méi yǒu kāishuǐ. There is neither beer nor boiled water.

**Exercise 7:** 1. Feng shui; Chinese geomancy (wind / water) 2. Kung fu; Chinese martial art (skill, accomplishment / man) 3. Qigong; work on vital energy field (air, breath / skill, accomplishment) 4. Tai chi; shadow boxing (supreme, ultimate / extreme, pole / fist)

**Exercise 8:** 1. 中国有绿茶. 2. 这里有可口可乐和啤酒. Or: 这里有可口可乐, 也有啤酒. 3. 这里没有水. 4. 这里也有花茶. 5. 这里有酒吗? 6. 没有, 这里没有开水, 也没有茶.

### Lesson 2

**Exercise 2:** Human being, person 亻

**Exercise 6:** 1. Nǐde diànhuà hàomǎ búshi líng yāo qī jiǔ sān bā liù èr wǔ sì èr. Your telephone number is not 0179-3862542. 2. Běijīng zài Zhōngguó. Beijing is (located) in China. 3. Mǎ xiānsheng chī wǒde Běijīng kǎoyā, hē wǒde píjiǔ. Mr. Ma is eating my Peking duck and drinking my beer. 4. Nǐ hē shénme? What are you drinking? 5. Wǒ zài zhèli. I am here.

**Exercise 7:** 1. Mao Zedong/Tse-tung (surname; hair / shine / east) 2. Deng Xiaoping (surname / small / peace) 3. Jiang Zemin (surname; river / shine / people) 4. Hu Jintao (surname; beard / bright / wave)

**Exercise 8:** 1. 他吃北京烤鸭, 喝花茶. 2. 他喝什么啤酒? 3. 王女士不喝酒. 4. 我在中国也吃北京烤鸭. 5. 我没有电话. 6. 这里有电话吗? 7. 李先生在.

### Lesson 3

**Exercise 1:** 30; 56; 999; 450; 8008; 603; 812; 5007; 1800; 250

**Exercise 2:** Food, nourishment 饣

**Exercise 6:** 1. Wǔge bāozi duōshǎo qián? How much do five yeast dumplings (baozi) cost? 2. Sānliǎng jiǎozi bākuài qián. 150 grams of jiaozi cost 8 yuan. 3. Nǐ mǎi shénme? What are you buying? 4. Wǒ qǐng nǐ chīfàn. I'm inviting you to a meal. 5. Wáng xiǎojie hē shénme chá? What kind of tea is Ms. Wang drinking? 6. Qǐng nǐ piányi yìdiǎn! Please, make it cheaper!

**Exercise 7:** 1. Breakfast (early / boiled rice) 2. Lunch (midday / boiled rice) 3. Dinner (late / boiled rice)

**Exercise 8:** 1. 二两饺子多少钱? 2. 一笼有几个包子? 3. 一笼有十个包子. 4. 三两饺子七块五. 5. 一个北京烤鸭十二美元. 6. 在中国一个北京烤鸭一百一十块人民币.

### Lesson 4

**Exercise 2:** Fire 火, 灬

**Exercise 6:** 1. Qǐng wèn, Lǐ xiānsheng hǎo ma? Excuse me, how is Mr. Li? 2. Nǐmende miàntiáo hěn hǎochī. Your noodles taste very good. 3. Jīntiān zhōngwǔ wǒ qǐng nǐ chīfàn. I'm inviting you to lunch today.

**Exercise 7:** 1. Complete chaos (confused / seven / eight / miserable state) 2. Massacre at Tiananmen Square (six / four / movement) 3. Five-spice powder (five / scent) 4. Small Chinese vehicle for carrying loads (three / wheel / vehicle) 5. 20% discount (eight / break away; discount)

**Exercise 8:** 1. 我一九八八年七月二十五号出生. 2. 北京烤鸭贵吗? 3. 你好吗? 4. 祝你生日快乐! 5. 我今天晚上七点半过生日. 6. 你过生日吗? 7. 请喝茶!

## Lesson 5

**Exercise 1:** 1. yìbēi píjiǔ 一杯啤酒
2. liǎngpíng pútaojiǔ 两瓶葡萄酒
3. Sānbēi báipútáojiǔ 三杯白葡萄酒
4. liǎngbēi hēipí 两杯黑啤 5. sìpíng Déguóde báipútáojiǔ 四瓶德国的白葡萄酒 6. yìbēi Yīngguóde píjiǔ 一杯英国的啤酒 7. liùpíng Měiguóde hóngpútáojiǔ 六瓶美国的红葡萄酒

**Exercise 2:** Language, to speak 言，讠

**Exercise 6:** 1. Nǐ shi Déguórén háishi Měiguórén? Are you a German or an American? 2. Měiguó de báipútáojiǔ hé Zhōngguóde báijiǔ hěn hǎohē. American white wine and Chinese distilled spirits (baijiu) taste very good. 3. Wǒmen qù hē jiǔ. We're going out to have a drink. 4. Tāmen sìgerén hē yìpíng pútaojiǔ. The four of them are drinking a bottle of wine. 5. Tā hē yìbēi kěkǒu kělè. She is drinking a glass of Coca-Cola.

**Exercise 7:** 1. Red envelope with gifts of money (red / wrap up) 2. Sugar (white / sugar) 3. Black market (black / market)

**Exercise 8:** 1. 你是中国人吗? 2. 我从美国来. 3. 请你写中文! or 请你用中文写! 4. 我喝德国的红葡萄酒.有吗? 5. 今天晚上我们去中国饭馆吃饭. 6. 德国的黑啤好喝，也不贵. 7. 在中国吃早饭不太贵. 8. 你今天下午去哪里?

## Lesson 6

**Exercise 1:** 1. Qǐng gěi wǒ càidān! 请给我菜单! 2. Qǐng lái yìpíng píjiǔ! 请来一瓶啤酒! 3. Qǐng lái liǎngbēi hóngpútáojiǔ! 请来两杯红葡萄酒! 4. Qǐng lái sānwǎn mǐfàn! 请来三碗米饭!

**Exercise 2:** Mouth 口

**Exercise 6:** 1. Wǒ zài zhèli kěyi bù kěyi yòng Rénmínbì mǎi cài? Can I shop for groceries here with renminbi? 2. Duìbuqǐ,

nǐ néng gěi wǒ diǎn píjiǔ hé èrliǎng jiǎozi ma? Excuse me, could you order beer and two liang of jiaozi for me? 3. Xièxie, wǒ bù hē jiǔ. No thank you, I don't drink alcohol. 4. Qǐng nǐ shuō Pǔtōnghuà! Please, speak Standard Chinese (Mandarin)! 5. Wǒ xǐhuan chī Déguócài, gèng xǐhuan chī Zhōngguócài. I like to eat German cooking, but I prefer to eat Chinese foods.

**Exercise 7:** 1. Recipe (food / list) 2. Vegetable market (vegetables / market) 3. Rice bucket; "big eater" (boiled rice / bucket)

**Exercise 8:** 1. 请给我英文菜单! 2. 我很好.你呢? 3. 请你给我一点绿茶! 4. 对不起，我的汉语不太好. 5. 能不能便宜一点? 6. 你想吃什么肉? 7. 我不能吃辣! 8. 你今天晚上想吃什么? 9. 你今天晚上想去哪里吃饭. 10. 我最喜欢吃饺子和包子.

## Lesson 7

**Exercise 1:** 1. 左边 2. 左边的银行 3. 银行的左边 4. 右边 5. 右边的汉字 6. 汉字的右边

**Exercise 2:** Water 水，氵

**Exercise 6:** 1. Shànghǎide xiǎolóngbāo lǐmiàn yǒu ròu, yě yǒu cài. In the Shanghai "xiaolongbao," there's both meat and vegetables. 2. Qǐng nǐ zài mǎi yìzhāng piào, wǒ yě yào qù. Please buy another (one more) ticket; I want to go there, too. 3. Duìmiànde fànguǎn méi yǒu hǎochīde cài. The restaurant opposite has no good food.

**Exercise 7:** 1. Yangtse, Long River (long / river) 2. Yellow River (yellow / river) 3. Pearl River (pearl / river) 4. Mekong River (billow, wave / dark blue water / river)

**Exercise 8:** 1. 我们今天去哪里吃饭. 2. 左边的词典是我的. 3. 茶馆在银行的对面. 4. 要不要给你打包? 5. 下午四点半再见. 6. 请你不要再来!

# Answers

## Lesson 8

**Exercise 2:** Bamboo 竹

**Exercise 6:** 1. Mǎ xiānsheng duì Lǐ xiǎojie hěn gǎn xìngqù. Mr. Ma is very interested in Miss Li. 2. Wǒmen chángcháng qù càishì mǎi shūcài, dòufu hé miàntiáo. We often go to the vegetable market to buy vegetables, tofu, and noodles. 3. Dào fànguǎn nǐ yào wǎng qián zǒu. To get to the restaurant, you have to go straight ahead!

**Exercise 7:** 1. (Still) Camera (expose / appearance / device) 2. Cell phone (hand / device) 3. Calculator (calculate / calculate / device)

**Exercise 8:** 1. 我们去吃饭吧! 2. 请你往北走. 3. 我对中国很感兴趣. 4. 我对酒过敏. 5. 我不能抽烟. 6. 请你写一下. 7. 对面是什么?

## Lesson 9

**Exercise 2:** Woman 女

**Exercise 6:** 1. Zǎoshàng Měiguórén yìbān hē kāfēi, bù hē píjiǔ. In the morning, Americans usually drink coffee and not beer. 2. Lǐ nǚshi zài xiūxi, Mǎ xiǎojie zài chōuyān. Mrs. Li is resting, and Ms. Ma is smoking. 3. Kāfēiguǎn lǐmiàn méi yǒu Běijīng kǎoyā. Nǐ kàncuòle! In a café, there are no Peking ducks. Your eyes deceived you!

**Exercise 7:** 1. Table tennis, Ping-Pong (ping / pong / ball) 2. Tennis (net / ball) 3. Basketball (basket / ball)

**Exercise 8:** 1. 你看一下吧! 2. 等一下!我还在吃早饭. 3. 你今天晚上还要跟你(的)女朋友一起过她的生日吗? 4. 你一定要给我介绍你的中国朋友! 5. 对不起, 我说错了. 6. 从你那里到我这里要花多少时间?

## Lesson 10

**Exercise 1:** 1. Rat 2. Ox 3. Tiger 4. Rabbit 5. Dragon 6. Snake 7. Horse 8. Goat (sheep, ram) 9. Monkey 10. Rooster 11. Dog 12. Pig (boar)

**Exercise 2:** Heart 心, 忄

**Exercise 6:** 1. Wǒ xiǎng yào dà yìdiǎnde fángjiān! I would like a larger room! 2. Nǐmen hái yǒu biéde fángjiān ma? Do you have any other rooms? 3. Wǒmen xiǎng zhù liǎngge wǎnshang. We would like to stay for two nights.

**Exercise 7:** 1. Television (electricity / see) 2. Table (table / suffix) 3. Bed 4. Air conditioning (empty; room / regulate)

**Exercise 8:** 1. 你别跟我说英语了! 2. 除了英文以外我还会说汉语. 3. 中国人说汉语说得很快. 4. 你还有便宜一点的房间吗? 5. 我想从三月十五号到(三月)二十号住这间房间. 6. 我们付钱付得太多. Or: 我们付了很多钱. 7. 我给你打电话.

## Lesson 11

**Exercise 2:** To walk, run 辶

**Exercise 6:** 1. Wǒyào mǎi liǎngzhāng dào Shànghǎide huǒchēpiào. I want to buy two train tickets to Shanghai. 2. Wǒmen zài nǎli shàngchē? Where do we board? 3. Tāmen zuò fēijī qù Zhōngguó, wǒ zuò huǒchē qù. You're flying to China; I'm going there by train.

**Exercise 7:** 1. Travel bag, carryall (trip / bag) 2. Travel agency (trip / association) 3. Tour group (trip / group) 4. Tour guide (trip / compass)

**Exercise 8:** 1. 从火车站到飞机场多远? 2. 我走错了. 3. 请你慢一点开车! 4. 我不能在这里等你. 5. 请你给我开张发票.

## Lesson 12

**Exercise 2:** Hand 手，扌

**Exercise 6:** 1. Nǐ péngyoude Hànyǔ shuōde hěn búcuò. Your friend doesn't speak Chinese badly. 2. Wǒmen bù chī zhūròu, yě bù hē píjiǔ. We don't eat pork and don't drink beer. 3. Tāmen xīngqīwǔ qù qīngzhēnsì. They're going to the mosque on Friday.

**Exercise 7:** 1. Office (handle / jointly / room) 2. Handle/take care of formalities (handle / hand / continue) 3. Handle matters (handle / matters)

**Exercise 8:** 1. 你说汉语说得很流利. 2. 在中国西部能吃烤包子. 3. 我们明天几点钟去清真寺? 4. 你什么时候给我买背包? 5. 对不起.请问，不戴帽子可不可以进清真寺? 6. 我想跟我的朋友一起吃清真菜!

## Lesson 13

**Exercise 2:** Illness, disease 疒

**Exercise 6:** 1. Qǐng bié gěi wǒ dǎzhēn! Please don't give me a shot! 2. Wǒ yào chī Xīyào, bú chī Zhōngyào! I want to take Western medicines, not traditional Chinese ones! 3. Wǒ zuótiān bù shūfu, xiànzài hǎo le. Yesterday I didn't feel well; now I'm okay again.

**Exercise 7:** 1. Acupuncture and moxibustion (needle / moxa, mugwort herb) 2. Anesthesia (anesthesia / drunk) 3. Antibiotic (offer resistance / bacteria / element) 4. Acupressure massage (push / hold)

**Exercise 8:** 1. 我这里疼. 2. 我想对大夫说. 3. 我对鸡蛋过敏. 4. 按摩以后我去吃饭了. 5. 只头疼，我不去看大夫. 6. 我小的时候，常常肚子疼. 7. 我什么时候可以看大夫.

## Lesson 14

**Exercise 2:** Clothing 衣，衤

**Exercise 6:** 1. Déguóde zhàoxiàngjī shi zuì hǎode. German cameras are the best. 2. Wǒmen duō chuān yìxiē yīfu qù lǚxíng. We'd best put on a little more clothing for the trip. 3. Yīngguóde báijiǔ bǐ Zhōngguóde báijiǔ là. English distilled spirits are stronger than Chinese distilled spirits (baijiu).

**Exercise 7:** 1. West; Occident (west / direction) 2. Western-style suit (west / clothing) 3. Tomato (west / red / persimmon)

**Exercise 8:** 1. 有没有更好的? 2. 我喜欢这条裤子. 3. 这个照相机跟那个一样贵. 4. 还有黑的吗? 5. 太贵.我不要了. 6. 有一点小，不合适.

## Lesson 15

**Exercise 2:** Sun, day 日

**Exercise 6:** 1. Yǒu wèntí, qǐng lái zhǎo wǒ! Please get in touch with me if there are problems! 2. Wǒ bànde liǎo. I can handle it (be able). 3. Yǒu guānxi jiù kěyǐ yáncháng qiānzhèng. If you have connections, you can extend the visa.

**Exercise 7:** 1. Company ID card 2. Permit, license 3. Identification card

**Exercise 8:** 1. 那个警察说我的签证过期了. 2. 麻烦你一下，你能不能帮助我延长签证? 3. 我现在没有空跟我的老板说话. 4. 我找不到我的照相机了. 5. 我说的你听见了吗?

# List of Words

List of Words

10 cents jiǎo 角 (3)

10 cents (colloq.) máo 毛 (3)

a little bit yìdiǎn 一点 (3)

abdomen, belly dùzi 肚子 (13)

absolutely; by all means yídìng 一定 (9)

address dìzhǐ 地址 (7)

after that; later, afterward; after yǐhòu 以后 (13)

again zài 再 (7)

airplane fēijī 飞机 (11)

airport fēijīchǎng 飞机场 (11)

alcohol jiǔ 酒 (1)

all dōu 都 (8)

all/everything together yìqǐ 一起 (9)

allergy guòmǐn 过敏 (8)

alone yígerén 一个人 (8)

also, too yě 也 (1)

America Měiguó 美国 (5)

and …? … ne? … 呢? (6)

and hé 和 (1)

anger, annoyance máfan 麻烦 (15)

animal dòngwù 动物 (10)

apple píngguǒ 苹果 (14)

approximately zuǒyòu 左右 (9)

arrive; to … dào 到 (7)

ask wèn 问 (4)

aspect particle guo 过 (10)

aspect particle le 了 (9)

at midday zhōngwǔ 中午 (4)

at one's discretion suíbiàn 随便 (13)

at the time of, when/ whenever … 的时候 (12)

attributive particle de 的 (2)

backpack bēibāo 背包 (12)

baggage; travel equipment xíngli 行李 (11)

ban yínháng 银行 (7)

baozi, Shanghai style xiǎolóngbāo 小笼包 (7)

be allergic to … duì … guòmǐn 对 … 过敏 (8)

be born chūsheng 出生 (4)

be called (surname only) xìng 姓 (9)

be called; call jiào 叫 (9)

be hungry dùzi è 肚子饿 (13)

be hungry è 饿 (13)

be in progress/going on zài 在 (9)

be inflamed fāyán 发炎 (13)

be interested in … duì … gǎn xìngqù 对 … 感兴趣 (8)

be located at a place, in, at zài 在 (2)

be missing/lacking, shortly before chà 差 (4)

be on a par with … gēn … yíyàng 跟 … 一样 (14)

be shì 是 (2)

be sick; sickness; defect bìng 病 (13)

be thirsty kě 渴 (13)

be thirsty kǒukě 口渴 (13)

because, since yīnwèi 因为 (8)

beer (dark) hēipí 黑啤 (5)

beer píjiǔ 啤酒 (1)

Beijing, Peking Běijīng 北京 (2)

bicycle zìxíngchē 自行车 (11)

big; old dà 大 (4)

bill, tab, invoice mǎidān 买单 (9)

birthday shēngrì 生日 (4)

black hēi 黑 (5)

boiled rice mǐfàn 米饭 (6)

boiled water kāishuǐ 开水 (1)

boss, proprietor lǎobǎn 老板 (15)

boyfriend nánpéngyou 男朋友 (9)

bread miànbāo 面包 (12)

breakfast zǎofàn 早饭 (5)

bring (here) dàilái 带来 (13)

broken; have spoiled huàile 坏了 (13)

but, however dànshì 但是 (7)

buy mǎi 买 (3)

calculate suàn 算 (9)

camera (still) zhàoxiàngjī 照相机 (14)

can huì 会 (6)

can; be able sein néng 能 (6)

can; be allowed kěyǐ 可以 (6)

Cantonese Guǎngdōngrén 广东人 (10)

celebrate the New Year guònián 过年 (4)

celebrate; cross guò 过 (4)

cell phone shǒujī 手机 (14)

cent fēn 分 (3)

cheap piányi 便宜 (3)

cheaper piányi yìdiǎn 便宜一点 (3)

cheers, to your health gānbēi 干杯 (11)

chess xiàngqí 象棋 (10)

chicken jī 鸡 (6)

China Zhōngguó 中国 (1)
Chinese characters Hànzì 汉字 (7)
Chinese Hànyǔ 汉语 (5)
Chinese Zhōngwén 中文 (5)
chopsticks kuàizi 筷子 (6)
Christmas shèngdànjié 圣诞节 (4)
clear, plain; understand míngbái 明白 (15)
clock diǎn 点 (4)
close, near jìn 近 (11)
clothes yīfu 衣服 (14)
Coca-Cola kěkǒu kělè 可口可乐 (1)
coffee kāfēi 咖啡 (9)
coffeehouse, café kāfēiguǎn 咖啡馆 (9)
cold lěng 冷 (14)
come across/over guòlái 过来 (13)
come from ... cóng ... lái 从 ... 来 (5)
come lái 来 (5)
compare bǐ 比 (14)
complete(ly), entire(ly) wánquán 完全 (12)
consult a physician; treat sick people kànbìng 看病 (13)
credit card xìnyòngkǎ 信用卡 (14)
cubed chicken jīdīng 鸡丁 (6)
day; sun rì 日 (4)
deep-fried, salted dough strip yóutiáo 油条 (9)
delicious (beverages) hǎohē 好喝 (4)
delicious (foods) hǎochī 好吃 (4)
desert shāmò 沙漠 (12)

dialect dìfānghuà 地方话 (7)
dictionary cídiǎn 词典 (7)
dim sum; snack diǎnxīn 点心 (10)
dinner wǎnfàn 晚饭 (5)
doctor, physician dàifu 大夫 (13)
drink alcohol hē jiǔ 喝酒 (2)
drink hē 喝 (2)
drive, steer; depart kāi 开 (11)
dumpling made of noodle dough jiǎozi 饺子 (3)
eat chī fàn 吃饭 (2)
eat chī 吃 (2)
eat food of animal origin chī hūn 吃荤 (6)
eat soup hē tāng 喝汤 (7)
eat vegetarian food chī sù 吃素 (8)
eight bā 八 (1)
England Yīngguó 英国 (5)
English Yīngwén 英文 (5)
English Yīngyǔ 英语 (5)
enter, go in jìn 进 (4)
euro ōuyuán 欧元 (3)
except, besides chúle ... yǐwài 除了 ... 以外 (10)
excuse me, sorry duìbuqǐ 对不起 (6)
expensive guì 贵 (3)
expire, run out, be overdue guòqī 过期 (15)
extend yáncháng 延长 (15)
extremely, unusually fēicháng 非常 (10)
(eye)glasses yǎnjìng 眼镜 (13)
eyes yǎnjing 眼睛 (13)
face miànzi 面子 (12)
family, home jiā 家 (9)

far from ..., away from ... lí 离 (11)
far yuǎn 远 (11)
fast, quick kuài 快 (6)
firm, company gōngsī 公司 (15)
fish yú 鱼 (8)
fit, suit héshì 合适 (14)
five wǔ 五 (1)
flavored tea huāchá 花茶 (1)
fluid, fluent liúlì 流利 (12)
food, groceries, kitchen cài 菜 (6)
for forming the complement of degree (CoD) de 得 (15)
for forming the CoP and CoD de 得 (15)
for forming the CoP liao 了 (15)
for forming the CoR and CoP dào 到 (15)
for forming the CoR and CoP dòng 动 (15)
for forming the CoR and CoP dǒng 懂 (15)
for forming the CoR and CoP jiàn 见 (15)
for wèi ... 为 ... (11)
forget wàng 忘 (10)
four sì 四 (1)
free time kòng 空 (15)
Friday xīngqīwǔ 星期五 (4)
friend péngyou 朋友 (9)
from; away from cóng 从 (5)
fruit shuǐguǒ 水果 (14)
fry in a wok, pan-stir chǎo 炒 (8)
gamble, bet xià 下 (10)
generic, most common measure word (MW) gè 个 (2)

# List of Words

German Déyǔ 德语 (5)

Germans Déguórén 德国人 (5)

Germany Déguó 德国 (5)

get in line; stand in line páiduì 排队 (11)

get in, board shàng chē 上车 (11)

get off, get out, disembark xià chē 下车 (11)

get to know rènshi 认识 (9)

gift, present lǐwù 礼物 (14)

girlfriend nǚpéngyou 女朋友 (9)

give a massage; massage ànmó 按摩 (13)

give an injection dǎzhēn 打针 (13)

give back, bring back tuì 退 (11)

give; for gěi 给 (6)

gladly, with pleasure gāoxìng 高兴 (9)

go with; travel by zuò ... 坐 (11)

go; go there qù 去 (5)

good hǎo 好 (4)

good looking hǎokàn 好看 (14)

good-bye zàijiàn 再见 (7)

green tea lǜchá 绿茶 (1)

Guangdong Province Guǎngdōng 广东 (10)

guest kèrén 客人 (8)

half bàn 半 (4)

hand shǒu 手 (12)

handbag, purse shǒutíbāo 手提包 (14)

handicraft shǒugōng 手工 (14)

happy, cheerful kuàilè 快乐 (4)

"hard sleeper"; sleeping car compartment yìngwò 硬卧 (11)

have a cold gǎnmào 感冒 (13)

have diarrhea lā dùzi 拉肚子 (13)

have fever fāshāo 发烧 (13)

have time yǒu kòng 有空 (15)

have, there is/are yǒu 有 (1)

he tā 他 (2)

head covering màozi 帽子 (12)

head tóu 头 (13)

health jiànkāng 健康 (11)

hear, listen (to) tīng 听 (9)

help bāngzhù 帮助 (15)

hen egg jīdàn 鸡蛋 (9)

her (poss. pron.) tāde 她的 (2)

here (North Chin.) zhèr 这儿 (1)

here (South Chin.) zhèli 这里 (1)

his (pers. pron.) tāde 他的 (2)

horse mǎ 马 (11)

hospital yīyuàn 医院 (13)

hot pot huǒguō 火锅 (11)

hot-and-sour soup suānlàtāng 酸辣汤 (7)

hotel, restaurant fàndiàn 饭店 (11)

hour xiǎoshí 小时 (11)

how far? duōyuǎn 多远 (11)

how long? duōshǎo shíjiān 多少时间 (11)

how many kilometers? duōshǎo gōnglǐ 多少公里 (11)

how many? jǐ 几 (2)

how much does it cost? duōshǎo qián 多少钱 (3)

how much? duōshǎo 多少 (2)

how old? duōdà 多大 (4)

how? zěnme? 怎么？ (6)

hundred bǎi 百 (3)

hurt, ache téng 疼 (13)

I wǒ 我 (2)

in front qián 前 (8)

in the afternoon xiàwǔ 下午 (4)

in the evening wǎnshang 晚上 (4)

in the morning zǎoshang 早上 (4)

in the morning, A.M. shàngwǔ 上午 (4)

inside, within, in lǐmiàn 里面 (7)

interest xìngqù 兴趣 (8)

interrogative particle ma 吗 (1)

introduce oneself; explain jièshào 介绍 (9)

Islamic, Muslim qīngzhēn 清真 (12)

it doesn't matter méi guānxi 没关系 (15)

it would be better; rather háishi 还是 (15)

joke, fun wánxiào 玩笑 (14)

just briefly, for a second yíxià 一下 (8)

key wǎn 碗 (6)

key yàoshi 钥匙 (10)

kick; play tí 踢 (10)

kilometer gōnglǐ 公里 (11)

know zhīdao 知道 (11)

lamb, mutton yángròu 羊肉 (12)

language -yǔ 语 (5)

language yǔyán 语言 (5)

large size; size dàhào 大号 (14)

largest unit of currency yuán 元 (3)

largest unit of money kuài 块 (3)

leg tuǐ 腿 (13)

Li (Chin. surname) Lǐ 李 (2)

like xǐhuan 喜欢 (6)

little, few shǎo 少 (2)

live, reside zhù 住 (10)

long cháng 长 (14)

long live ... wànsuì 万岁 (11)

lose diū 丢 (12)

lunch wǔfàn 午饭 (5)

Ma (Chin. surname) Mǎ 马 (2)

mahjong májiàng 麻将 (10)

make a phone call dǎ diànhuà 打电话 (10)

make jokes kāi wánxiào 开玩笑 (14)

make out receipts kāi 开 (7)

make zuò 做 (6)

market shìchǎng 市场 (14)

matter, affair shì 事 (15)

may I ask ... qǐng wèn 请问 (4)

meaning yìsi 意思 (15)

meat cut into strips ròusī 肉丝 (6)

meat ròu 肉 (6)

medications (trad. Chin.) Zhōngyào 中药 (13)

medications (trad. Chin.) Zhōngyī 中医 (13)

medications (Western) Xīyào 西药 (13)

medications (Western) Xīyī 西医 (13)

medications yào 药 (13)

melon xīguā 西瓜 (14)

menu càidān 菜单 (6)

method, ways and means bànfǎ 办法 (12)

minute(s) fēn 分 (4)

Miss xiǎojie 小姐 (2)

mixed shíjǐn 什锦 (8)

mixed vegetables sùshíjǐn 素什锦 (8)

modal particle for commands, requests, etc. ba 吧 (8)

money qián 钱 (3)

month; moon yuè 月 (4)

more, even more gèng 更 (6)

mosque qīngzhēnsì 清真寺 (12)

mountain shān 山 (12)

mouth kǒu 口 (13)

Mr., husband xiānsheng 先生 (2)

Mrs., Ms. (form of address) nǚshì 女士 (2)

much duō 多 (2)

Muslim cuisine qīngzhēncài 清真菜 (12)

must; need, requite děi 得 (8)

MW for an indefinite number of things xiē 些 (14)

MW for bottles píng 瓶 (5)

MW for bound writings like books běn 本 (7)

MW for flat things like tickets zhāng 张 (7)

MW for glasses, goblets, and cups bēi 杯 (5)

MW for long things like pants and skirts tiáo 条 (14)

MW for tops like sweaters and T-shirts jiàn 件 (14)

my, mine wǒde 我的 (2)

name míngzi 名字 (9)

nearly, almost chàbuduō 差不多 (11)

need, require xūyào 需要 (11)

nine jiǔ 九 (1)

no, not bù 不 (2)

noodle made of wheat flour miàntiáo 面条 (4)

normally, usually yìbān 一般 (9)

North Chinese, Northerners běifāngrén 北方人 (10)

not (have) méi 没 (1)

not bad búcuò 不错 (10)

not supposed to be bié 别 (10)

not have, there isn't/aren't; without méi yǒu 没有 (1)

not often bùcháng 不常 (5)

now xiànzài 现在 (4)

number hào 号 (4)

number hàomǎ 号码 (2)

oasis lǜzhōu 绿洲 (12)

often, frequently chángcháng 常常 (5)

on foot bùxíng 步行 (11)

(on the) left zuǒbiān 左边 (7)

(on the) right yòubiān 右边 (7)

one yī 一 (1)

(one)self zìjǐ 自己 (13)

only, merely zhǐ 只 (7)

opposite, across (from) duìmiàn 对面 (7)

or háishi 还是 (5)

order diǎn 点 (6)

other biéde 别的 (10)

our wǒmende 我们的 (3)

outside wàimiàn 外面 (14)

overall yígòng 一共 (9)

# List of Words

pants, trousers kùzi 裤子 (14)

passport hùzhào 护照 (15)

pay fù qián 付钱 (9)

pay with ... yòng ... fùqián 用 ... 付钱 (14)

Peking duck, Běijīng kǎoyā 北京烤鸭 (2)

person, human being rén 人 (5)

phonetic transcription; spell Pīnyīn 拼音 (7)

place, locality dìfāng 地方 (7)

play dǎ 打 (10)

plural suffix men 们 (3)

point in time shíhou 时候 (10)

police officer jǐngchá 警察 (15)

police station gōng'ānjú 公安局 (15)

pork zhūròu 猪肉 (12)

porridge made of rice and water zhōu 粥 (9)

pound jīn 斤 (14)

precept, principle dàoli 道理 (12)

present arguments jiǎng dàoli 讲道理 (15)

previously; formerly; before yǐqián 以前 (13)

probably kěnéng 可能 (9)

profession, occupation zhíyè 职业 (15)

quality zhìliàng 质量 (14)

quarter of an hour yíkè 一刻 (4)

question, problem wèntí 问题 (15)

real(ly), genuine zhēn 真 (10)

receipt fāpiào 发票 (7)

red hóng 红 (5)

relationship guānxi 关系 (15)

renminbi (RMB) Rénmínbì 人民币 (3)

repair xiū 修 (13)

request; invite; please qǐng 请 (3)

reserve, preorder yùdìng 预订 (10)

restaurant fànguǎn 饭馆 (5)

ride a horse/bike qí 骑 (11)

right away, at once jiù 就 (8)

right, correct duì 对 (8)

roast duck kǎoyā 烤鸭 (2)

room fángjiān 房间 (10)

run; walk zǒu 走 (8)

seafood hǎiwèi 海味 (8)

seat, place zuòwèi 座位 (11)

see; look at; read; visit kàn 看 (9)

seek, seek out, contact zhǎo 找 (15)

seem; apparently hǎoxiàng 好象 (13)

serve shàng 上 (9)

seven qī 七 (1)

Shanghai cuisine Shànghǎicài 上海菜 (7)

Shanghai dialect Shànghǎihuà 上海话 (7)

Shanghai Shànghǎi 上海 (7)

sharp, spicy là 辣 (6)

she tā 她 (2)

shop for groceries mǎi cài 买菜 (8)

shop mǎi dōngxi 买东西 (14)

short duǎn 短 (14)

should; must yīnggāi 应该 (7)

sing chànggē 唱歌 (10)

sing karaoke chàng KǎlāOK 唱卡拉OK (10)

sit, sit down zuò 坐 (4)

six liù 六 (1)

slow màn 慢 (6)

small/loose change língqián 零钱 (11)

smoke chōuyān 抽烟 (8)

so-so mǎmǎhūhū 马马虎虎 (10)

soccer zúqiú 足球 (10)

some, several yìxiē 一些 (15)

soup tāng 汤 (7)

sour suān 酸 (7)

South Chinese, Southerners nánfāngrén 南方人 (10)

speak, say shuō 说 (5)

speak, tell jiǎng 讲 (15)

specialty tècān 特餐 (10)

spend money huā qián 花钱 (9)

spend time on something huā shíjiān 花时间 (9)

Spring Festival chūnjié 春节 (4)

Standard Chinese/Mandarin Pǔtōnghuà 普通话 (7)

steamer that fits over a pot lóng 笼 (3)

still hái 还 (6)

stomach wèi 胃 (13)

story, floor; multistory building lóu 楼 (10)

straight ahead; uninterrupted; always yìzhí 一直 (8)

street mǎlù 马路 (11)

sunglasses tàiyángjìng 太阳镜 (12)

supermarket chāoshì 超市 (14)

sweet tián 甜 (14)

syllable for forming superlative zuì 最 (6)

Szechuan cuisine Chuāncài 川菜 (13)

take a break xiūxi 休息 (8)

take, bring (with) … dài 带 (11)

take, grasp, hold ná 拿 (12)

taxi; rental car chūzū qìchē 出租汽车 (11)

tea chá 茶 (1)

teahouse cháguǎn 茶馆 (7)

telephone diànhuà 电话 (2)

telephone number diànhuà hàomǎ 电话号码 (2)

temple sì 寺 (12)

ten shí 十 (1)

ten thousand wàn 万 (11)

thanks; thank xièxie 谢谢 (6)

that (one over there) nà 那 (5)

that (one over there) nàge 那个 (5)

their (poss. pron., f. pl.) tāmende 她们的 (3)

their (poss. pron., pl.) tāmende 他们的 (3)

therefore suǒyǐ 所以 (11)

these zhèxiē 这些 (14)

they (f. pl.) tāmen 她们 (3)

they tāmen 他们 (3)

things dōngxi 东西 (14)

this zhè 这 (3)

this zhège 这个 (3)

those (over there) nàxiē 那些 (14)

thousand qiān 千 (3)

three quarters of an hour sānkè 三刻 (4)

three sān 三 (1)

throw up tù 吐 (13)

ticket (for travel) chēpiào 车票 (11)

ticket; banknote piào 票 (7)

tight, firm jǐn 紧 (14)

time measured in hours zhōng 钟 (4)

time shíjiān 时间 (9)

to; in the direction of wàng 往 (8)

today jīntiān 今天 (4)

tofu dòufu 豆腐 (8)

toilet cèsuǒ 厕所 (13)

tomorrow míngtiān 明天 (11)

too expensive tài guì 太贵 (3)

too, overly tài 太 (3)

tooth yá 牙 (13)

train huǒchē 火车 (11)

train station huǒchēzhàn 火车站 (11)

travel lǚxíng 旅行 (14)

turn off, turn into guǎi 拐 (8)

two èr 二 (1)

two; liang (50 grams) liǎng 两 (3)

understand dǒng 懂 (10)

unpleasant bù shūfu 不舒服 (13)

use; with, by yòng 用 (5)

vegetable market càishì 菜市 (8)

vegetables shūcài 蔬菜 (8)

vegetarian dish sùcài 素菜 (8)

vehicle chē 车 (11)

very hěn 很 (4)

visa qiānzhèng 签证 (15)

visit friends kàn péngyou 看朋友 (9)

wait děng 等 (8)

Wang (Chin. surname) Wáng 王 (2)

want; must; become yào 要 (6)

want; would like; think; guess xiǎng 想 (6)

warm nuǎnhuo 暖和 (14)

we wǒmen 我们 (3)

wear on one's back bēi 背 (12)

wear on one's hands tí 提 (12)

wearing of caps and glasses dài 戴 (12)

wearing of clothing chuān 穿 (14)

week xīngqī 星期 (4)

western part xībù 西部 (12)

what? what kind of … shénme 什么 (2)

when? shénme shíhou 什么时候 (10)

where? where to? nǎli? 哪里 (5)

where? where to? nǎr? 哪儿 (5)

which? nǎ 哪 (4)

white bái 白 (5)

who? shéi 谁 (10)

wine pútáojiǔ 葡萄酒 (5)

wish; congratulate zhù 祝 (4)

with; follow s.o. gēn 跟 (9)

wool sweater máoyī 毛衣 (14)

work gōngzuò 工作 (9)

wrap up, put in a bag/box dǎ bāo 打包 (6)

write xiě 写 (5)

written language; language -wén 文 (5)

wrong; mistaken cuò 错 (9)

# List of Words

year nián 年 (4)
year of age/life suì 岁 (4)
yeast bun mántou 馒头 (9)
yeast dumplings bāozi 包子 (3)
yesterday zuótiān 昨天 (13)
you nǐ 你 (2)
your nǐde 你的 (2)
your (pl.) nǐmende 你们的 (3)
your (poss. pron., pl.) nǐmen 你们 (3)

zero líng 零 (2)

... ne? ... 呢？ and ...? (6)
... de shíhòu ... 的时候 at the time of, when/whenever ... (12)

ànmó 按摩 give a massage; massage (13)

ba 吧 modal particle for commands, requests, etc. (8)
bā 八 eight (1)
bái 白 white (5)
bǎi 百 hundred (3)
bàn 半 half (4)
bànfǎ 办法 method, ways and means (12)
bāngzhù 帮助 help (15)
bāozi 包子 yeast buns (3)
bēi 背 wear on one's back (12)
bēi 杯 MW for glasses, goblets, and cups (5)
bēibāo 背包 backpack (12)
běifāngrén 北方人 North Chinese, Northerners (10)
Běijīng 北京 Beijing, Peking (2)

Běijīng kǎoyā 北京烤鸭 Peking duck (2)
běn 本 MW for bound writings like books (7)
bǐ 比 compare (14)
bié 别 not be supposed to (10)
biéde 别的 other (10)
bìng 病 be sick; illness, sickness; defect (13)
bù 不 no, not (2)
bù shūfu 不舒服 unpleasant (13)
bùcháng 不常 not often (5)
búcuò 不错 not bad (10)
bùxíng 步行 on foot (11)

cài 菜 food, groceries, kitchen (6)
càidān 菜单 menu (6)
càishì 菜市 vegetable market (8)
cèsuǒ 厕所 toilet (13)
chá 茶 tea (1)
chà 差 lack; shortly before (4)
chàbuduō 差不多 nearly, almost (11)
cháguǎn 茶馆 teahouse (7)
cháng 长 long (14)
chàng KǎlāOK 唱卡拉OK sing karaoke (10)
chángcháng 常常 often, frequently (5)
chànggē 唱歌 sing (10)
chǎo 炒 fry in a wok, stir-fry (8)
chāoshì 超市 supermarket (14)
chē 车 vehicle (11)
chēpiào 车票 ticket (for travel) (11)
chī 吃 eat (2)
chī fàn 吃饭 eat (2)

chī hūn 吃荤 eat food of animal origin (6)
chī sù 吃素 eat vegetarian food (8)
chōuyān 抽烟 smoke (8)
chuān 穿 wearing of clothing (14)
Chuāncài 川菜 Szechuan cuisine (13)
chúle ... yǐwài 除了 ... 以外 except (for), besides (10)
chūnjié 春节 Spring Festival (4)
chūsheng 出生 be born (4)
chūzū qìchē 出租汽车 taxi; rental car (11)
cídiǎn 词典 dictionary (7)
cóng 从 from; away from (5)
cóng ... lái 从 ... 来 come from ... (5)
cuò 错 wrong; mistaken (9)

dà 大 big; old (4)
dǎ 打 play (10)
dǎ bāo 打包 wrap up; put in a bag/box (6)
dǎ diànhuà 打电话 make a phone call (10)
dàhào 大号 large size, size (14)
dài 带 take with, bring with (11)
dài 戴 wearing of caps and glasses (12)
dàifu 大夫 doctor, physician (13)
dàilái 带来 bring (here) (13)
dànshì 但是 but, however (7)
dào 到 arrive; to ... (7)
dào 到 for forming the CoR and CoP (15)
dàoli 道理 precept, principle (12)

dǎzhēn 打针 give an injection (13)

de 的 attributive particle (2)

de 得 for forming the CoP and CoD (15)

de 得 for forming the complement of degree (CoD) (10)

Déguó 德国 Germany (5)

Déguórén 德国人 Germans (5)

děi 得 must; need, require (8)

děng 等 wait (8)

Déyǔ 德语 German (5)

diǎn 点 order (6)

diǎn 点 clock (4)

diànhuà 电话 telephone (2)

diànhuà hàomǎ 电话号码 telephone number (2)

diǎnxīn 点心 dim sum; snack (10)

dìfāng 地方 place, locality (7)

dìfānghuà 地方话 dialect (7)

diū 丢 lose (12)

dìzhǐ 地址 address (7)

dòng 动 for forming the CoR and CoP (15)

dǒng 懂 understand (10)

dǒng 懂 for forming the CoR and CoP (15)

dòngwù 动物 animal (10)

dōngxi 东西 things (14)

dōu 都 all (8)

dòufu 豆腐 tofu (8)

duǎn 短 short (14)

duì 对 right, correct (8)

duì ...gǎn xìngqù 对... 感兴趣 be interested in ... (8)

duì ... guòmǐn 对 ... 过敏 be allergic to ... (8)

duìbuqǐ 对不起 (I'm sorry) (6)

duìmiàn 对面 opposite, across (from) (7)

duō 多 much (2)

duōdà 多大 how old? (4)

duōshǎo 多少 how much? (2)

duōshǎo gōnglǐ 多少公里 how many kilometers? (11)

duōshǎo qián 多少钱 How much does it cost? (3)

duōshǎo shíjiān 多少时间 how long?, how much time? (11)

duōyuǎn 多远 how far? (11)

dùzi 肚子 abdomen, belly (13)

dùzi è 肚子饿 be hungry (13)

è 饿 be hungry (13)

èr 二 two (1)

fàndiàn 饭店 hotel, restaurant (11)

fángjiān 房间 room (10)

fànguǎn 饭馆 restaurant (5)

fāpiào 发票 receipt (7)

fāshāo 发烧 have fever (13)

fāyán 发炎 be inflamed (13)

fēicháng 非常 extremely, unusually (10)

fēijī 飞机 airplane (11)

fēijīchǎng 飞机场 airport (11)

fēn 分 cent (3)

fēn 分 minutes (4)

fùqián 付钱 pay (9)

gānbēi 干杯 cheers, to your health (11)

gǎnmào 感冒 have a cold (13)

gāoxìng 高兴 glad(ly), with pleasure (9)

gè 个 generic measure word (MW) (2)

gěi 给 give; for (6)

gēn 跟 with; follow someone (9)

gēn ... yíyàng 跟 ... 一样 be on a par with ... (14)

gèng 更 more; even more (6)

gōng'ānjú 公安局 police station (15)

gōnglǐ 公里 kilometer (11)

gōngsī 公司 firm, company (15)

gōngzuò 工作 work (9)

guǎi 拐 turn off, turn into (8)

Guǎngdōng 广东 Guangdong Province (10)

Guǎngdōngrén 广东人 Cantonese (10)

guānxi 关系 relationship (15)

guì 贵 expensive (3)

guo 过 aspect particle (10)

guò 过 celebrate; cross (4)

guò nián 过年 celebrate the New Year (4)

guòlái 过来 come across/over (13)

guòmǐn 过敏 allergy (8)

guòqī 过期 run out, expire, be overdue (15)

hái 还 still, yet (6)

háishi 还是 it would be better; rather (15)

háishi 还是 or (5)

hǎiwèi 海味 seafood (8)

Hànyǔ 汉语 Chinese (5)

Hànzì 汉字 Chinese characters (7)

hào 号 number (4)

hǎo 好 good (4)

hǎochī 好吃 delicious (4)

hǎohē 好喝 delicious (4)

hǎokàn 好看 good looking (14)

hàomǎ 号码 number (2)

# List of Words

hǎoxiàng 好象 seem; apparently (13)

hé 和 and (1)

hē 喝 drink (2)

hē jiǔ 喝酒 drink alcohol (2)

hē tāng 喝汤 eat soup (7)

hēi 黑 black (5)

hēipí 黑啤 dark beer (5)

hěn 很 very (4)

héshì 合适 fit, suit (14)

hóng 红 red (5)

huā qián 花钱 spend money (9)

huā shíjiān 花时间 spend time on something (9)

huāchá 花茶 flavored tea (1)

huàile 坏了 broken; have spoiled (13)

huì 会 can (6)

huǒchē 火车 train (11)

huǒchēzhàn 火车站 train station (11)

huǒguō 火锅 hot pot (11)

hùzhào 护照 passport (15)

jǐ 几 how many ?; some (2)

jī 鸡 chicken (6)

jiā 家 family, home (9)

jiàn 件 MW for tops like sweaters and T-shirts (14)

jiàn 见 for forming the CoR and CoP (15)

jiǎng 讲 speak, tell (15)

jiǎng dàoli 讲道理 present arguments (15)

jiànkāng 健康 health (11)

jiào 叫 be called; call (9)

jiǎo 角 10 cents (3)

jiǎozi 饺子 dumplings made of noodle dough (3)

jīdàn 鸡蛋 hen egg (9)

jīdīng 鸡丁 cubed chicken (6)

jièshào 介绍 introduce oneself; explain (9)

jìn 进 enter, go in (4)

jìn 近 near (11)

jǐn 紧 tight, firm (14)

jīn 斤 pound (14)

jǐngchá 警察 police officer (15)

jīntiān 今天 today (4)

jiù 就 immediately, right away (8)

jiǔ 酒 alcohol (1)

jiǔ 九 nine (1)

kāfēi 咖啡 coffee (9)

kāfēiguǎn 咖啡馆 coffee-house, café (9)

kāi 开 writing out receipts (7)

kāi 开 drive, steer; depart (11)

kāi wánxiào 开玩笑 make jokes (14)

kāishuǐ 开水 boiled water (1)

kàn 看 see; look at; read; visit (9)

kàn péngyou 看朋友 visit friends (9)

kànbìng 看病 consult a physician; treat sick people (13)

kǎoyā 烤鸭 roast duck (2)

kě 渴 be thirsty (13)

kěkǒu kělè 可口可乐 Coca-Cola (1)

kěnéng 可能 probably (9)

kèrén 客人 guest (8)

kěyǐ 可以 can; be allowed to (6)

kòng 空 free time (15)

kǒu 口 mouth (13)

kǒukě 口渴 be thirsty (13)

kuài 块 largest unit of money (3)

kuài 快 quick, fast (6)

kuàilè 快乐 happy, cheerful (4)

kuàizi 筷子 chopsticks (6)

kùzi 裤子 pants (14)

là 辣 sharp, spicy (6)

lā dùzi 拉肚子 have diarrhea (13)

lái 来 come (5)

lǎobǎn 老板 boss, proprietor (15)

le 了 aspect particle (9)

lěng 冷 cold (14)

lí 离 far from ..., away from ... (11)

Lǐ 李 Li (Chin. surname) (2)

liǎng 两 two; liang (50 grams) (3)

liao 了 for forming the CoP (15)

límiàn 里面 inside, within, in (7)

líng 零 zero (2)

língqián 零钱 small/loose change (11)

liù 六 six (1)

liúlì 流利 fluent, fluid (12)

lǐwù 礼物 gift (14)

lóng 笼 steamer placed on top of a pot (3)

lóu 楼 floor, story; multistory building (10)

lùchá 绿茶 green tea (1)

lǚxíng 旅行 travel (14)

lǜzhōu 绿洲 oasis (12)

ma 吗 interrogative particle (1)

Mǎ 马 Ma (Chin. surname) (2)

mǎ 马 horse (11)

máfan 麻烦 anger, annoyance (15)

mǎi 买 buy (3)

mǎi cài 买菜 shop for groceries (8)

mǎi dōngxi 买东西 shop, purchase (14)

mǎidān 买单 bill, tab, invoice (9)

májiàng 麻将 mahjong (10)

mǎlù 马路 street (11)

mǎmǎhūhū 马马虎虎 so-so (10)

màn 慢 slow (6)

mántou 馒头 yeast bun (9)

máo 毛 10 cents (3)

máoyī 毛衣 wool sweater (14)

màozi 帽子 head covering (12)

méi 没 not (have) (1)

méi guānxi 没关系 it doesn't matter (15)

méi yǒu 没有 not have, there isn't/aren't; without (1)

Měiguó 美国 America (5)

men 们 plural suffix (3)

miànbāo 面包 bread (12)

miàntiáo 面条 noodles made of wheat flour (4)

miànzi 面子 face (12)

mǐfàn 米饭 boiled rice (6)

míngbái 明白 clear, plain; understand (15)

míngtiān 明天 tomorrow (11)

míngzi 名字 name (9)

ná 拿 take, grasp, hold (12)

nà 那 that (one over there) (5)

nǎ 哪 which? (4)

nàge 那个 that (one over there) (5)

nǎli? 哪里 where?, where to? (5)

nánfāngrén 南方人 South Chinese, Southerners (10)

nánpéngyou 男朋友 boy-friend (9)

nǎr? 哪儿 where?, where to? (5)

nàxiē 那些 those (over there) (14)

néng 能 can; be able (6)

nǐ 你 you (2)

nián 年 year (4)

nǐ de 你的 your, their (2)

nǐmen 你们 your (pl.) (3)

nǐmende 你们的 much (3)

nuǎnhuo 暖和 warm (14)

nǚpéngyou 女朋友 girlfriend (9)

nǚshì 女士 Mrs./Ms. (form of address) (2)

ōuyuán 欧元 euro (3)

páiduì 排队 get in line; stand in line (11)

péngyou 朋友 friend (9)

piányi 便宜 cheap (3)

piányi yìdiǎn 便宜一点 cheaper (3)

piào 票 ticket; banknote (7)

píjiǔ 啤酒 beer (1)

píng 瓶 MW for bottles (5)

píngguǒ 苹果 apple (14)

Pīnyīn 拼音 phonetic transcription; spell (7)

pútáojiǔ 葡萄酒 wine (5)

Pǔtōnghuà 普通话 Standard Chinese/Mandarin (7)

qí 骑 ride a horse/bike (11)

qī 七 seven (1)

qián 钱 money (3)

qián 前 in front (8)

qiān 千 thousand (3)

qiānzhèng 签证 visa (15)

qǐng 请 request; invite; please (3)

qǐng wèn 请问 May I ask ... (4)

qīngzhēn 清真 Islamic, Muslim (12)

qīngzhēncài 清真菜 Muslim cuisine (12)

qīngzhēnsì 清真寺 mosque (12)

qù 去 go; go there (5)

rén 人 person, human being (5)

Rénmínbì 人民币 renminbi (RMB) (3)

rènshi 认识 get to know (9)

rì 日 day; sun (4)

ròu 肉 meat (6)

ròusī 肉丝 strips of meat (6)

sān 三 three (1)

sānkè 三刻 three quarters of an hour (4)

shāmò 沙漠 desert (12)

shān 山 mountain (12)

shàng 上 serve (9)

shàng chē 上车 get in, board (11)

Shànghǎi 上海 Shanghai (7)

Shànghǎicài 上海菜 Shanghai cuisine (7)

Shànghǎihuà 上海话 Shanghai dialect (7)

shàngwǔ 上午 in the morning, A.M. (4)

shǎo 少 little (2)

shéi 谁 who? (10)

shèngdànjié 圣诞节 Christmas (4)

shēngrì 生日 birthday (4)

# List of Words

shénme 什么 what?, what kind of ... (2)

shénme shíhou 什么时候 when? (10)

shí 十 ten (1)

shì 事 matter, affair (15)

shì 是 be (2)

shìchǎng 市场 market (14)

shíhou 时候 point in time (10)

shíjiān 时间 time (9)

shíjǐn 什锦 mixed (8)

shǒu 手 hand (12)

shǒugōng 手工 handicraft (14)

shǒujī 手机 cell phone (14)

shǒutíbāo 手提包 handbag (14)

shūcài 蔬菜 vegetables (8)

shuǐguǒ 水果 fruit (14)

shuō 说 speak, say (5)

sì 寺 temple (12)

sì 四 four (1)

suàn 算 calculate (9)

suān 酸 sour (7)

suānlàtāng 酸辣汤 hot-and-sour soup (7)

sùcài 素菜 vegetarian dish (8)

suì 岁 year of age/life (4)

suíbiàn 随便 at one's discretion (13)

suǒyǐ 所以 therefore (11)

sùshíjǐn 素什锦 mixed vegetables (8)

tā 他 he (2)

tā 她 she (2)

tāde 她的 her (2)

tāde 他的 his (2)

tài 太 too, overly (3)

tài guì 太贵 too expensive (3)

tàiyángjìng 太阳镜 sunglasses (12)

tāmen 他们 they (3)

tāmen 她们 they (3)

tāmende 她们的 their (pl.) (3)

tāmende 他们的 their (pl.) (3)

tāng 汤 soup (7)

tècān 特餐 specialty (10)

téng 疼 hurt, ache (13)

tī 踢 kick; play (10)

tí 提 carry in one's hands (12)

tián 甜 sweet (14)

tiáo 条 MW for long things like pants and skirts (14)

tīng 听 hear, listen (to) (9)

tóu 头 head (13)

tù 吐 throw up (13)

tuì 退 give back, bring back (11)

tuǐ 腿 leg (13)

wàimiàn 外面 outside (14)

wàn 万 ten thousand (11)

wǎn 碗 bowl (6)

wǎnfàn 晚饭 dinner (5)

Wáng 王 Wang (Chin. surname) (2)

wǎng 往 to; in the direction of (8)

wàng 忘 forget (10)

wánquán 完全 complete, entire (12)

wǎnshang 晚上 in the evening (4)

wànsuì 万岁 long live ... (11)

wánxiào 玩笑 joke, fun (14)

wèi 胃 stomach (13)

wèi ... 为 for ... (11)

–wén 文 written language; language (5)

wèn 问 ask (4)

wèntí 问题 question, problem (15)

wǒ 我 I (2)

wǒde 我的 my, mine (2)

wǒmen 我们 we (3)

wǒmende 我们的 our (3)

wǔ 五 five (1)

wǔfàn 午饭 lunch (5)

xià 下 gamble, bet (10)

xià chē 下车 get out/off (11)

xiǎng 想 want; would like; think; guess (6)

xiàngqí 象棋 chess (10)

xiānsheng 先生 Mr., husband (2)

xiànzài 现在 now (4)

xiǎojie 小姐 Miss, Ms. (2)

xiǎolóngbāo 小笼包 Shanghai-style baozi (7)

xiǎoshi 小时 hour (11)

xiàwǔ 下午 in the afternoon (4)

xībù 西部 western part (12)

xiě 写 write (5)

xiē 些 ZMW for an indefinite number of things (14)

xièxie 谢谢 thanks; thank (6)

xīguā 西瓜 melon (14)

xǐhuan 喜欢 like (6)

xìng 姓 be called (surname only) (9)

xíngli 行李 baggage; travel equipment (11)

xīngqī 星期 week (4)

xīngqīwǔ 星期五 Friday (4)

xìngqù 兴趣 interest (8)

xìnyòngkǎ 信用卡 credit card (14)

xiū 修 repair (13)

xiūxi 休息 take a break (8)

Xīyào 西药 medications (Western) (13)

Xīyī 西医 medicine (Western) (13)

xūyào 需要 need, require (11)

yá 牙 tooth (13)

yáncháng 延长 extend (15)

yángròu 羊肉 lamb, mutton (12)

yǎnjing 眼睛 eyes (13)

yǎnjìng 眼镜 (eye)glasses (13)

yào 药 medications (13)

yào 要 want; must; become (6)

yàoshi 钥匙 key (10)

yě 也 also, too (1)

yī 一 one (1)

yìbān 一般 normally, usually (9)

yìdiǎn 一点 a little (bit) (3)

yídìng 一定 absolutely; by all means (9)

yīfu 衣服 clothes (14)

yígerén 一个人 alone (8)

yígòng 一共 overall (9)

yǐhòu 以后 after that; later, afterward (13)

yíkè 一刻 quarter of an hour (4)

yīnggāi 应该 should; must (7)

Yīngguó 英国 England (5)

Yīngwén 英文 English (5)

yìngwò 硬卧 "hard sleeper"; sleeping car compartment (11)

Yīngyǔ 英语 English (5)

yínháng 银行 bank (7)

yīnwèi 因为 because, since (8)

yìqǐ 一起 all together (9)

yǐqián 以前 earlier, previously; before (13)

yìsi 意思 meaning (15)

yíxià 一下 just briefly, for a second (8)

yìxiē 一些 some (15)

yīyuàn 医院 hospital (13)

yìzhí 一直 straight ahead; uninterrupted; always (8)

yòng 用 use; with, on (5)

yòng ... fùqián 用 ... 付钱 pay with ... (14)

yǒu 有 have, there is/are (1)

yǒu kòng 有空 have time (15)

yòubiān 右边 (on the) right (7)

yóutiáo 油条 deep-fried, salted dough strip (9)

yú 鱼 fish (8)

-yǔ 语 language (5)

yuán 元 largest unit of currency (3)

yuǎn 远 far (11)

yùdìng 预订 reserve, preorder (10)

yuè 月 month; moon (4)

yǔyán 语言 language (5)

zài 在 be in progress/going on (9)

zài 在 be located at a place, in, at (2)

zài 再 again (7)

zàijiàn 再见 goodbye (7)

zǎofàn 早饭 breakfast (5)

zǎoshang 早上 in the morning (4)

zěnme? 怎么？ how? (6)

zhāng 张 MW for flat things like tickets (7)

zhǎo 找 seek, seek out, consult (15)

zhàoxiàngjī 照相机 (still) camera (14)

zhè 这 this (3)

zhège 这个 this (3)

zhèlǐ 这里 here (1)

zhēn 真 real, genuine (10)

zhèr 这儿 here (1)

zhèxiē 这些 these (14)

zhǐ 只 only, merely (7)

zhīdao 知道 know (11)

zhìliàng 质量 quality (14)

zhíyè 职业 profession, occupation (15)

zhōng 钟 time measured in hours (4)

Zhōngguó 中国 China (1)

Zhōngwén 中文 Chinese (5)

zhōngwǔ 中午 at midday (4)

Zhōngyào 中药 medications (traditional Chin.) (13)

Zhōngyī 中医 medicine (traditional Chin.) (13)

zhōu 粥 porridge made of rice and water (9)

zhù 住 live, reside (10)

zhù 祝 wish; congratulate (4)

zhūròu 猪肉 pork (12)

zìjǐ 自己 (one)self (13)

zìxíngchē 自行车 bicycle (11)

zǒu 走 run; walk (8)

zuì 最 syllable for forming the superlative (6)

zuò 做 make (6)

zuò 坐 sit, sit down (4)

zuò ... 坐 go with; travel by ... (11)

zuǒbiān 左边 (on the) left (7)

zuótiān 昨天 yesterday (13)

zuòwèi 座位 seat, place (11)

zuǒyòu 左右 approximately (9)

zúqiú 足球 soccer (10)

# The Audio CDs

## Contents of the Audio CDs

CD 1:

Track

CD 2:

Track